Cimarrón Pedagogies

Yolanda Medina and Margarita Machado-Casas
General Editors

Vol. 25

The Critical Studies of Latinxs in the Americas series
is part of the Peter Lang Trade Academic and Textbook list.
Every volume is peer reviewed and meets
the highest quality standards for content and production.

PETER LANG
New York • Bern • Berlin
Brussels • Vienna • Oxford • Warsaw

Lidia Marte

Cimarrón Pedagogies

Notes on Auto-ethnography as a Tool for Critical Education

PETER LANG
New York • Bern • Berlin
Brussels • Vienna • Oxford • Warsaw

Library of Congress Cataloging-in-Publication Data
Names: Marte, Lidia, author.
Title: Cimarrón pedagogies: notes on auto-ethnography as a tool for
critical education / Lidia Marte.
Description: New York: Peter Lang, 2020.
Series: Critical studies of Latinxs in the Americas; vol. 25
ISSN 2372-6822 (print) | ISSN 2372-6830 (online)
Includes bibliographical references.
Identifiers: LCCN 2019049911 | ISBN 978-1-4331-7536-7 (hardback: alk. paper)
ISBN 978-1-4331-7535-0 (paperback: alk. paper) | ISBN 978-1-4331-7537-4 (ebook pdf)
ISBN 978-1-4331-7538-1 (epub) | ISBN 978-1-4331-7539-8 (mobi)
Subjects: LCSH: Ethnology. | Research—Methodology. | Critical pedagogy. |
Educational anthropology.
Classification: LCC GN316 .M367 | DDC 305.8—dc23
LC record available at https://lccn.loc.gov/2019049911
DOI 10.3726/b16284

Bibliographic information published by **Die Deutsche Nationalbibliothek**.
Die Deutsche Nationalbibliothek lists this publication in the "Deutsche
Nationalbibliografie"; detailed bibliographic data are available
on the Internet at http://dnb.d-nb.de/.

The paper in this book meets the guidelines for permanence and durability
of the Committee on Production Guidelines for Book Longevity
of the Council of Library Resources.

© 2020 Peter Lang Publishing, Inc., New York
29 Broadway, 18th floor, New York, NY 10006
www.peterlang.com

All rights reserved.
Reprint or reproduction, even partially, in all forms such as microfilm,
xerography, microfiche, microcard, and offset strictly prohibited.

Printed in the United States of America

Dedication

I dedicate this book to my mother, Silvia Angélica de la Cruz, for her fierce *cimarrón* commitment to learning and to her children's education, and for migrating to the North so I could have access to a higher education that she could not obtain for herself. I am paying with this book a debt of gratitude to her irreverent attitude and her life-sustaining teachings. To my sister Silvia Argentina Marte, who picked up the task where my mother left it, who have continued taking care of my wellness where ever I happen to live, and now here in San Juan, Puerto Rico; for her delicious foods, moral support and the example of her strength and dignity even under the most un-auspicious circumstances. I also dedicate this book *in memoriam* to my beloved Brian Stross, for his anthropological teachings, his humor, love of food and music, for his commitment to social justice and for his unconditional friendship. This book is in part a response to Stross who (in different occasions and in different ways) asked me why I cared so much about teaching, and I could not answer him coherently at the time. Even though it is too late now for him to read this book, I feel at peace now with my answer.

With this book, I am paying a debt of gratitude also to my formal and informal teachers and mentors, who have taught me how to learn throughout my life. I am grateful for the tools they shared, which further individual and collective liberations, critical consciousness and radical imagination. I thank them for challenging me to recognize my power to produce small spaces of autonomy for myself and others, to re-invent a more dignified life and to represent and create archives of my own history. Thanks to Eugenio García Cuevas, who first exposed me in the 1980s to critical tools and political economy, and introduced me to the work of Aníbal Ponce, who has become, ever since, a model and avatar for my teaching. I dedicate also this book to an unsuspected mentor, to Jormiguita, for her twin flame friendship and for the jewel of her children's stories, which I consume avidly. I am learning through her stories to teach without teaching, and to say so much with the sharp precision of less words. I dedicate lastly and *in memoriam, to* Christopher Heath, a dear friend, brilliant artist and photographer, who taught me to refine my graphic arts skills and to be *in-place*, through our long photo-walking routes through the shores and streets of Staten Island, Brooklyn and Manhattan.

Table of Contents

Acknowledgments   ix

Introduction: Mapping Educational Contexts, Relations and Histories   1
Chapter One: What Is Ethnography? Qualitative Methodologies
    and Academic Narratives   11
Chapter Two: Critical Auto-ethnography: Mapping Personal Root and Routes
    through "Native" Ethnography   35
Chapter Three: Critical Auto-ethnography in the Classroom:
    Auto-ethnographic Projects, Toolkit for Critical analysis
    and Course Design   57
Chapter Four: *Cimarrón* Pedagogies: Marronage, Critical Education
    and Liberation Paths   91

Bonus Track: Mapping the Calendars of My Educational Roots and Routes   119
Appendix: Teaching Resources   139

Acknowledgments

I am grateful to my dearest friend and colleague, Natalia Biani, for being a compassionate witness, first reader and first editor of this book manuscript; without her enthusiasm for the contents, unconditional support, bilingual expertise and insights this work would have not existed. To the series editor at Peter Lang, Yolanda Medina, for her support and editing help since the book prospectus stages. I thank her for believing in the potential of this book and in my ability to complete it. I thank Peter Lang Publishers, for the risk and vision to publish this kind of work. I am grateful to my current and former students; without them this book would have not been necessary; I thank them for helping me remain a student and for inspiring me to continue teaching. I thank those who gave me permission to use samples of their work and evaluations. I thank all of those who did not drop my courses, being open minded and courageous to try the tools I offer, for letting me be a witness to their visions, struggles and cultural histories, and for nurturing hope, the certainty that new generations will help us create more sustainable, just and joyful worlds. Thank you to colleagues who read the manuscript and gave their endorsements.

Thanks to the Department of Sociology & Anthropology (DSA), University of Puerto Rico (Rio Piedras Campus), for support with accommodating schedules and course-load negotiations to have the time-space to focus on the completion of my work. Gracias and bows of respect to our DSA chairs over these years, Jorge Giovannetti, Jaime Pérez (an ethnographer who teaches constantly through his kindness, humor and humbleness), and Lanny Thompson. To the chairs' sidekick angels, administrative assistants, Mildred, Denise and Mari Carmen, for their kind help and for saving us from going mad with paperwork. Thanks to Dr. Ana Maritza Martinez, at one point, dean of the School of Social Sciences, for her time and kind support in moments of job crisis. Kind thanks to Bárbara Abadía-Rexach, innovative scholar, dedicated teacher and friend, for the collaboration to visit mutually our classes, learning from each other's teaching styles. I am grateful to colleagues in the Comité de Personal of the DSA (especially to Jorge and Juan José), who—unbeknown to them—helped me return to Puerto Rico to complete my healing and to fine-tune my teaching. Thanks to Carlos Guilbe, a brilliant geographer with an ethnographer's heart, for his support of my work, for his inspiring commitment to his teaching, for his friendship and refreshing sense of humor. Thanks to Viviana de Jesús, Paola Schiapacasse and other colleagues whose names are many to list, and to the "sin par" Donato, at the LabCAD. Thanks to Isar Godreau and Mariluz Franco, for their anti-racist and de-colonizing work that we have been using at UPR to further pedagogies of liberation, and for offering mentoring resources for undergraduate research. Thanks to the cleaning and maintenance crew and administrative staff from different schools and departments, for their work, and for their contribution to help create a community of solidarity in campus. I will be forever grateful to Carole Counihan, Samuel Wilson, Jonathan Shannon and Deborah Kapchan, for their mentoring and support all these years. Many years ago, Val Episcopo, at St. Edwards University (Austin, TX), asked me to explain my approach to using auto-ethnography in the classroom, to her also goes my gratitude, and here is my answer.

Gracias, to my family, who from their dispersed geographies, offer me their love and moral support, even when they don't quite understand what is it that I do. Thanks to old and new dear friends, for their moral and survival support Dina, Lucia, Teresa, Eugenio and Lidia (la Camarada Reyes), Pamela, and to Elba Paoli (my middle school teacher and dear friend), among others. Thanks to Ana, for being the best neighbor and friend anyone could have, for feeding me and helping me to re-adapt to Puerto Rico, for teaching me to appreciate tropical place-making, for her kind humanity and her joyful disposition. I thank anyone else who directly or indirectly gave me help and moral support throughout the manuscript writing and completion process for this book.

I am grateful to the beautiful soundtrack that helped me to complete this book (especially during challenging days), in particular, in this ritual recurrence: Sona

Jobarteh & Band-*Kora Music from West Africa* (Gambia-London), Alí Farka Touré, *The River* (Mali), *Irak Instrumental Music* (Doha, Qatar), Coltrane (US, My Favorite Things), *Bonga 1974* (Senegal), Cesarea Evora (Cape Verde), Ska-Reggae (mixed) and Nneka (*Live in Berlin*). The diversity of music and foods we have created makes life in this Planet delicious, and it reconciles me with my humanity.

Introduction: Mapping Educational Contexts, Relations and Histories

We have to talk about liberating minds, as well as liberating society.

Angela Davis

Framings and Common Grounds

What we do in the classroom is not a rehearsal; it is real life. Learning happens spontaneously in everyday life; it is through such ongoing process of socialization that we are "domesticated" into becoming culturally specific humans. Formal education, however, happens mostly through "conscious" learning efforts and through problematic and contested institutional spaces, sites of great vulnerability, but also of great opportunity, especially for college students "of color." The structure, disciplining practices and ideologies that circulate—and are reproduced—through these spaces shape profound transformations in our ways of perceiving, understanding and taking action.

The practices of a "banking education" identified by Paulo Freire (2000) are the standards in most college classrooms, where the student is a passive being to be molded, or a recipient to be filled with information, to later regurgitate in an exam. These practices are costly and ineffective for all students and are particularly damaging and catastrophic for students who come from marginalized communities, all minorities, queer groups, immigrant communities, and for students coming from any colonized memory-histories. Students who come from such communities or "minoritized" social groups, frequently find, in the colleges they attend, a toxic environment of rejection where they do not feel valued but rather pathologized; this is usually expressed through stereotypes, prejudices and racist micro-aggressions (see Duncan 2005, Yosso 2005, Delgado 2013). These conditions aggravate their already challenged sense of self-worth and trust in their intelligence, capacities and talents. Self-esteem, in this sense, is rather a socio-cultural and historical issue rather than only a psychological one. Opposed to this ethnocentric and colonial pedagogy, Freire—and many others after him—proposed a *critical pedagogy praxis*, where being awake and responsive is the start of participatory learning and a democratic dialogue. Rather than discarding previous experience and cultural knowledge, a critical pedagogy creates space to first discover what kinds of filters students bring to class, to identify, evaluate, integrate and help transcend—through radical imagination—existing limitations, gaps and boundaries, according to the students' abilities, interests and life projects.

Yet, like going to the bathroom, no one can teach anyone critical (or creative) thinking; all we can do is to identify certain tools and resources to share with students, create spaces of dialogue in the classroom to allow for understanding to happen, explain how to apply certain concepts to interpret our everyday realities, create assignments through which students have a chance to test-drive those tools, evaluate their learning process, and then, hope for the best. Only students themselves can test-drive the new tools and knowledge, so they can get to know and modify them according to their educational goals, to their own needs and current challenges. We cannot liberate anyone either, from external or internal oppressions, but we can share with students the legacy and strategies of those who have found a way to de-colonize their minds and their personal lives, and who have joined others in collective liberations. We, as teachers, need to learn to trust our students' capacity to find—and hold with passion to that—what they most need to learn for their own projects of liberation.

Giving students the opportunity to explore where they are located as social agents *in-place* and how to examine and value their experiences, help them generate skills to navigate the private-public thin divide through which all humans negotiate our survival and our life projects. Researching *where* and *when* they are, recognizing the macro-narrative frames that shape their micro-narratives and ideologies, and practicing documenting the cultural histories that made them possible, help them obtain the mastery of what we want them to learn, but through a different route, a personal grounded investment, which has more profound and lasting benefits. Thus, we can help students discover their strength and their "marronage potential" even under the most restricted and challenging situations. Yet, before new knowledge can be integrated, and new methods and theories mastered, students need to develop "a critical praxis" (an embodied new perspective, not only a mode of "thinking," as if they were an isolated brain). Learning is a synergistic process of experience, of feeling, thinking and imagining.

The suggestive framing of this book as "*cimarrón* pedagogy," proposes going beyond critical education, to a radical strategy of engagement beginning from the personal grounds of where our students are. This approach is a way of recycling and celebrating ethno-historical strategies of liberation, as an ongoing project for which much work is still needed, including traveling the long global history of Afro-diasporic communities in their educational struggles and contributions. The word *Cimarrón* (maroon) was used in the Hispanic Caribbean to name run-away goats, pigs, enslaved indigenous groups and later enslaved indigenous Africans and their descendants brought to the Americas in the Atlantic Slave Trade. Likewise, cimarronaje/marronage was used to name any *petit* or *grand* act of resistance to colonial rule. Extending marronage as a historical instance, we can use this term as a metaphor to speak of our intentions for a liberation pedagogy.

Given the conditions in most colleges and schools where we teach and the prevailing banking education visions in our societies, creating more safe spaces for dialogue, human dignity and liberation in our classrooms is a *cimarrón* act. I echo bell hooks' calling for finding pleasure and excitement in teaching for liberation, to which I would add the necessity of humor and poetics when teaching difficult matters. This approach balances the burden of addressing so much suffering, trauma and violence, but it also best represents the contradictory complex politics of our human experiences.

The hegemonic discourses of a western education imposed in the Americas had their inherent cultural ethnocentrisms, their symbolic violence and their class marks. Trying to create a space of human dignity and liberation in our classrooms is, hence, a *cimarrón* de-colonizing first step into practicing—until we get it right—viable forms of participative democracy and new forms of learning communities.

Seeds of the Book: Genesis and Motivations

The book *Cimarrón Pedagogies* is a testimonial account and evaluation of the Critical Auto-ethnography methodology that I have used in my classroom as main resource to teach a variety of Anthropology and General Education college courses. This book offers description, evaluation and examples of how to use Auto-ethnography as main strategy for undergraduate research projects. Researching the ground of student's everyday experiences through their personal perspectives, is a form of engaged pedagogy utilizing experiential, project-based and place-based assignments, as well as other experimental strategies (such as use of media, popular culture extra-curricular activities). Maybe the best way to summarize this approach is through the feminist phrase "the personal is political" (and vice versa); through an auto-ethnographic project this phrase is *felt*, not just pondered, researched and theorized. During the research process and the writing of their final reports, students not only learn how to generate their own research question and answered it, they also discover their own power to rename and narrate their own cultural histories. Through this testimony I wish to share the usefulness of auto-ethnography to help teachers–students research topics of significance to their lives and concerns, paying attention to the diverse composition of the classes, the type of institutions and the places where they are located. This pedagogical approach is a form of *marronage*, that help us create—at least in the classroom and for one semester—small liberated spaces, bridging the individual and the collective, private and public, past and present, the poetic and the political, and the local/global negotiations in our students' lives.

My use of auto-ethnography in the classroom came about initially as an outcome of challenges with Internal Review Boards [IRBs] that regulates field research (permit for conducting research with human subjects required in the social sciences), particularly in my teaching of anthropology courses. The paperwork and complexity of this kind of application cannot be completed in one semester, and the process is challenging for undergraduate students (many of whom have never done any kind of research, nor heard about ethnography). Given this limitation, and because of my commitment to ethical research, I began assigning in my courses only auto-ethnographic field projects that they could complete in one semester, with a basic training in ethics. Since they worked with themselves as main center of their projects and collected only one oral history from a person known to them, they could get the research training and experience I wanted them to have. Students' topics, research questions, their challenges and success in the completion of their auto-ethnographic projects were evidence that this approach was working. And, more important, they have produced original knowledge that inspired them to continue their education and their research projects or to continue documenting their family histories. The consistent harvest of good work that my students have produced over the years has revealed to me the power of auto-ethnographic methodologies, for anyone, to develop personally grounded projects with relevance to their local lives, without ignoring the macro-context and global webs that condition our lives. In the case of the Caribbean, such global interconnections (of ethno-historical accidents and imperial oppressions) dates back as far as the 16th century.

I have been using this auto-ethnographic project-based approach since 2008, in Austin, TX, in New York City, and now in San Juan, Puerto Rico, with a wide range of diverse students and different general education courses, not only in anthropology. My students at the University of Puerto Rico, where I teach now, have shown me the other side of the Puerto Rican diaspora that I taught at CUNY-Brooklyn College; in both sides I have been witness to the power of auto-ethnography to help them understand where they are, and how they got to be there.

This book is also a closure harvest for me; there are many (and old) personal and professional motivations for this book, as will become clear later to the readers, but the actual *written* seed that launched the book as a viable project was planted through a paper that I presented at the conference *African Diasporas Old and New*, at the University of Texas at Austin (Marte 2014). That paper focused on these questions: Can we teach about the Caribbean without addressing Africa? and how do African Diaspora paradigms help us do this? This concern emerged from the challenges in my experience teaching Caribbean courses (in both anthropology and general education), in classrooms full of overt and subtle racism, and on the rewards of helping students acquire the basics of a racialization literacy. Beyond the paper, the audience for our panel was attentive and generous; after my presentation (with music soundtrack and interactive mappings) they gave me encouraging feedback, had many questions and a desire to know more about what it is, that I actually do, in the classroom. I hope that seed has grown now into a nice tree to answer some of their questions, and that it might give others new seeds for their teaching and for their own auto-ethnographic explorations.

Description of Contents and Summary of Chapters

The contents of the book are organized into chapters; the first two chapters give an overview discussion of ethnographic methodologies, and the last two chapters ground that discussion through testimonial accounts of my use of auto-ethnography, of research-centered teaching and my approach to critical education. The Appendix offers examples of teaching materials, for those who wish to test-drive some of these tools. Below I share a summary of each chapter to help readers locate materials of their interest. It is my hope that each chapter could stand on its own, but also to work as complement with each other. Although certain points of discussion return in all chapters, this is not a repetition but rather a reiteration in a different way of areas that are related. The very core of this book rests on the use of an auto-ethnographic perspective, hence all throughout, I use first person voice to ground more academic discussions through my own testimonial narratives.

Chapter One: "What is Ethnography? Qualitative Methodologies and Academic Narratives." The focus of this chapter is to explain, for a broader audience, what is ethnography. I begin with basic definitions and characteristics of ethnographic fieldwork and describe, from my perspective as a critical feminist ethnographer, some of the most relevant transformations of this methodology, through a discussion of genealogy of scholars who have been important in my own formation as an anthropologist. This chapter is necessary to understand the development and current status of auto-ethnography.

Chapter Two: "Critical Auto-ethnography: Mapping Personal Root and Routes through 'Native' Ethnography." In this chapter I explain some basic definitions of auto-ethnography as a fieldwork methodology and the most basic approaches to its use. I include a brief review of scholars and examples of works using this methodology, particularly those articles that I assign in my courses. I offer also a discussion of my own definitions and approaches to auto-ethnography as a perspective and a political project and evaluate what I believe are its contributions to my teaching. In closing, I discuss research-centered and place-based education, as necessary context to help students produce grounded auto-ethnographic projects and more critical personal narratives.

Chapter Three: "Critical Auto-ethnography in the Classroom: Auto-ethnographic Projects, Toolkit for Critical analysis and Course Design." This chapter describes the auto-ethnographic project that I assign, how it is completed throughout the semester, and evaluates the significance of students' final reports. I also include three more sections related to course design: (a) Discussion of theoretical concepts that I teach, to help students engage in critical analysis of their auto-ethnographic data and to produce final reports that go beyond personal narratives; (b) Description of the supporting coursework and classroom dynamics that support the completion of the projects; (c) Testimony of my experiences using auto-ethnographic methods to teach different courses, in different kinds of colleges, and to diverse groups of students, as well as outside formal education. The overall goal of this chapter is to evaluate the use of the auto-ethnographic methodology, how it helps in meeting SLOs (Student Learning Objectives) for courses, for students to value their own personal histories, develop critical and scholarly skills, as well as "social capital" to know their civil rights and to engage more effectively with political issues in their localities.

Chapter Four: "*Cimarrón* Pedagogies: Marronage, Critical Education and Liberation Paths." In this chapter I explain what is meant by the book's title and the term *cimarrón*, offering a brief overview of the ethno-historical context of plantation slavery that framed marronage in the Caribbean, and the significance of an African Diaspora and racial literacy to best engage with radical post-colonial pedagogies. I offer a sort of genealogy of teacher-mentor-scholars who, through their work and example, helped me to develop and to commit to an eco-feminist pedagogy. I close with some reflections on my auto-ethnographic "*cimarrón*" strategy, and why this approach results in a critical education, with potential for healing and liberation.

Bonus Track: "Mapping the Calendars of My Educational Roots and Routes," as the title suggests, it could be an optional reading, yet it offers a detailed explanation of the genesis of my teaching approach, and is a good example of "memory-data" for a potential auto-ethnographic project centered in the topic of education. I have included this part for those readers that might want a more direct grounding of my own educational history. These fragmented auto-ethnographic vignettes trace some *roots* (origins or earlier educational experiences in DR) and some *routes* (educational trajectories in Puerto Rico and United States). Warning: This is not a full auto-ethnographic account, since I have not done the research required for such a project, it is rather a collection of "landmark" moments in my formation as a student, teacher and artist-scholar. This piece shows the kinds of—literal and symbolic—movements in how I learned how to learn. I highlight resources, experiences and encounters with my mentors through informal and formal education, to show how I became a college professor, and in a sense, showing the personal reasons for why I use auto-ethnography in my teaching.

Appendix: Teaching Resources, this part contains a sampler of resources that I use in college classrooms, for diverse courses, but all centered around an auto-ethnographic research project. The resources are: auto-ethnographic research project guides, rubrics for assignments, teaching materials, in-class workshops, website links and examples of students' works. I have also included few handouts, part of the *Toolkit for Critical Analysis*, that I assign to students, to teach them theoretical concepts useful for the analysis of their auto-ethnographic project data. This appendix is provided to support the discussion in Chapter Three, and to give access to readers/users to teaching materials. These could be simplified and tailored to particular needs, if someone wish to test-drive auto-ethnographic approaches (an email address is also provided, if they wish to share feedback about their experiences).

Significance and Contributions

This book contributes to the use of interdisciplinary qualitative research methods in the classroom, especially to further undergraduate research. Indirectly this work contributes to anthropology of education and to new trends in Latino Critical

Studies. Through this book, I want to contribute to further research-centered teaching and place-based education (this later used mostly in biology and ecology education), by enriching these approaches with the use of auto-ethnographic methodologies (formerly practiced by minority, "native" and feminist teachers). This bricolage is a powerful combination of tools for a radical liberation pedagogy, which has been nurtured from Freire's early work to most current experimental teaching practices, such as the "flipped classroom" (Keengwe 2014) and "critical citizenship" (Johnson & Morris 2010). These methods, and the transdisciplinary techniques we might add to them (such as mapping methods), are suitable because they begin where it matters; the social and ecological relations of *where* and *when* students are, *what* they are *doing* and with *whom*, and how they are narrating their experiences.

The main intention for this intervention in a public dialogue about education (from my non-expert perspective), is to promote more experiments and renewing of commitment to an "engaged pedagogy," one that could help teachers, students and their communities, to regain some joy and investment in the very process and fruits of learning. Another intention is to inspire an active production of interdisciplinary knowledge *by* and *for*, not just *about* the diversity of "localities." The concept of "place-memory" (Hayden 1997) encapsulates for me the need for local, native, auto-ethnographic research focused on the' infra-politics' of everyday life, on local micro-histories. Through these shifting intimate scales, which are the most immediate grounds of our individual and collective survival, we keep learning how to find (and to create) a sense of "home" in this strange and beautiful Planet. These immediate realms help us generate relevant questions about our cultural coordinates, from the most concreted economic and embodied negotiations, to our most radical collective hopes.

References

Delgado, R. (2013). Storytelling, counter-storytelling and naming one's own reality: Oppositionists and others plea for Narrative. In Delgado, Richard and Jean Stefancic (Eds.), *Critical race theory: The cutting edge* (3rd ed., pp. 71–80). Philadelphia: Temple University Press.

Duncan, G. A. (2005). Critical race ethnography in education: Narrative, inequality and the problem of epistemology. *Race, Ethnicity and Education, 8*(1), 93–114.

Freire, P. (2000). *Pedagogy of the oppressed*. New York: Bloomsbury.

Hayden, D. (1997). *The power of place: Urban landscapes as public history*. Cambridge, MA: MIT Press.

Johnson, L., & Morris, P. (2010). Towards a framework for critical citizenship education. *The Curriculum Journal, 21*(1), 77–96.

Keengwe, J. (Ed.). (2014). *Promoting active learning through the flipped classroom model.* Hershey, PA: IGI Global.

Marte, L. (2014, April 4). *Afro-Caribbean Pedagogies: Can we engage African Diaspora paradigms without addressing Africa?*. Paper presented at African Diasporas Old and New, University of Texas at Austin-Africa Conference –History Department and CAAAS– (Center for African & African American Studies).

Yosso, T. (2005, March). Whose culture has capital? A critical race theory discussion of community cultural wealth. *Race, Ethnicity and Education, 8*(1), 69–91.

CHAPTER ONE

What Is Ethnography?

Qualitative Methodologies and Academic Narratives

The time is gone when anthropologists could find solace in the claim that our main civic duty [...] was the constant reaffirmation that the Bongobongo are "humans just like us" [...] Too many of the Bongobongo are now living next door, and a few of them may even be anthropologists presenting their own vision of their home societies, or studying their North Atlantic neighbors.

Michel-Rolph Trouillot (In *Global Transformations*, 2003)

Framings, Scope and Limitations

Ethnography has been considered a marker of anthropology since the early institutionalization of the discipline in the 19th century in the US. Yet, this is specifically a methodology used by socio-cultural anthropology, a sub-field of anthropology. Anthropology is a social science that proposes to holistically study human diversity and the human experience past and present, from diverse dimensions, mainly through four sub-fields: archeology (the long pre-historic past) which focuses on the societies, landscapes and artifact traces left by human groups; physical or biological anthropology, focuses on the evolutionary and physiological aspects of human species and primates; linguistic anthropology, focuses on communication, language and representational practices. Socio-cultural anthropology (my area of training), in its most basic form, aims to research and understand the diverse social processes and cultural practices of living human groups in their diversity, and the experience of being human in our times, with all its complexities. It is important to clarify that *cultural* anthropology is the term used in the US academic tradition, and *social* anthropology refers to the European (in particular UK) academic tradition. In this book I use the term *socio-cultural* anthropology as used in Puerto Rico and in some Latin American countries. Yet I want to clarify that my discussion does not engage anthropology as practiced in Latin America, Africa, Asia and other regions. My focus for the debates and publications discussed below come from the US tradition, for which the concept of "culture" is privileged as a useful distinction. This is the current in which I was trained and is what shapes and informs my anthropological practice.

The purpose of this chapter is to explain what *Ethnography* is, its emergence and moments of transformations within and outside of anthropology, classical and more recent ways of practicing it, the implications it has as an academic tool for our present times, and its central role in the development of auto-ethnographic methodologies. The intention of this chapter is to offer a wider vision of ethnography, with a narrow focus on particular aspects that are relevant to understand the subsequent discussion of auto-ethnography in Chapter Two. The academic resources discussed are meant to support the more *experiential* contents of the other chapters, by discussing the potential and limitations of ethnographic tools for academic research and for informing teaching practices. This is not a literature review, a history of ethnography, nor a genealogy of the main debates. Many other perspectives can be found in the literature by scholars with the expertise in this topic (I highly suggest Michael Agar's works—in particular 1996—for an accessible in-depth overview of ethnography). My suggestion is to use this, and Chapter Two, as references to clarify doubts about ethnography and auto-ethnography, especially when reading Chapter Three. I hope that these resources are also useful for readers who wish to explore these topics in more depth (hence, I have included in the references, works not discussed, for readers who want to explore issues that I don't address fully here).

The views of ethnography that I am offering respond to my situated interpretations, according to my own academic formation and to the particularities of my vision and experiences. My discussion begins with definitions and explanations of what ethnographers do during fieldwork. I discuss then moments of transformation and critiques of the ethnographic practices. I conclude with a genealogy of sorts, of currents and scholars that were important to me during my graduate training and later through my research (indirect mentors); hence, this chapter is filtered through a first person auto-ethnographic voice, which honors the main proposal of this book.

What Is Ethnography?

Before we get tangled with academic jargon and lost into conceptual abstractions, I offer the punchline: Ethnography is a methodology, that utilizes mixed field methods, to design research projects and to conduct research. Ethnography is also considered a genre of writing, due to the particular narrative style to report research findings. As a methodology, ethnography is a kind of *qualitative methodology* (in contrast to quantitative) that requires fieldwork. The knowledge produced from ethnographic research, aims at understanding and explaining present human experience within a particular topic, from the grounded perspective of particular social groups, and through their cultural practices. Ethnography, as a constantly evolving genre or writing style, ranges from texts centered in narratives and descriptive passages about a particular group way of life, to more theoretical analysis of social phenomena, and includes also more researcher-centered self-reflections. Ethnography is used in Anthropology, other social sciences and, increasingly, in many other kinds of academic research, such as in art and humanities, education and health related fields. In this sense, this interdisciplinary use becomes an ideological choice or *perspective* from where to question and to understand the poetics and politics of our complex human condition. In the more than 150 years of anthropological publications, ethnography has become a kind of cultural production in its own right, that has amazed a remarkable textual and visual archive of the human experience, from the perspective of diverse anthropologists and scholars, in the context of their own historical times.

Just as when defining what is life, sometimes it is best to focus on characteristics rather that attempting a coherent definition. Ethnography as a methodology involves conducting fieldwork research with living human groups, in everyday settings, rather than in labs or controlled experiments (calling this "natural" settings is problematic). Given the complexity of our human lives, ethnographers focus on a particular topic, and generate specific research questions to guide their focus during fieldwork, but trying to take in, holistically, all the rest. The main method of fieldwork is *participant-observation*, acquiring original knowledge from interactions with particular people, in specific places, to produce primary sources by documenting (through fieldnotes and audiovisual recordings) ordinary behavior, communication, practices, artifacts, and gathering narratives, oral histories, informal interviews, elicitation of vernacular knowledge, questionnaires, among other qualitative instruments. As any other research involving interactions among humans, the ethnographic fieldwork is a process that requires ethical training and compliance. The central ethical and legal mandate, as it is supposed to be in medicine, is first "doing no harm," to interact in respectful and patient ways, regardless of what is going on.

Through ethnographic fieldwork research, we try to understand the individual and group experiences in their own cultural specificity and simultaneously in the shared grounds of our humanity; how we do, perceive-think, speak-communicate, and create the marvelous and weird things we do as well as the tensions, conflicts and negotiations that ensue. Yet no social group is homogeneous, and no individual human is generic; hence, ethnographers need to document behaviors and events from culturally specific points of view, angles or perspectives of particular people, in particular geographic places at particular space-times, and in specific local-global relations. As ethnographers we are aware that many points of view or perspectives [henceforth POVs] are needed for a wider vision of the human condition, so generalizations from our data is not the main aim, that is why the sampling is valid even if it focuses on a small group, one family or even one single individual (as Ruth Behar has done). Like a close-up photo, we narrow the human unity to get a more depth of understanding of differences, to feel-hear-see-touch-taste what it means for the participants in our studies to be human (this is what we call the "emic" or inside POV). We also do more classical bibliographic and archival research about our project's community and field-site, to locate them in historical context and current statistical data, and to find out about the current state of academic understanding about the particular topic of our research project. This goal of this bibliography is to create an "etic" understanding from the "outside" POV of the researcher, and to inform the analysis and interpretation of the field data.

Of course, this kind of research, as any other qualitative methodology, is not clear cut, nor is a smooth going somewhere and "gathering data." As will become evident in further discussions below, these clear-cut steps and tasks (as practiced mostly before the 1980s) are still one of the major problematics of ethnographic research, that have driven critiques, transformations and refinements of this tool from within and outside anthropology (and these limitations is what auto-ethnography puts, so powerfully, in evidence). More simply put, ethnographers gather stories in the context where they occur. We listen, ask (and respond if prompted), observe and participate in what is going on. Ideally, we are supposed to be fully *present*, engaged in the measure that collaborators in our studies allow us to participate and to share their worlds. Ideally also, this process happens in a non-judgmental space of acceptance and appreciation of differences, aware of our own ethnocentrism, this is, consciously examining the influences of our own cultural filters. Through fieldwork many challenges and micro-political negotiations occur; yet, this method also renders marvelous mutual insights and discoveries. In this sense, ethnography is a space of intercultural and interpersonal encounters and exchanges, as complex, contingent and "real" as our everyday interactions. To me, these experiential aspects of our human interactions are what makes ethnography a needed tool for qualitative research.

To conduct ethnographic research and to understand what ethnography is, we need to address the term *culture*. Widely varied definitions of culture have been proposed, and their implications have been debated since the 19th century (in their 1952 book, anthropologists Kroeber and Kluckhohn gathered more than 200!), and the problematics of its essentialized usage has been questioned and denounced (see Stocking 1996). The concept of "culture," so central in US anthropology, was also transformed during the 1980s "crisis" within the discipline; culture went from a concrete "reality" out there, that can be easily identified as an avocado in a tree (bounded "culture areas" or studying "a culture," for example) to an abstract concept in its *adjective* form ("cultural" practices), this is the version that most ethnographers use commonly today. The following is an idiosyncratic, yet useful metaphor for "culture": "... *But it was fitting me like a tight chemise. I couldn't see it for wearing it. It was only when I was off in college, away from my native surroundings that I could see myself like somebody else and stand off and look at my garment. Then I had to have the spy-glass of Anthropology to look through that.*" It was subtly proposed by a US Black woman anthropologist, Zora N. Hurston, in her book *Mules and Men* (1935). Such *subtlety* was maybe needed, not to be accused of theorizing or interpreting her data, which was not well seen in ethnographic works of the 1930s, and much less to be taken seriously from a black woman in the segregated and sexist society of that time. This indirect theorization is useful and revealing of how this scholar was already using a "critical" conception of "culture," bounded more by historical and political conditions than by purely geographical and natural "culture area." Hurston was also writing from an auto-ethnographic perspective, not only looking at her Black community in Florida as an objective detached observer.

Chang's book about *Autoethnography as Method* (2008) includes a wonderful chapter called "The Web of Culture," which my students reported to be useful to grasp this slippery, yet productive concept of culture. The author asks, early on in the chapter, provocative philosophical questions, such as "where is culture located?" or is it individual or collective? Using a "web" metaphor, she manages to describe the many matrixes and interconnections of the "cultural" in our human experience. She also clarifies that individuals are social agents, yet interdependent of others as social species and shaped by the context of their survival. Humans are not puppets of culture, but rather imaginative beings that have created remarkable complexities, beauty and terrors throughout our history. In particular, I appreciate how Chang makes emphasis on migration and cultural change, to understand social transformations across generations, as this is also a foundational phenomenon that I teach in almost all my courses: the centrality of movements and diasporas in our becoming the kinds of humans we are today, but also in re-inventing our cultural histories. It is through "culture," as a human evolutionary tool, that we have amazed our staggering diversity of material culture and archives of representation (these archives are strategic memory-work that have given us hegemony as a species).

In my basic anthropology courses, I briefly teach the concept of culture debate, then proceed to give students a *working definition* of "culture" in quote, which includes these characteristics, culture is: Learned from our surroundings (indirectly and directly), interpretive and contested, placed and historical, experienced individually and negotiated collectively, and expressed through material culture and through our bodies and minds. For example, nothing places the diversity and significance of particular *cultural practices* in stark light as situations of conflict, violence and wars. After an initial confrontation, most of the damage comes from misunderstandings and mutual ethnocentrisms; each one is an enemy to each other, who needs to be categorized fast, as they are trying to impose their own way of life or POV on the other (be it through borders, resources, religious and political ideologies, etc.). Ethnocentrism, believing that our way of life is normal and superior, is an inescapable tendency of all humans, but when not questioned and named is used to defend a "right" to hegemony, our own group cultural practices as the best, and our truths as the only objective reality. These "reality" claims are at the core of how we have been not only domesticated, this is *socialized* as generic humans, but simultaneously *enculturated* (e.g., to speak a specific language, perceive the world and behave in particular ways, acceptable to our place and historical context). This useful ethnocentric socialization is also a weapon, used individually and collectively, which have led humans into despicable exploitation, violence, and discriminatory practices (of humans and of other species) based on the long shelf-life prejudices of differences. Ironically, it is this same ethnocentrism that gives us the particularities of our unity as a species (we are the only animal who cooks its food and invest heavily on the differences of our culinary cultures).

Paradigm Shifts: Ethnography Roots, Routes and Transformations

The definitions of ethnography—offered above—correspond loosely to contemporary ways of practicing anthropological research. Yet, ethnography as a methodology has undergone many transformations since its emergence and as it was first use by early scholars in the 19th and 20th centuries in the US (see Boas 1966, 1989, Malinowski 2002, Rochner 1966). The refinement and transformation of ethnographic tools span the foundational uses by Boas, Malinowski and the first women anthropologists such as Ruth Benedict (2005), Margaret Mead (1963) and Zora N. Hurston (1935), the classical positivist ethnography practiced until approximately the 1970s to the watershed moments of the "crisis" of representation and the "reflexive turn," critical ethnography between 1990s and 2000s, and more recent post-critical ethnography (post-colonial) and diverse contemporary experimental approaches (for an overview of this see Foley 2002). Rather than a comprehensive history of its development, I offer below a discussion of few moments, movements and works (practices, debates, publications), about ethnography, otherness, boundaries of the "field," what is considered "data," paradigms of objectivity-subjectivity and issues of ethics in the process of transformation from the first uses by Boas (1966) in the 1890s to the current era of post-critical ethnography (Noblit et al. 2004).

The classical iconic image of an anthropologist used to be a white Euro-American upper middle-class male, working in remote "tribal" jungles, with dark-skinned natives, for years on end. Their reports of findings, in many cases, were based on conversing with a few top-ranking males in the community and then writing an "ethnography" (what was supposed to be a full realistic description of an entire society (e.g., "the" Nuer by Evans-Pritchard 1940 or Malinowski's "the" Trobianders published in 1922). These ethnographies were not only accepted as scientific data, they were also supposed to describe and catalog, once and for all, unchanging, bounded "cultures," their behavior, how they thought, ways of life and cosmovision of the world, in an unquestioned homogeneity. This huge colonial generalization of human groups has also given way to classical iconic images of what an anthropologist was supposed to look like. From these full ethnographies to what we modestly call today "ethnographic accounts," there is a huge epistemological gulf; anthropological writing became acknowledged as provisional, partial interpretations of a particular human group at a specific historical place-time, based on partial perspectives of some of the members of a community, as interpreted by particular anthropologists, who came from specific countries.

The major changes in practice and theory within Anthropology, and the changes in how ethnography as a methodology has been used between the 1920 until today, respond, in part, to how anthropology keeps re-inventing itself, through *external* pressures, forced by changing geopolitical landscapes, by communities themselves that have been objects of its studies, by other disciplines critiques and attacks (see Min-ha 1989, Stocking 1996), but also through a commendable constant *internal* critique since its institutionalization, by its progressive practitioners, about the present and future political implications of the discipline and its engagement with living populations. The external pressures came concretely through the transformations of colonial territories and of the very empires and countries from where the earlier anthropologists were coming from. The internal transformations we further nurture by new "minority" and "native others" who increasingly were able to enter PhD anthropology programs in the US in great numbers, especially after the 1980s.

Social sciences explanatory models, or what it is called a paradigm, were also shifting, generating neo-Marxist theoretical frameworks after the 1960s, that moved the social sciences analysis from *positivist* science (reality is knowable, measurable and science is objective and value free) to *critical theory* focused not on neutral science or objective epistemologies but on power and historical praxis with political dimensions for all kinds of knowledge creation. These conditions of production (Kuhn's scientific revolutions) have implications for how we name and perceive "realities" (for a good discussion of this shift and of social theory as a European post-war academic and cultural movement see Denzin 1999, Ortner 1984, 2006, Foley 2002). Among the most influential theoretical frameworks shaping most productively a paradigm shift in social sciences and humanities were structuralism (the work of Edward Sapir and Levi-Strauss as iconic representatives), Marxism (dialectical materialism), which entered anthropology much earlier yet became most visible in publications during the 1970s and 1980s. It was as a response to these critical intellectual movements that methodological tools were transformed resulting in post-structuralist and post-colonial critiques, beyond the more visible and amorphous discourses of post-modernity, which were coming mostly from the humanities (see Marcus & Clifford, 1986).

This upheaval included further interdisciplinary nurturing from new conceptions of power beyond Antonio Gramsci and Michel Foucault, which focused on feminist concerns with "theories of practice" (see Rich 1984, Ortner's 2006 critique of Bourdieu). The more vocal trends were moving from a conception of power as force, control and domination to a fuzzier matrix of situated relations, fluid processes of negotiations, micro an infra-politics beyond resistance-accommodation, and new performative identity politics at diverse scales and dimensions (see Spry 2006). Simultaneously—and more prominently today—further theoretical and methodological contributions came from Black feminist theory (Hill-Collins 2002), Critical Race Theory (Delgado & Stefancic 2001) and feminist political ecology (Fraser 1990, Duncan 1996). In particular, feminist theory and methodologies had tremendous influence in furthering critical analysis and refining theories of practice and power in feminist scholarship and beyond (see Hess-Biber et al. 1999). The works of Faye Harrison (1991, 1993, 1997, 2008), specifically, Harrison's proposal for de-colonizing anthropology and calling for an anthropology of liberation, had a significant impact, especially among minority and other non-traditional anthropologists in the US and beyond, as it showed us, in practice, how to do critically engaged ethnographic research.

Social Darwinism and other deterministic dichotomies of self/other, us/them, home/field, object/subject were hence questioned and de-centered in ethnographic discourses and practices. This was being done from inside and outside, in particular, ethnography has been re-shaped by the contributions of many interdisciplinary feminist women scholars, for example, the concept of "situated knowledge" (Haraway 1988) became widely used as a trendy garnish in feminist anthropology and other disciplines. Yet, it had profound implications for questioning objectivity and giving ethnographers permission to continue using this tool, in spite of its problematic partiality. The putative "crisis of representation" that Marcus and Fisher identified in their also seminal publication *Anthropology as Cultural Critique* (1986) was an internal crisis for those that could afford amnesia, that considered themselves unmarked, and held as true the myth of bounded cultural areas and fixed fields of research, but this was not the case for the new kinds of anthropologists entering US academia as minorities, immigrants or indigenous "others," nor was this the case for those early US women anthropologists, who were also marked by a gendered and racial otherness.

As can be noticed from the discussion above, *Ethnography* is not a neutral methodology, cooked in isolation by a rational discipline looking for the best tools to create scientific knowledge. In a sense, similar curiosity and approaches to discover human diversity were common centuries before anthropology existed as a profession (from Herodotus to Spanish priests in the 16th century). The origins of ethnography could be found in precursors archival practices such as travel narratives and colonial chronicles, as well as early literary and historical narratives (see Clifford & Marcus 1986). Early Europeans' travel accounts, documentation of conquest, colonial records and chronics were initially used to help manage the colonial enterprises of grabbing, mapping and classifying lands, resources, people, their labor and the wealth of artifacts-artistic productions of these new territories. These practices helped colonial authorities in the Americas to "know the other" with less conflict and resistance, to train and survey native allies as "cultural brokers" and to impose their language, religion and ways of life with less bloodshed and more cooperation from locals. No total control needs to be assumed, or mean intension a priori, as for example, many individual missionaries turned themselves into the first ethnographers. They were a more benign kind of cultural brokers who made, in fact, remarkable contributions to understand indigenous populations, including the writing of first grammars of unknown indigenous languages (mostly in Africa and México). In some cases, these "unintentional" ethnographers demanded human rights for the indigenous communities they worked with, as the case in the Caribbean of the catholic priest Fray Ramón Pané and father Bartolomé de las Casas in the island of Hispaniola (today Dominican Republic and Haiti).

Hence, claiming a purity or respectable "objective" tradition of *doing ethnography*, reflects a lack of awareness of this problematic ethno-historical context, which the Haitian anthropologist Michel-Rolph Trouillot has examined, in a seminal article about the "savage slot" or otherness trope in anthropology (2003). Trouillot traces and analyses how anthropology was made possible by the colonial enterprise as well as by intellectual trends of institutionalization in the social sciences, which needed Sociology and other disciplines to focus on Western societies and its "civilized" internal others in the emergent capitalist system between the 16th and 19th centuries, while anthropology was to take care of the uncivilized colonial others. Trouillot concept of "colonial discursive fields" is useful in this regard to understand how scientific-academic knowledge is produced in very specific ethno-historical contexts, and the fact that he made his critique from inside the anthropological discipline, gives it a very particular taste of poetic justice. He was part of a new generation of minority and indigenous scholars needed to carve out—from the inside—spaces from where their very presence and the validity of their research were possible. As Trouillot suggest, they needed first to problematize and change the ethnographic "savage slot" tropes—*where* the field is, and who the *objects* of study could be for this discipline. They also needed to question ethnographic objectivity claims, the "common sense" of colonial western rationality, and the notion of a fixed lineal development of human societies and progress, in which white supremacy and other Euro-centric tenets were privileged.

The critique of classical ethnography that I have offered above, is not meant to invalidate the work of any scholars or to propose discarding anthropology as a valid career choice. I consider anthropology one of the most promising academic fields, of crucial relevance for our current predicaments in this century and in the future. Yet, I am aware of the problematic origins of this discipline as a colonial tool and of its complicity with the exploitation and violence—direct and symbolic—of capitalism by Euro-American imperial regimes. The fact that I became an anthropologist—as an "other," a Caribbean immigrant woman—unthinkable even for 1960s academic contexts in the US, is a sign of my trust and hope on the liberation potential of this practice and on its usefulness to help us create more just and sustainable worlds, where human differences are not just tolerated but recognized, understood, protected and celebrated.

On the Uses of Ethnography: Feminist, Critical and Post-Colonial Ethnographies

Contemporary ethnography exhibits a wide and diverse range of fieldwork methods mixtures (from applied action research to digital ethnography), and also a diversity of narrative styles in the production and dissemination of academic findings (from self-reflexive, postmodern hybrid texts to performance and ethnographic exhibitions). Critical ethnography and Post-Critical Ethnography refer to post-structural, post-colonial and feminist ethnographic praxis, informed by performance and gender/sexuality theorizations coming from diverse disciplines, which had their boom since the 2000s (see Foley 2002, Ortner 1996). Yet, this kind of radical critical ethnographic approach is still not the mainstream in the practice of anthropology, nor among many ethnographers in the US and beyond. The post, in post-critical ethnography (see Noblit, Flores & Murillo 2004), points to the need of an anthropology relevant to understand a post 1990s world, but sadly, given 911 legacies and more recent events in US political "devolvement" (such as the Trump administration), it becomes even more needed now.

Concrete and virtual fields have fuzzy boundaries of where/when "home" and the "field" begin and end (see Gupta & Ferguson 1997). Our experience as ethnographers is shaped by who we are as specific humans, that is why our cultural history needs to be taken into consideration in the research design, during fieldwork and data gathering, since this affects how we interpret data, and the kinds of narratives and representations of "others" we create when sharing our academic findings with particular publics. A critical ethnographer is always interdisciplinary, concerned with a wider global vision, yet, invested in the local narrow focus of cultural specificity. This wider vision is basic to understand the unity of our shared human experiences, and the narrow focus help us dislodge essentialized determinisms to show situated experiences, from particular perspectives, evidencing the diversity as inseparable from our unity. For example, as a critical feminist ethnographer, I design research projects that ask open-ended *how* and *what* questions. There are some ethno-historical *whys*—in conversation with the ethnographic present—that arise out of answering *what* and *how* types of questions that can be proposed as possible interpretations, and it is from there that I generate theoretical contributions.

Investing time to choose ethically our toolkits for research help us design projects that are valid, relevant, situated, engaged and grounded on process—fieldwork as cultural encounter—as well as in the more general outcomes and implications of our topic of analysis. As the main instruments of research, ethnographers are immersed in the same matrixes of power and cultural ethnocentrisms as the study participants, although occupying different power locations. Feminist critical ethnographers focus, hence, on understanding the embodied experiences of our collaborators, not abstract a priori identities, but practices performance and narratives, places-environments-relations, communicative interactions and silences, mapping routes and movements, as well as the materiality—objects of daily use—of ordinary as well as sacred artifacts (from cooking pots to the cell phone). The naming of the individuals we work *with* is also important for a feminist critical ethnographer; from the use of "informants" we have moved to participants or "collaborators." The term informant was widely used in early anthropology and later by the CIA in his undercover surveillance, aptly referring to individuals that in one way or another informed on their people to those that were paying them. Changing the way we name the people we work with is not a semantic frivolity, but an alignment with the shift from "objects" of study to "subjects" that are social agents, whose willingness to work with us and their invaluable help are essential for the completion of any ethnographic project. This part of our ethical mandate honors the dignity of these humans and help us keep re-inventing an ethnographic practice that could be useful beyond academia.

This kind of ethnographic intervention is more a "caring-witnessing" and an engaged practice that requires also a new name, hence I use the term "deep hanging-out" (this is a form of critical "observant-participation," as Joao Costa Vargas suggests). For example, during fieldwork my intention is to be aware and attentive to an embodied field practice that foregrounds place, spatial relations of bodies, communication and practices, material culture and movements. Through narrative-focused elicitation, dialogue and oral histories, I document my collaborators perspectives, while participating and learning the local daily choreographies that they follow throughout a day. This renaming is more widely used among feminist anthropologists, as does the often used "rich point" (a challenging moment of research through which we find a new insight to redirect the project, see Agar 2006, 2004, 1986, for a discussion of this). Rich points are many and useful, and go beyond re-directing the course of our projects, it is inseparable from the micro-politics of fieldwork, and how the personal becomes essential to take into account in project design and in the process of fieldwork. For example, Caribbean food practices and cuisine are by-products of the "Columbian exchange" and colonization, as well as of the plantation slavery regime. It would be hard to understand and explain the ethno-present of *bacalao* (Norwegian dried-salted codfish) consumption in the communities I work with as a cultural "choice." But it is my "native" status, my familiarity with the Caribbean, with its colonial ethno-history and cultural practices, as well as knowing the actual taste of bacalao, what allows me to make to make fine-grained observations during fieldwork and later careful analysis of the food data.

"Theory in the Flesh": Genealogies for a Critical Ethnographic Praxis

Ethnography has been test-driven, revised, and refined by many within and outside anthropology, and there are diverse genealogies according to our training and to the scholarly works that each anthropologist was exposed to during their graduate training. It is important to clarify that methodological choices are never separated from theoretical framings, nor from the wider vision we hold for the kinds of work we wish to create; this means that *how* we perceive the people, places and topics we are researching will have a direct effect how we conduct our research and the tools we select for fieldwork.

I would have not learned to be the kind of ethnographer that I am, without the interdisciplinary—and somehow chaotic—theoretical and methodological formation that I created by chance and intention. Hence, the genealogy that I share below includes sources that go beyond ethnography or qualitative methodologies. I have chosen some landmark experiences, in my own graduate education, which helped me develop a toolkit to design my dissertation project, and ever since marked profoundly research and my teaching practice. As students we are not a tabula rasa; we already bring knowledge, skills and the cultural capital of experiences that have shaped who we are becoming. I brought also resources to graduate school, acquired during my undergraduate education in Puerto Rico that also influenced the kind of academic literature that was more appealing to me. For example, I had been exposed to the powerful writings of Caribbean and Latin American scholars who had a tremendous influence in my commitment to critical research and academic writing, among them Aníbal Ponce, Eduardo Galeano, Franz Fanon, Aimée Cesaire, and Emeterio Betances, among others. I do not discuss the contributions of these "teacher-mentors" here (for details about my educational routes, see Chapter Four and the Bonus Track). Below I discuss authors that I encountered during the completion of my graduate studies in anthropology at the University of Texas at Austin.

Among the classical anthropologists, Claude Levi-Strauss (1963) was the most readable for me; I enjoyed learning about his Marxist-structuralism legacy that has been so powerful and necessary for us to get to the post-structural and post-colonial de-centering of western grand narratives. He was not, however, interested in ethnography per se, but his brilliant insights in other areas compensated for that. Clifford Geertz's concept of "thick description," proposing the need for interpretive analysis of fieldwork data and deeper contextualization of the "realist" storytelling aspect of ethnography, had a tremendous impact in ethnographic research and writings, and was hopeful to me (see 1973). I appreciate also the way he paid attention to the "trifles" of everyday life in his fieldwork, as necessary for "thick description" (2008), and for his poetic interpretations in reporting his ethnographic findings. He published also a book (strangely invisible in debates) about the anthropologist as creative author (see 1988). It was, however, a series of chance encounters with certain authors that marked my decision to complete my degree in anthropology. As it has probably become obvious, those years of my anthropology and ethnography training were very intense; indeed, there was a lot of crying and existential crisis, that helped me grow tremendously, and for which I am deeply grateful today.

The seminal article by the Mexican-American anthropologist Renato Rosaldo (1983) about headhunters' rage (when loosing a dear person in war), was an important landmark in my formation. In that article he reflected about his own rage about the death of his wife, during his fieldwork research with the Illongots in Luzon, Philippines in the 1960–1970s. This moving and poignant self-reflection made a great impact in my conception of the separation between "field" and "home," and about ethnographic narratives. I saw an example of the powerful writing that can be produced when the ethnographer (who is the main instrument of research and not an objective, neutral machine) becomes a visible aspect of reporting our research findings. Dorinne Kondo's works were a revelation to me, through her *Crafting Selves* book, and especially, through reading her reflexive journal article "Dissolution and reconstitution of self" (1986), both based on her fieldwork research on gender and power in a Japanese workplace. Her Japanese-American experience in the country of her parents, her approach to ethnography and her powerful writing voice, had a crucial impact in my understanding of the complexity of ethnography, in my research practice, as well as in my writings. Kirin Narayan, an Indian-American anthropologist, through one of her self-reflexive articles (1993), helped me question our roles as "native" anthropologists, who study in communities with whom we share a common language and cultural history, and to understand critically our assumptions about difference and familiarity, and how false dichotomies of self/other, home/field are even more problematic for those of us in such positions (see also Jacob-Huey 2002). In a similar fashion, the problematizing of Kamala Visweswaran (1994) of the micro-politics of fieldwork for feminist anthropologists warned me of the dangers of assuming commonalities a priori, and the need to be critical of power differences, in spite of shared women's experiences, in and outside of the "field."

By a citation chance, I came across the work of Ruth Behar, a Jewish-Cuban-American anthropologist, through her book *Translated Woman* (1993) and her article about "anthropology that breaks your heart" (1996), based on her fieldwork with Esperanza (an ethnographic project focusing on only one person, but crowded with other humans surrounding her), taught me the benefits of an extreme form of focused "deep hanging-out," and about the challenges of validity when our research sampling is very small (for further discussion of this see 1999). I also found in her work an echo of how emotionally challenging is to do work with marginalized individuals, to feel our impotence to help, and the delicate ethical negotiations of doing so even if we could. Other works, found through my graduate courses, have also been significant for designing my feminist critical ethnographic practice. The fierce poetics in the queer writings of Jafari Allen (2007), Audre Lorde (1984) and bell hooks (2000), taught me to dare to express my ethnographic voice, beyond a mere academic reflexivity, and to have the courage to also admit my limitations, contradictions and vulnerabilities, so the reader could best judge the accountability of my work.

Important also for my ethnographic understanding and practice were the work of Faye Harrison (see 1991, 1997), her radical approach to de-colonize anthropology and ethnographic practice and her focus on Afro-diasporas in the Caribbean. In fact, I assign now to my graduate students the article "ethnography as politics" (1991) as the best training ground before they go "into the field." In the work of Haitian anthropologist Gina A. Ulysse (2007) I found a wonderful example of radical, post-colonial and critical feminist ethnography, that showed me the path to finish my dissertation. The book of Arlene Davila, *Latinos Inc* (2006), was crucial for me to understand the media production apparatus going beyond a semiotic analysis of representations, as well as to understand how and when Dominicans in NYC engaged with this pan-ethnicity label, and the role of media in identity politics. I later found other relevant works of hers, in particular related to Latinx ethnic enclaves or barrios (2003) and language and culture of Latinx in media (2000), as I had noticed that many ads and programs used food as metaphor. Davila helped me understand the complexity of ethnicity as cultural identity, specifically the emergence and transformations of the "Hispanic" and "Latino" labels, as problematic pan-ethnicity claims agglutinating a great diversity within immigrant populations and their descendants, as well as those "Hispanics" who resided, for example in New Mexico and other states which used to be part of México until the 19th century, when the US took over those territories ("we didn't cross the border, the border crossed us").

Since audiovisual data was central to my project and to my approach to research, I searched related methods and found visual anthropology. The focus of this fringe sub-field was on ethnographic films (produced mostly by professional filmmakers in collaboration with ethnographers), it was a bit disappointing to me. However soon I found works by anthropologists that used audiovisual methods as central part of their ethnographic fieldwork (see Pink 2013, 2015). I found, as well, critiques of visual anthropology that open other doors unknown to me and that became, eventually, important in my teaching also. For example, the work of Faye Ginsburg I found by accident, and then kept looking for more. I had to show the film *Atanarjuat* (The Long Runner) for a course where I was the teaching assistant. I didn't know anything about that film or indigenous media, and I watched in awe.

I began looking for references, to help me understand what I had just watched, and found Ginsburg article (2003) and then her other writings on indigenous media and visual anthropology (see 1997 and 1998) . I have since found also her work with Rayna Rapp (an early feminist anthropologist that I had read before) on disability, and this work I assign now in some of my courses.

Other complementary sources were also needed, which I found through interdisciplinary works such as Donna Haraway (1988). For problematizing issues of "home" an article by Chandra Mohanty and Emily Martin (1986) and the work of Sarah Ahmed (1999) were significant for me, as they addressed clearly through their arguments concerns that I had in researching migrant senses of home. I rejoiced when I found memory studies scholars, such as Maurice Hallbachs (1992), Pierre Nora (1989) and Henri Lefebvre (1991), but it was the book *Cultural Memory: Recall from the Present* (see Bal et al. 1999), that gave me the critical understanding I needed on cultural memory and memory-work. I found the *grounding* I was looking for in place/space through two edited volumes, one by the anthropologist Setha Low (2003) and another by Gupta and Ferguson (1997). Yet it was through the more radical approaches of feminist political ecologists such as Dorine Massey, Nancy Fraser and Nancy Duncan (see Duncan 1996, for a discussion of the basics of this approach) that the relevance of these dimensions became clear to me and gave me the tools to analyze critically the place-data. I felt that I still needed more concrete methodological ways of researching place/space dimensions during fieldwork, which were not a focus in the anthropology courses I was taking. That is when I found the work of Maria Elisa Christie, a cultural geographer doing ecological mappings of house gardens in Mexico (see Christie 2003 and 2004), by taking a course in the geography department (where she was an instructor). Christie's work echoes the 'sensual ethnography' first proposed by Stoller (1989).

As I continued expanding my searches, to best design my ethnographic projects, I found many other authors, unsuspected mentors, who helped me gather and develop my own toolkits and approaches to fieldwork. The food research of anthropologist Carole Counihan taught me how to foreground gendered labor with the richness of her ethnographic accounts, and her scholarly contributions have become for me a "founding mother" legacy that I teach students through my food courses. Her humbleness and accessibility in mentorship of new food scholars is also legendary; I have seen many young faces illuminated with gratitude at the sole mention of her name. Without Counihan and Penny Van Esterik (1997) pioneering work on food, body and gender many of us would have had to re-invent the wheel. The book *Tangled Routes* by Deborah Barndt (2002), about the tomato trail (from production to consumption) and the Mexican women workers lives invested in that chain), came late into my life, as a gift of my mentor Polly Strong upon passing my dissertation defense. This book has become very influential for refining my food mapping method and one chapter Whose Choice? has become a "staple reading" that I assign regularly in my food courses (according to their testimony, my students benefit greatly from her style of analysis).

Through the Center for African & African-American Studies, I found how crucial African Diaspora paradigms were for understanding the Caribbean and its diasporas in the US (I discuss this further in Chapter Four). The work of Kevin Yelvington is crucial to understand the global social formations and racialization from and of the Caribbean, yet it was one article in particular "The anthropology of Afro-Latin America and the Caribbean: diasporic dimensions" (2001), that helped me to understand intersections of race, gender, class and national formations in the region. Although a long and rich work to digest (and difficult essay for undergraduate students to decipher, as I have found out), it works well as a literature review about African diasporas in the Americas, an argument for the significance of the Caribbean for anthropology and a discussion about the wider US debates on Blackness. Mintz and Price's *The birth of African-American culture: An anthropological perspective* (1976), helped me understand the multi-dimensional complexities of Caribbean cultural formations beyond a simplistic creolization or African survival debate, showing that the Caribbean was "… a unique region where people under the stress of slavery had to improvise, invent and literally create [new] forms of human [socio-cultural organization]…" (1976: 84).

The work of Aisha Khan was a breath of fresh air, her understanding of the significance of the Caribbean for anthropological studies and for understanding a globalized planet, is best expressed through her own words, "the world is catching up to the Caribbean" (2001: 1) and for her attention to food in the Caribbean (see 1994). The works of Michel-Rolph Trouillot, Kevin Yelvington and Sidney Mintz became pieces of a puzzle that I needed to make sense of, to produce the kind of research I wanted to develop around food, place-memory and Dominican migration to New York City. These works influenced my research and my teaching ever since, as they helped me clarified my focus on the Caribbean, its significance to understand processes of globalization and the contribution of the region to an anthropology of the African Diaspora in the Americas. Trouillot's book *Silencing the Past* (1995), specifically his theorizations of power and the "silences" of archives, gave me the first clues to historical imagination in the Caribbean and to ethno-history as sources I needed for my work (together with his writings on anthropology and the "savage slot" already discussed). These works have become regular staples also in my teaching, as I assign them at the least provocation. Even though I read other works of Trouillot (e.g., his work about the Haitian Diaspora in NYC), I was not impressed by its ethnographic approach or the writings of such accounts, as I found them surprisingly dull and devoid of the powerful wit and sharpness of his more critical ethno-historical writings.

Sidney Mintz's remarkable work about sugar, plantation slavery and power (1986) as a global staple beyond the Caribbean, helped me recognize the necessity of an ethno-historical analysis to understand the "ethnographic present" of Caribbean diasporas in the United States. Mintz shows as a good teacher, rather than directly theorized; he sprinkled his analysis with tiny ethnographic gems from his fieldwork in the Caribbean. The work of Mintz has become central to my food research but also in my teaching of food and Caribbean related courses. In particular, I appreciate his analysis of plantation slavery through food production, as it foregrounds the implications of the centrality of time, labor and geopolitics for theorizing negotiations of power under the new Capitalist mode of production (which had its first experiments precisely in the Caribbean). His beautiful chapter "Tasting food, tasting freedom" (1996), moved me deeply, and it became a watershed to clarify my desire for a critical food studies approach, and for the kinds of methodological contributions that I wanted to make to this field. Rarely do we get to cry reading academic writings ... I cried reading this chapter, stopping and re-reading, as if to make sure I was not hallucinating ... someone had already saved me so much work by analyzing the tremendous significance of food globally and in Caribbean histories and experiences, the emergence of a creative and new regional cuisine, and its connection to slaves and their descendants' struggle for survival, freedom and dignity. Mintz gave me also so many clues through this work, to understand the continuing racialization of this food-memory-history in the Caribbean present, the struggles and hopes of Dominican migrant women in NYC, and why they cherished their hard-earned foods, and for understanding even my own family food practices ... what a gift!

I encountered Critical Ethnography late in my training. It was, in fact, through the publications and contributions of education and rhetoric scholars that I was first exposed to this version of ethnographic fieldwork (see Anderson 1989, Foley 2002). In 2006, the anthropologist Soyini Madison's *Critical Ethnography and Performance* book was first published. By then, I have been gathering trends and fragments of a critical toolkit to guide me in the kind of engaged feminist and post-colonial work that I wanted to produce. My early *bricolage* of many disparate strands was promising, yet unwieldy. Finding that there was already a community of scholars, with new approaches to ethnography and to other qualitative methodologies, who also addressed many of my theoretical concerns, was a gift. This discovery helped me to focus my contributions on refining my interdisciplinary approaches, cooking up into that mixture the visual methodologies from my previous training, as well as mapping methods, relevant to develop critical food research (which lead me eventually to develop *foodmaps* method). It was from this experience that I began channeling those insights into my teaching practice, choosing an auto-ethnographic project-based and place-based approach. Initially, when exposed to classical ethnographic works in my graduate courses, in spite of appreciating their contributions, I mostly learned from them what I did not want to do and how I would not want to write about my research findings. These older ethnographic styles made me doubt if anthropology was for me, and if I wished to use a tool soiled with such colonial prejudices. Fortunately, I found other interdisciplinary works, which taught me to question the potential and limitations of ethnography as a methodology, and clarified how I could develop a form of engaged scholarship committed to ethical fieldwork and critical cultural analysis, and this eventually had an effect on my choosing a teaching style that foregrounds commitment to civil rights, respect for differences, and struggles for social justice locally and globally.

Many of the authors discussed in this informal genealogy were considered "minorities" due to their own cultural histories or diasporic origins and, hence, their mere existence influenced how I perceived my own problematic relationship to anthropology, my presence in this discipline and in academia, more broadly, since I was also an outsider, a working-class Dominican immigrant studying, of all places, in Texas. These outsider-within scholars represented for me a sense of hope and relief, a certainty that I was where I should be. The scholars discussed in above, and many more that I had to leave out, inspired a commitment to keep refining my ethnographic approach, to engaged scholarship and ethics, and a desire to produce powerful writings whenever I share my research findings. These authors have been mentors-teachers to me, even if, in the majority of cases, we have never met; in a sense, this is a thank you and homage to them, for what they have done, through their work, for me and for other minority scholars. Although some authors who I have discussed are not ethnographers, and the reader might be asking, what do those works have to do with ethnography? I hope it has become clear, that ethnography is an interdisciplinary praxis, and that, in order to be a good critical ethnographer "in the field," we need to also become a critical scholar outside of it. In sharpening our understanding of the human condition, we sharpen also our "ethnographic eye."

References

Agar, M. (2006, September). An ethnography by any other name ... *Forum Qualitative Sozialforschung/Forum: Qualitative Social Research*, 7(4).

Agar, M. (2004). We have met the other and we're all nonlinear: Ethnography as a nonlinear dynamic system. *Complexity, 10*(2), 16–24.

Agar, M. (1996). *The professional stranger: An informal introduction to ethnography*. New York: Academic Press.

Agar, M. (1986). *Speaking of ethnography* (Vol. 2). Newbury Park: Sage.

Ahmed, S. (1999). Home and away: Narratives of migration and estrangement. *International Journal of Cultural Studies, 2*(3), 329–347.

Allen, J. S. (2007). Means of desire's production: Male sex labor in Cuba. *Identities: Global Studies in Power and Culture, 14*(1–1), 183–202.

Anderson, Gary. (1989, Fall). Critical ethnography in education: Origins, current status, and new directions. *Review of Educational Research, 59*(3), 249–270.

Bal, M., Crewe, J. V., & Spitzer, L. (1999). *Acts of memory: Cultural recall in the present*. Hanover: Upne.

Barndt, D. (2002). *Tangled routes: Women, work, and globalization on the tomato trail*. Lanham: Rowman & Littlefield.

Behar, R. (1993). *Translated woman: Crossing the border with Esperanza's story*. Boston: Beacon Press.

Behar, R. (1996). *The vulnerable observer: Ethnography that breaks your heart*. Boston: Beacon Press.

Behar, R. (1999). Ethnography: Cherishing our second-fiddle genre. *Journal of Contemporary Ethnography, 28*(5), 472–484.

Benedict, R. (2005). *Patterns of culture* (Vol. 8). Boston: Houghton Mifflin Harcourt.

Boas, F. (1989). *A Franz Boas reader: the shaping of American anthropology, 1883–1911*. Chicago: University of Chicago Press.

Boas, F., & Codere, H. (1966). *Kwakiutl ethnography*. Chicago: University of Chicago Press.

Brown, S. G., & Dobrin, S. I. (2004). *Ethnography unbound: From theory shock to critical praxis*. Albany: SUNY Press.

Chang, H. (2008). *Autoethnography as method: Developing qualitative inquiry series*. Walnut Creek, CA: Left Coast Press.

Clifford, J., & Marcus, G. E. (Eds.). (1986). *Writing culture: The poetics and politics of ethnography*. Berkeley: University of California Press.

Christie, M. E. (2003). *Kitchenspace: gendered spaces for cultural reproduction, or, nature in the everyday lives of ordinary women in central Mexico* (UT-Austin, Doctoral dissertation).

Christie, M. E. (2004). Kitchenspace, Fiestas, and Cultural Reproduction in Mexican Houselot Gardens. *Geographical Review, 94*(3), 368–390.

Counihan, C., & Van Esterik, P. (Eds.). (1997). *Food and culture: A reader* (1st ed.). New York: Routledge.

Counihan, C. M., & Kaplan, S. L. (2003). *Food and gender: Identity and power*. London: Routledge.

Dávila, A. (2006). *Latinos, Inc.: The marketing and making of a people*. Berkeley: University of California Press.

Dávila, A. (2003, spring). Dreams of place: Housing, gentrification, and the marketing of space in El Barrio. *Centro Journal, XV*. Accessed at: http://www.redalyc.org/articulo.oa?id=37715106

Dávila, A. (2000). Mapping Latinidad: Language and culture in the Spanish TV battlefront. *Television & New Media, 1*(1), 75–94.

Delgado, R., & Stefancic, J. (2001). *Critical race theory: An introduction.* New York: New York University Press.

Denzin, N. K. (1999). Interpretive ethnography for the next century. *Journal of Contemporary Ethnography, 28*(5), 510–519.

Duncan, N. (1996). *BodySpace: Destabilizing geographies of gender and sexuality.* Psychology Press.

Evans-Pritchard, E. E. (1940). *The nuer* (Vol. 940). Clarendon: Oxford.

Foley, D. E. (2002). Critical ethnography: The reflexive turn. *International Journal of Qualitative Studies in Education, 15*(4), 469–490.

Fortier, A. M., Ahmed, S., Castaneda, C., & Sheller, M. (2003). *Uprootings/Regroundings: Questions of home and migration.* New York: Berg.

Fraser, N. (1990). Rethinking the public sphere: A contribution to the critique of actually existing democracy. *Social Text,* (25/26), 56–80.

Geertz, C. (1988). *Works and lives: The anthropologist as author.* Stanford: Stanford University Press.

Geertz, C. (2008). Thick description: Toward an interpretive theory of culture. In Timothy Oakes, & Patricia L. Price (Eds.), *The cultural geography reader* (pp. 41–51). New York: Routledge.

Ginsburg, F. (2003). Atanarjuat off-screen: From "media reservations" to the World stage. *American Anthropologist, 105*(4), 827–831.

Ginsburg, F. (1998) Institutionalizing the unruly: Charting a future for visual anthropology. *Ethnos, 63*(2), 173–201. doi: 10.1080/00141844.1998.9981571

Ginsburg, F. (1997). "From little things, big things grow": Indigenous media and cultural activism. In D. Fox, & O. Starn (Eds.), *Between resistance and revolution.* New Brunswick: Rutgers University Press.

Gupta, A., & Ferguson, J. (1997). *Anthropological locations: Boundaries and grounds of a field science.* Berkeley: University of California Press.

Gupta, A., & Ferguson, J. (1997). *Culture, power, place: Explorations in critical anthropology.* Durham: Duke University Press.

Halbwachs, M. (1992). The social frameworks of memory. In L. Coser (Ed.), *On collective memory* (pp. 35–189). Chicago: University of Chicago Press.

Haraway, D. (1988). Situated knowledges: The science question in feminism and the privilege of partial perspective. *Feminist Studies, 14*(3), 575–599.

Harrison, F. V. (2008). *Outsider within: Reworking anthropology in the global age.* Urbana: University of Illinois Press.

Harrison, F. V. (1993). Writing against the grain: Cultural politics of difference in the work of Alice Walker. *Critique of Anthropology, 13*(4), 401–427.

Harrison, F. V. (1991). Ethnography as politics. In *Decolonizing anthropology: Moving further toward an anthropology for liberation* (pp. 88–109). Virginia: American Anthropological Association.

Harrison, F. V. (1997). *Decolonizing anthropology: Moving further toward an anthropology of liberation.* Arlington, VA: Association of Black Anthropologists, American Anthropological Association.

Harrison, F. V. (1991). Women in Jamaica's urban informal economy. In *Third world women and the politics of feminism* (Vol. 632, p. 173). Bloomington: Indiana University Press.

Hesse-Biber, S. N., Gilmartin, C. K., & Lydenberg, R. (1999). *Feminist approaches to theory and methodology: An interdisciplinary reader.* New York: Oxford University Press.

Hill-Collins, P. (2002). *Black feminist thought: Knowledge, consciousness, and the politics of empowerment.* New York: Routledge.

Hirsch, M., & Spitzer, L. (2002). We would not have come without you: Generations of Nostalgia. *American Imago, 59*(3), 253–276.

Hoelscher, S., & Alderman, D. H. (2004). Memory and place: Geographies of a critical relationship. *Social & Cultural Geography, 5*(3), 347–355.

hooks, b. (2000). *Feminism is for everybody: Passionate politics.* London: Pluto Press.

Hurston, Z. N. (1935). Mules and men, Florida: J. B. Lippincott Company.

Kroeber, A. L., & Kluckhohn, C. (1952). *Culture: A critical review of concepts and definitions.* Papers. Peabody Museum of Archaeology & Ethnology, Harvard University.

Jacobs-Huey, L. (2002). The natives are gazing and talking back: Rewriting the problematics of Positionality, voice, and accountability among 'native' ethnographers. *American Anthropologist 104*(3) 791–804.

Khan, A. (2001). Journey to the center of the earth: The Caribbean as master symbol. *Cultural Anthropology, 16*(3), 271–302.

Khan, A. (1994). Juthaa in Trinidad: Food, pollution, and hierarchy in a Caribbean diaspora community. *American Ethnologist, 21*(2), 245–269.

Kincheloe, J. L., & McLaren, P. (2011). Rethinking critical theory and qualitative research. In *Key works in critical pedagogy* (pp. 285–326). Rotterdam: Sense Publishers.

Kondo, D. K. (1986). Dissolution and reconstitution of self: Implications for anthropological epistemology. *Cultural anthropology, 1*(1), 74–88.

Lefebvre, H. (1991). *The production of space* (Vol. 142). Oxford: Blackwell.

Lévi-Strauss, C., & Layton, M. (1963). *Structural anthropology* (Vol. 1, pp. 213–216). New York: Basic books.

Lorde, A. (1984). *Sister outsider: Essays and speeches.* New York: Crossing Press.

Low, S. M. (2003). *The anthropology of place.* Oxford: Blackwell.

Madison, D. S. (2006). *Critical ethnography: Method, ethics, and performance.* Thousand Oaks: Sage.

Malinowski, B. (2002). *Argonauts of the Western Pacific: An account of native enterprise and adventure in the archipelagoes of Melanesian New Guinea.* London: Routledge. [first published in 1922].

Malinowski, B. (1967). *A Diary in the strict sense of the term.* New York: Harcourt, Brace, and World.

Marcus, G. E., & Fischer, M. M. (1999). *Anthropology as cultural critique: An experimental moment in the human sciences.* Chicago: University of Chicago Press.

Martin, B., & Mohanty, C. T. (1986). Feminist politics: What's home got to do with it? *Feminisms: An anthology of literary theory and criticism,* 293–310.

Mead, M. (1963). *Sex and temperament in three primitive societies* (Vol. 370). New York: Morrow.

Minh-Ha, T. T. (1989). *Women, native, other. Writing, Post-coloniality and Feminism.* Bloomington: University of Indiana Press.

Mintz, S. W. (1996). *Tasting food, tasting freedom. Tasting food, tasting freedom: Excursions into eating, culture, and the past.* Boston: Beacon Press.

Mintz, S. W. (1986). *Sweetness and power: The place of sugar in modern history.* New York: Penguin.

Mintz, S. W., & Price, R. (1976). *The birth of African-American culture: An anthropological perspective* (Vol. 2). Boston: Beacon Press.

Mohanty, C. T. (2003). *Feminism without borders: Decolonizing theory, practicing solidarity.* New Delhi: Zubaan.

Narayan, Kirin. (1993, September). How "native" is a 'native anthropologist? *American Anthropologist,* New Series, 95(3), 671–686.

Noblit, G. W., Flores, S. Y., & Murillo, E. G. (2004). *Post-critical Ethnography: Re-inscribing Critique.* New York: Hampton Press.

Nora, P. (1989). Between memory and history: Les lieux de mémoire. *Representations,* 26, 7–24.

Ortner, S. B. (2006). *Anthropology and social theory: Culture, power, and the acting subject.* Durham: Duke University Press.

Ortner, S. B. (1996). *Making gender: The politics and erotics of culture.* Boston: Beacon Press.

Ortner, S. B. (1995). Resistance and the problem of ethnographic refusal. *Comparative Studies in Society and History,* 37(1), 173–193.

Ortner, S. B. (1984). Theory in anthropology since the sixties. *Comparative Studies in Society and History,* 26(1), 126–166.

Pink, S. (2015). *Doing sensory ethnography.* London: Sage.

Pink, S. (2013). *Doing visual ethnography.* Los Angeles: Sage.

Rich, A. (1984). Notes towards a politics of location. In *Feminist postcolonial theory: A reader* (pp. 29–42).

Rohner, R. P. (1966). Franz Boas: Ethnographer on the northwest coast. In *Pioneers of American anthropology* (pp. 149–212).

Rosaldo, R. (1994). Cultural citizenship and educational democracy. *Cultural Anthropology,* 9(3), 402–411.

Rosaldo, R. (1989). Introduction: Grief and a headhunter's rage. In *Culture and truth: The remaking of social analysis* (pp. 1–21). [first published in 1983 in Am anthropologist]

Rosaldo, R. (1983). Grief and the Headhunters' Rage. In E. M. Bruner (ed.), *Text, play and story*. Washington, DC: American Anthropological Association.

Spry, T. (2006). A "performative-I" co-presence: Embodying the ethnographic turn in performance and the performative turn in ethnography. *Text and Performance Quarterly, 26*(4), 339–346.

Stocking, G. W. (Ed.). (1996). *Volksgeist as method and ethic: Essays on Boasian ethnography and the German anthropological tradition* (Vol. 8). Madison: University of Wisconsin Press.

Stoller, P. (1989). *The taste of ethnographic things: The senses in anthropology*. Philadelphia: University of Pennsylvania Press.

Trouillot, M. R. (1995). *Silencing the past: Power and the production of history*. Boston: Beacon Press.

Trouillot, M. R. (2003). Anthropology and the savage slot: The poetics and politics of otherness. In *Global transformations* (pp. 7–28). New York: Palgrave Macmillan.

Ulysse, G. A. (2007). *Downtown ladies: Informal commercial importers, a Haitian anthropologist and self-making in Jamaica*. Chicago: University of Chicago Press.

Vargas, J. H. C. (2006). *Catching hell in the City of Angels: Life and meanings of blackness In South Central Los Angeles* (*critical American studies*). New York: University of Minnesota Press.

Visweswaran, K. (1994). *Fictions of feminist ethnography*. Minneapolis: University of Minnesota Press.

Yelvington, K. A. (2001). The anthropology of Afro-Latin America and the Caribbean: diasporic dimensions. *Annual Review of Anthropology, 30*(1), 227–260.

CHAPTER TWO

Critical Auto-ethnography

Mapping Personal Root and Routes through "Native" Ethnography

The Personal is Political

(Feminist saying)

Introduction and Framings

Similarly of what I did in Chapter One, my intention is to use this more "academically informed" chapter, as a reference aid for readers to understand terms used in Chapter Three. In contrast to Chapter One, which is about *Ethnography*, this chapter is about *Auto-ethnography*; my focus in this chapter is to explain basic definitions and characteristics of auto-ethnography, with a brief tour of its emergence and development within and outside of anthropology, and its current status as an interdisciplinary methodology and narrative genre. I offer also my own definitions, based on the tailored version of *critical auto-ethnography* that I have been using in the classroom. In addition, I explain how I use auto-ethnographic projects to support a project-based, research-centered and place-based critical pedagogy practice. I conclude with a discussion of some theoretical framings (such as intersectional analysis, critical race theory, and ethno-semiotics) that are necessary to turn biographic data, from memoirs into auto-ethnographic critical cultural analysis that goes beyond the personal to the political.

The phrase "the personal is political" could be the most appropriate way to open this chapter on Auto-ethnography methodology, a research approach that places the researcher at the center of an investigation, and a writing style that openly uses the first person voice to report research findings. This now popular saying is usually associate with second wave feminist movements and publications of the 1970s; of uncertain origins, it is usually attributed to Carol Hanisch, due to her essay in 1970, in which she used it as a title, but the meaning implicated was discussed before and after by many other authors. Basically, it refers to how personal experiences (not only those of women) are shaped by the social locations that individuals occupy within systems of power relations. It foregrounds the significance of the social to understand the self, the collective to understand the individual, and vice versa, how the "public" is implicated in the "private," and how all humans are social agents actively engaged within a matrix of power relations. As I say to my students, the private is so crowded, it is scandously public (as sodomy laws so clearly reveal), and public is always lived by particular subjects, from their individual locations (as an individual decision by a senator or a governor in office can reveal). Auto-ethnography is a methodology that allows us to map, concretely and symbolically, the personal roots and routes of a particular of how a particular topic (such as foodways or gendered identity) have unfolded in our lives, and the significance of that journey for our present experiences. In this sense it is centering the personal, the private self, to examine the public, the wider social contexts that have made possible an individual life. Because auto-ethnographic fieldwork research is done from wherever we are, it is always a form of "native" ethnography, this means it is done from our the local grounds of where we live, how we earn our living, our family and community networks, and place-making, the ways we navigate local place.

As the reader might already suspect, auto-ethnographic methodologies have been more easily embraced by interdisciplinary scholars of any field, that come from specific social locations, such as Indigenous, Africa-American, Latinx, Queer, functionally diverse scholars and other *alter-native* ethnographers entering the "fields" of academia as a profession. They (we) are the "others" who come from communities that used to be the usual *objects* of study of mainstream ethnographers. As part of these grouping of scholars, my understanding and evaluation of auto-ethnography are not meant to be authoritative. In a sense, these are my own auto-ethnographic (pun intended) interpretations shaped by the particularities of my academic training, my research and teaching praxis and my own cultural history. Many other possible stories of auto-ethnography can be traced from other perspectives (henceforth POVs), shaped as well by other authors' own social locations and histories.

What Is Auto-ethnography?

This is not bad for a Wikipedia definition: "Autoethnography is a form of qualitative research in which an author uses self-reflection and writing to explore their personal experience and connect this autobiographical story to wider cultural, political, and social meanings and understandings" (accessed May 2017). Ellis et al. (2011: 3) have a more academic definition: "Autoethnography is an approach to research and writing that seeks to describe and systematically analyze personal experience in order to understand cultural experience. This approach "challenges canonical ways of doing research and representing others and treats research as a political, socially-just and socially-conscious act [...], thus, as a method, autoethnography is both a process and a product." (2011: 3). Anderson (2006) offers a distinction between *analytic and evocative autoethnography*; he supports the more analytic form in which researchers are insiders of the research group or place, are committed to theoretical understandings of the topic and propose a critical analysis (2006: 373). Ellis and Bochner (2011) propose this methodology as "...an autobiographical genre of writing that displays multiple layers of consciousness, connecting the personal to the cultural" (2011: 739). From these multiple—and sometimes confusing—definitions found in the literature, the one I find the most useful is this one from Chang (2008), which I reproduce at length: "Autoethnography is a methodology and inquiry that utilizes autobiographic materials of the researcher as primary data. Differing from other self-narrative writings such as autobiography and memoir, autoethnography emphasizes cultural analysis and interpretation of the researcher's behaviors, thoughts, and experiences in relation to others in society. The [product] should be ethnographical in its methodological orientation, cultural in its interpretations and autobiographical in its contents." This is one of the definitions I emphasize the most with my students, as it is accessible, yet complete enough to unpack during class discussions. This one coincides with the most widely cited definition of Reed-Danahay (1997 and 2009), who in her book goes beyond a definition, as she explains in detail the completion of an auto-ethnography, from project design, writing and analysis, to final presentation of a public report, and evaluates the critiques and multiple reactions to auto-ethnographic accounts from inside and outside the academia.

All the definitions above are valid and useful, I suggest, however, defining *Auto-ethnography* by what it is not: it is not a biography, a memoir, a form of self-flagellation, a navel gazing ego-alienation trip, nor a realistic account of a person's "true" self. I define critical auto-ethnography as a methodology (many methods can be include under this umbrella), a narrative style or writing genre, a cultural project, a perspective, a form of personal liberation path, and a way of making-place and making communities across diverse boundaries *glocally* (I will return to my *bricolage* definition later in this chapter, when I explain how I use it the classroom). Auto-ethnographies begin with a personally relevant issue that one wishes to understand in more depth and, in most cases, is associated with an area or point of tension or challenge in our personal lives, our family, community or, more broadly, through our shared human experience. As a form of qualitative methodology, it is very similar to ethnography in terms of design and implementation of qualitative research projects. It requires defining a topic, formulating research questions, doing fieldwork, identifying a specific field-site and relevant community (or in-groups), gathering primary sources (personal memory-data and written fieldnotes of field observations and reflections), and secondary sources (academic references to understand the topic, to guide the analysis, and to give ethno-historical context). It requires also organizing, editing and analyzing the data found, drafting written reports answering the research questions, and sharing research findings with publics (in writing or through other media platforms). The research project can take 6 months to a year. Sometimes, in part due to "vulnerability" issues, it could stretch over years, before an author decides to stop research, write an account and to publish the findings.

Although auto-ethnographic research requires gathering memory-data and personal documents as forms of self-reported reflections, and family archives related to the topic chosen for the project, it also requires fieldwork, as it is a research of the *present*, from the present (this is what makes it *ethnographic*). Hence doing fieldwork (participant-observation) is not optional, but central. It seems to me that the term "deep hanging-out" with yourself (this is, spending quality time with self and others, being fully present and engaged, and writing fieldnotes of the observations and discoveries) is more appropriate and suitable for obvious reasons. As I explain to my students, the "self," besides being a moving target, is multiple, layered and very crowded. Concrete and virtual fields have also fuzzy boundaries in auto-ethnographic research, at even more extreme degrees than ethnography. As stated above, auto-ethnographic research is always a form of local and "native" ethnographies, or insider scholarship, because the data is generated around a specific individual embodied experience "from the present," and everyone is an insider or member of a particular group and a resident of a particular locality. The field-site and community of research becomes hence the local life, place and relations of the researcher, in particular those aspects of daily life related to the topic being researched.

In describing the project that they will embark on to my students, I teach them to think of auto-ethnographic fieldwork as "deep-hanging-out" with yourself. The term "deep-hanging-out," sometimes used to refer to informally to ethnography fieldwork (participant-observation), is of uncertain origins; James Clifford mentions that he heard it from Clifford Geertz, and Geertz alludes to how he heard it from Renato Rosaldo. I came into this term while a graduate student, it was used by a professor in a feminist anthropology seminar, and I have not found as of yet, any proper definition of it, and the tree authors mentioned above, dislike and dismiss this term as too informal and irreverent. I fell in love, instantly, with this concept, because I felt (after my first fieldwork experience) that it described much better than any of the other academic sounding term, what we actually do as ethnographers; we hang-out with people. As I explain to my students, this hanging-out could be so extended, so emotionally close and so deep, to affect a researcher's physical and emotional health; many ethnographers have been murdered in the field, have died of accidents, have been captured and kidnapped as suspect belonging to leftist guerrillas or to the CIA, and some others had to make tough decisions of how deep to go, how far to "participate" and collaborate, for example. when doing fieldwork among police, gangs or drug addicts. In auto-ethnographic fieldwork the hanging-out is also deep, as profound, revelations and traumas are discovered, and doing the oral history with people close to them emotionally could be very, at times, tense and conflicting, but also healing (for concrete examples, see Chapter Three).

To analyze auto-ethnographic data effectively, and to be able to contextualize the personal experiences that are central to auto-ethnographic projects is necessary to gain an understanding of the socio-cultural and historical dimensions that frame our daily experiences in a particular place. When time for writing report and sharing findings come, I remain students that besides writing a first person narrative, researchers need to be careful to avoid sentimentality and confessional nostalgia, especially when it comes to the memory-data. To help them deal with this challenge, over my years of teaching I have developed a grouping of basic concepts to help students acquire critical skills, to be able to interpret their data and write about their findings critically in their final reports. I call these interdisciplinary concepts a *Toolkit for Critical Analysis*; some of the most basic terms are ethnocentrism, power—in its many forms—political economy, intersecting identities, identity politics, situated knowledge, etc.). The concepts in the Toolkit are linked to particular theoretical frameworks such as Post-colonial and Post-structural analysis, Black feminist and Queer theory, Critical Race Theory, through authors that have been key in my own research (such as the authors discussed in Chapters One and Four). These approaches are chosen not only because they are the most contemporary or "cutting edge" ones, but also because of my academic formation and my political and poetic dispositions. These theoretical currents and concepts have been the most useful for teaching students how to critically analyze and contextualize their auto-ethnographic data, to be able to produce more in-depth narratives. To avoid distracting the discussion of auto-ethnography, here I give only this brief notice of the academic sources from where I have taken these concepts; the practical uses and modified definitions of each are further described in Chapter Three.

"We Are All Ethnic": Auto-ethnography Roots, Routes and Transformations

If we take sincerely the proposal of Trouillot (discussed in Chapter One) to problematize the "West" tropes of "the savage slot" by mapping ethno-historically the "discursive field" of the "other" from before the institutionalization of anthropology (which he sets back to the colonial encounter in the Americas after 1492), we could then include as earlier precursor Fray Ramón Pané. His self-reflexivity could be conceived as contributing to one of the first insider ethnography and even auto-ethnography in the New World. As a catholic priest during the first years of the Spanish colonization in the Americas, Pané's (1999), took upon himself, to get to know the indigenous people he was obligated to convert to Christianity. In his brief account about the "Tainos" in the Caribbean, he showed his effort to train himself in the language they spoke (diverse dialects of Arawak) and to understand their mythology and ways of life. In this document, he highlights poetically (and indirectly politically) the tribulations of ethnographers and the limitations of the ethnographic methodology, quite a few centuries before the invention of anthropology (see Arrom 1992, Cattan 2013). Feeling the weight of the micro-macro-politics of his fieldwork (a true colonial "deep hanging-out") with indigenous Caribbean communities in the 16th century, he recognizes that he might fail in his attempt to understand and to translate these unknown ways of life. Besides the uncertainty about available sources and "informants," his openly admitted rudimentary language skills, and the ad hoc nature of his "scholarly" part-time pursue, I imagine that the tensions and effects of the violent colonial context on the lives of his collaborators—enslaved under the yoke of *encomiendas*—powerfully influenced his research and his writings. Pané's doubts pointed—centuries in advance—to the weird role of an ethnographer; we, as ethnographers, are the problematic instrument of knowledge production, bounded by our own cultural filters, histories, circumstance, personal locations and power agendas. As Marx would say, making our histories—and being witness to others' struggles to make theirs—happens within geopolitical contexts "not of our own choosing."

Taking a huge jump, from this early precursor in the 16th century Caribbean, we land in the 20th century US. The ethno-historical context in the emergence of auto-ethnography proper, has few landmark points between the 1930s and the 1970s, and moments of boom between the 1990s and 2000s as well as in the present. A quick timeline of this methodology in US anthropology is found since its early practitioners; this is the case of Zora N. Hurston's auto-ethnography, *Mules and Men*, published in 1935. This timing is not accidental; it responds to the depression era and to the context of racial segregation in the US during the 1920s and 1930s, when this Black woman anthropologist was conducting her graduate research under the mentorship of Franz Boas (see Dorst 1987). In the introduction to that book she wrote: ".... But it [culture] was fitting me like a tight chemise. I couldn't see it for wearing it. It was only when I was off in college, away from my native surroundings that I could see myself like somebody else and stand off and look at my garment. Then I had to have the spy-glass of Anthropology to look through that." This is quite a concise definition of culture, a contribution that was not acknowledged by Boas in his preface, but that it has become fuel for feminist anthropologists (especially for women of color) interested in self-reflexive and experimental writing methods.

Without the more radical version of *critical ethnography* (discussed in Chapter One), auto-ethnography would have remained a fringe praxis, and without the *critical* part, auto-ethnography would not have its sharp power to help us question concepts such as what is considered valid data, the boundaries and micro-politics of fieldwork, dichotomies of objectivity-subjectivity, self-other, individual-collective, and to deal with the ethical challenges of working with "human subjects" who increasingly refuse (with good reasons and valid resistance) to sign the consent forms we present to them during fieldwork. Women feminist anthropologists, "minority," indigenous and other assorted native and insider scholars have been liberating space and offering critiques of the subjective nature of ethnographic fieldwork since the beginning of the institutionalization of anthropology. After the 1980s self-reflexivity essays and integrated reflexivity first person voice vignettes, began appearing in ethnographic works (mostly by women, "minority" and diasporic anthropologists, such as Dorinne Kondo, Kamala Narayan, and Michelle Rosaldo among many others before them, who, as Zora N. Hurston, have declared their researcher positions since the beginning of anthropology as a discipline.

It seems that the major contributions to the development of auto-ethnography into an *almost*—not quite yet—legitimate tool of research and publications come from outside anthropology and its mainstream ethnographic practice, in fields that range from communication studies, health and nursing to education (Banks & Banks 2000, Foster & O'Brien 2006, Adams 2012, Block & Weatherford 2013,

Acosta, Goltz & Goodson 2015). Other diverse authors from multiple disciplines ranging from social sciences to literature and film, have also examined their personal roles in research and made critiques of traditional ethnography (see Min-Ha 1982, Hills-Collins 1986, Martin and Mohanty 1986, Narayan 1993, hooks 2000, McClaurin 2001, Alexander 2005, Allen 2011, Danticat 2011, Moraga and Anzaldua 2015, among others).

There is an increasing acceptance and appreciation of auto-ethnographic methodologies within and outside anthropology and academia (e.g., the *Journal of Contemporary Ethnography*). This aperture is due, in part, to what Hanson (2004) calls "the narrative and reflexivity turns" in the social sciences and, in part, attuned to the zeitgeist of our times, resonating with an age characterized by individualism and a re-centering of the "self." A renewed interest in auto-ethnography is also part of a revaluation of qualitative methodologies in contemporary scholarship across the social sciences, humanities, communication, education, rhetoric and composition, psychology, nursing and related health fields. In an era of mistrust and tensions, when many marginalized and indigenous communities are refusing to give anthropologists and other social researchers permission to work with them and their communities, when many displaced groups, refuges and migrants have undocumented status, auto-ethnography seems more appealing. The book, *Ethnography unbound: Power and Resistance in the City* (Burawoy et al. 1991), is an excellent book from scholars in the fields of Education and Rhetoric using ethnographic methods in their classrooms, and they include examples of passages from students' essays that are auto-ethnographic. Another important book to understand the interdisciplinary breath in the use of auto-ethnographic methods is Brown and Dobrin (2004), a good introduction to the use of critical ethnography in the classroom, that also addresses the general debates about the validity of self-reflexive ethnography and engaged scholarship. Chang's *Auto-ethnography as Method* (2008) is an excellent book about this methodology; includes definitions, practical applications and examples of steps in the process of conducting auto-ethnographic fieldwork and cultural analysis of the data.

Compilations of auto-ethnographies have become more frequent, such as Boylorn and Orbe who have published an excellent interdisciplinary volume in their book *Critical Autoethnography* (2014). The featured ethnographic accounts range from struggles with cancer, first generation college student status, coming out as gay or lesbian to challenges with disabilities. Two chapters in particular offer rich narratives; in chapter 5 *Performing fortune cookie,* Hao, a Chinese immigrant man in the US, researches the invention of fortune cookies and (beautifully illustrated with some of his father's responses, "It is just something they eat out here") and his own experiences and struggles of transculturation. Hao analyzes the mainstream construction of "chineseness," using Paul Gilroy's (1993) definition of diaspora as "a process of becoming rather than being," and how is diversely experienced, accepted and resisted by particular communities and individuals within the Chinese and Chinese-American population. In chapter 10 Morella-Pozzi (2014) discusses the social and cultural discrimination and micro-aggressions that people *differently able* (formerly called disabled) receive daily in the name "I am just trying to *help* you." The author relates how tiny details could become unnecessary obstacles, as she discusses her experiences as a graduate student, and how she needed to endure delays and bureaucratic hoops just to get a textbook in a readable format. Yet she also turns her sharp critique around to analyze a prevalent victim-hood mentality; to analyze this part of her auto-ethnographic data she refers to Freire's critical pedagogy approach, showing how "we suffer from and participate in our own oppression."

The editor of this volume, Robin Boylorn (an interpersonal communications scholar) in her article about black feminist blogging discusses the intersections of gender, class, race and feminist auto-ethnography. She proposes that auto-ethnographic blog narratives have served for her as a strategy to navigate the public and private spheres of belonging as a Black woman academic and as a member of her family and community. She suggests examining "lived experiences" using creative research methods and writing techniques—such as blogging—to "make sense of cultural phenomena". She uses the term "astigmatism" ("no seeing yourself clearly"), showing the need to use new lenses (beautiful echoes of Hurston), as she walks us through her own journey into feminist praxis. She states "auto/ethnography as a method allows me to write (about/for) my life and to make sense of it: Blogging allows me to do that in a more open space, which jeopardizes my anonymity but creates a larger public space for the kinds of conversations auto/ethnography should instigate." (2013: 76). Although I have assigned occasionally in my courses some of the examples discussed above, there are as well other auto-ethnographic writings that are regular fare in my courses, as these give students a sense of the potential of ethnographic writings, in its most political and poetic sense.

The article "Dancing the Beloved Children" (2009), Jafari Allen presents a poetic, fine-grained analysis of individual desire, autonomy and community in a Black queer dance club in the US, and the emergence of new forms of communal spirituality through clubs, as sacred spaces compensating for black homes as unsafe spaces for gender/sexual diversity. His auto-ethnographic writing is very cinematic, *showing* rather than just writing about queer time and place reading, in the way gay and lesbian writers struggles in NYC on "the page" and on the "canvas" of everyday life. As Allen puts it, "You got to get your life before it can be transformed"

(2009: 318). Another example is Mari-Luz Esteban (2004) article, where she analyzes gender, health and embodiment through her auto-ethnographic research about her body image and obesity. This essay is, besides a well-structured narrative, embedded with critical theoretical analysis, yet without excess jargon, and it is very accessible to students at the University of Puerto Rico (as it is published in Spanish). Another piece that I have assigned for few years is Chavez (2012) discussion of her experiences in higher education as a working-class Brown Chicano woman has consistently a powerful effect on my students, they seem to get, from this article, what I am asking from them, and offers them, as well, a chance to reflect about their own educational routes.

Lastly, Gina A. Ulysse in her article "Papa, patriarchy and power" (2006) examines her gendered resistance to her father's patriarchal rules before and after migration between Haiti and NYC. This is also a very engaging and accessible example for students. Ulysse is an anthropologist and a performance ethnographer, she narrates her experiences in a vivid way. Through what she calls an "auto-ethnographic montage," she reconstructs and de-constructs her perspective, and in the process frames her family's migrant history, and the experience of a girl's development of a Black feminist consciousness, in conversation and resistance with her father's patriarchal power. By examining intersections of gender, migration and race grounded in an auto-ethnographic narrative, the shifting grounds of "home" become evident, pointing to the domestic/private micro worlds in relation to the huge scale of wider issues in Haitian ethno-history (such as the Duvalier dictatorship), while revealing how complex subjectivities are produced through Haitian women "counter-narratives." For anthropology courses I assign Dorinne Kondo's powerful self-reflexive article (1986) about the micro-politics of ethnographic fieldwork, the delicate boundaries between self-other and her experiences of "going native" (describing brilliantly the "rich point" of this realization) while doing research in Japan, as a Japanese-American woman. There are also other powerful self-reflexive passages embedded in Kondo's more mainstream ethnographic accounts that I also use to show students examples of critical auto-ethnographic writings.

Teaching Critical Auto-ethnography: Personal Mappings of Local Roots and Routes

Critical Auto-ethnography is deeply linked to Critical Ethnography (see Ellis & Bochner 2011), a contemporary feminist approach to ethnographic methodology that aims to pay "critical" attention to our closest relations of local home; since, in the process of mapping the alliances and tensions of our local "home" routes, we will have also traveled the globe. Critical Auto-ethnography is was re-shaped by this current and its contributions also promotes socio-cultural awareness of contexts, relations and histories. This methodology is not only for "native" or insider anthropologists, "minority scholars," feminists, queers, or women. It is a good departure for teaching not only contents but ways of doing and ways of engaging the social through something that obsesses people, in particular young generations, themselves. In this sense, auto-ethnography is a kind of *selfie*-ethnography, a *fast-food* ethnography for our times. Auto-ethnography, when done critically (taking into account the micro-and-macro political implications of a single human life), becomes a very radical and powerful form of *selfie*, one that does show a kaleidoscopic *facing* and engagement with our multiple intersecting worlds. This methodology gives students tools to examine how they are mapped *in* and *out* in their society and local communities; it helps them question how they position themselves and negotiate concrete and metaphoric boundaries in their taken-for-granted familiar worlds. The aim is for students to understand how their individual experiences are interdependent and inseparable from the social collective histories and conditions that frame their lives.

In my own bricolage version of critical auto-ethnography, that I teach in the classroom, I make emphasis on project design, by first choosing a topic and then formulating an answerable, open-ended, research question of personal and social significance. Then the process of research becomes a journey to answer that question, through the use of multiple sources of data to triangulate. The research extends to one semester of fieldwork, grounded in students' immediate localities, which includes the routes they travel to get to the campus (and when relevant their translocal networks). Besides writing the "memory-data" and researching the ethno-historical global context that frame localities, auto-ethnographers focus on the present of their daily lives, to preserve the "ethnographic" in this methodology, which means to do fieldwork with themselves in relation to the issue being researched. Students need to gather additionally one oral history (to get a contrasting perspective in relation to their own experiences), and to do hand-drawn mappings of routes and movements to ground their research *in-place*. The outcome of the project is the writing of a final report about their findings. For this final product critical cultural analysis is not optional (regardless if they wish to share their report in a video or digital media or a graphic—comic—book form), but an integral part of their narrative.

It is through this empirical experience that students come to learn, not just abstractly, but to *feel*, that *the personal is always political and vice versa*, that subjectivity and community are mutually arising and require constant negotiation and questioning. In my experience, it works for the short-attention-span generations, but also with older students, and even for the most positivist-minded students coming from the natural sciences, in spite of their initial reluctance. As any pilot study, an auto-ethnographic study lasting one semester is a pilot project, as such it cannot be expected to have the depth and development of a more advanced academic research with a full year of fieldwork. The idea is to let students test-drive this tool, to use the skills and experiences they gain to become more aware of what is going on in their personal lives. As it happens, some students acquire a taste for the potential and freedom of auto-ethnographic methodologies and seek further training and experience (when this occur, some ask for an independent studies course, to continue working on a project).

Many reasons justify the choice of using auto-ethnographic methods in my classroom, for example: (1) confronting students to ask, why should we trust your ethical ways if you don't know what it means to be a subject of your own research?; (2) generating research that responds to students' personal and career interests, goals, and cultural histories; and (3) recognizing our changing times, the molding of new technologies, and our difficulties finding readers of academic works (publications proliferate but those who wish to read do not have the time or inclination for "serious, detached, boring works"). Thus, we need to make room for reporting the outcomes of research in alternative formats, and to disseminate knowledge re-inventing ancient forms (such as storytelling, testimonies and chronicles) to make contents appealing to new audiences. Regardless of how long we still have to go in our understanding of why we humans love stories so much, the fact remains that we seem to place great emphasis on narratives and storytelling, regardless of their quality or truth. Even in our virtual-simulacra 21st century, the power of stories masks itself through the database (YouTube videos compilations that stitch together weeding bloopers, animal amazing behaviors, violent incidents in global school grounds, squirrel chasing humans, among others). Stories help us, especially in educational settings, "to dislodge taken for granted and naturalized mind-sets instead of blaming or wasting energy attacking particular groups as oppressors" (see Harris 2006 through Delgado 2012).

My pedagogical approach is research-centered and place-based education, organized around experiential assignments; it is hence project-based, using the auto-ethnographic project discussed above, as the central work of the semester. To teach using auto-ethnography is to me a way to engage with the inseparability of theory and practice; research-centered teaching (project-based) and place-based learning (experiential focus on localities and communities) are two approaches that have been helpful to achieve this integration, to create a *praxis of liberation* that students can take with them once the course has ended. Such pedagogical approaches are productive and exciting, yet they also require intense time-investment and commitment on the part of both teachers and students, and intense emotional investment. The related classroom assignments also require lots of writing, which implies lots of grading (most of the time without teaching assistants). Yet, it seems necessary and worth the extra-work; liberation does not just happen, it is an investment, it requires collaborative work.

I discovered research-centered teaching and place-based education, in part, influenced by my food research and the methodology I had to create to do the kind of projects I wanted to complete about food, memory and diaspora of Dominicans in the US. One of the strongest influences on my research focus on place and memory I owe to the work of Dolores Hayden (1997a). But it was indeed through my practice of teaching and through the students I had to work with, that I decided to use a semester long auto-ethnographic research project that is place-based, responding to immediate issues of my students' locality. It was only during this last year—and through this book—that I found academic publications that explained these strategies, which offer validation and evidence for my approach. For example, McInerney (2011) argues how critical pedagogy and place-based education complement each other through the grounding of students' experiences in their localities, and Gruenewalt proposes a "critical pedagogy of place" (2003). The more accessible books by Sobel (2004) in the *Nature Literacy Series* of the Orion Society give guidelines, examples and evaluations of how to use place-based education to connect classrooms and communities. Although the series is addressed to teachers of middle school and K–12, and is focused on ecological education and sustainability, the pedagogical strategies they share go beyond this aim, having implications for writing across the curriculum, for the history of places and for researching social aspects of the children's local communities. Dalton focuses on media studies, rather than place, which is a good example of how to use personal narrative within a critical pedagogy approach, as a form of "emancipatory praxis" across all disciplines (2003). Dalton, among other authors (see Camangian 2010, Warren 2011) offer us good examples of how to turn the lens towards us as teachers, by using auto-ethnography to evaluate our own practice. Enns and Sinacore (2005) have a good discussion of multicultural and social justice approaches in feminist classrooms using teaching material very similar to place-based and auto-ethnographic methodologies.

The challenges of teaching all, but in particular marginalized and "minority" students, in institutions with questionable teaching resources (and not always under fair labor or working conditions), taught me how much more needed is teaching *with*, rather than teaching *to;* this teaching *with* and *for*, is a must in critical pedagogy, particularly the kind that is informed by feminist praxis (as will be discussed in Chapter Four). These books and articles are inspiring and hopeful for those of us interested in grounding our teaching practice *in-place* and from the experiential poetics and politics of students' local lives. These works are still new to me, I need to read and re-read them again to choose new resources to update the use of auto-ethnography in my teaching.

Creating Better Auto-ethnographic Accounts: Critical Analysis & Contextualization

As with any research tool, even critical auto-ethnography has its limitations and pitfalls, which I address below, yet there are ways to recognize and work *with* these challenges (necessary "rich points") to continue refining further our critical tools for understanding the internal and external worlds we inhabit. Hanson (2004), and earlier Hayano (1979) examined the pitfalls and challenges of auto-ethnography, among these the issues of validity, accountability, the dangers of turning the report into a memoir or congratulatory and sentimental biographical narrative, and the vulnerability risks in the sharing in public of such personal narratives. These warnings are indeed valid, and I make sure we have class discussions about them. Yet these challenges and risks are not less common with more traditional forms of ethnography (and even with other qualitative methods, such as surveys or structured interviews, which are not "raw data" of what people really think or do, but representations of what study participants think the researchers are looking for). To write a compelling first person narrative, based on memory-data, is not enough, indeed.

There are many ways to meet the challenges of producing better auto-ethnographic accounts, and to face the critiques of the biographical sentimentality and validity that are directed at this methodology. One of the ways to meet these challenges is to make sure auto-ethnographic accounts include centrally (as Chang and Reed-Danahay recommend) critical cultural analysis and contextualization of personal experiences. Following this advice, I discovered early on in my using of this methodology in my courses, that is was necessary then, to train students to effectively analyze auto-ethnographic data and to contextualize the personal experiences within wider socio-cultural and historical dimensions. With this aim in mind, and over the years, I have developed a grouping of basic concepts to help students acquire such critical skills. These theoretical concepts have been the most useful for teaching students how to critically analyze, interpret and contextualize their auto-ethnographic data and to apply them in the writing of their final report narratives.

The practical uses and working definitions of many of these concepts are further described in Chapter Three, in this chapter I only point to their theoretical origins and my reasons for using these particular concepts, instead of others. I found these concepts through authors who became key references in my own research (these authors were discussed in Chapter One, and others will be discussed in Chapter Four). These concepts have been crucial in my academic formation in graduate school and are linked to particular theoretical frameworks such as Post-colonial and Post-structural analysis, Black feminist and Queer theory, Critical Race Theory. These frameworks are chosen not only because they are the most contemporary or "cutting edge," but also because of the political and poetic affinities that I have to them. The concepts included in my *Toolkit for Critical Analysis* are interdisciplinary and are grouped into short handouts which contain brief definitions and summaries for each concept. The concepts in the readings are: ethnocentrism, prejudice, discrimination, stereotype, code-switching, matrix of power (diverse forms of power, including hegemony-consensus, agency, etc.), political economy (labor, geopolitics, colonization, globalization), situated knowledge, difference-normativity, intersecting Identities, identity politics, feminisms, queer theory, representation and ethno-semiotics. These concepts are useful for questioning where we are, what is going on, how this varies according to diverse perspectives and social locations, how to interpret daily life and social interactions and to question who is asking, looking, writing and from where; this is, to take responsibility, to be accountable for what students, as researchers, are proposing as interpretations of their data and experiences.

For the concept of power, meaning a matrix of negotiations and political economy, I rely on a bricolage of my understanding of Antonio Gramsci (1997, 2000), Michel Foucault (1980), feminist theories of practice (Mohanty 2003, Ortner 2006). For an ethno-historical concept of power Sidney Mintz (1986) and Michel-Rolph Trouillot's (1995)'s contributions are crucial for a post-colonial critique, to de-center the "West" and to understand the production of power after the 1492 colonization of the Americas. To understand the nuances of power as agency, even among the most marginalized, such as working class, welfare recipients and even the homeless, the work of James Scott (1990) and Robin Kelley (1996) were tremendously significant for teaching students the subtleties of "micro-politics" and "infra-politics" of everyday life through what appears as individual and isolate actions. Basic concepts such as culture, ethnocentrism, discrimination and others related to intercultural communication, come from cultural anthropology, for intersecting identities, identity formations and identity politics I use the Black feminist Intersectional model of analysis (Hill-Collins 1986, Crenshaw 1991,

McClaurin 2001). For representation I rely Marita Sturken (1997), Sturken and Cartwright (2001), Paul Gilroy (1993), and James Clifford (1988, 1997), but especially on Stuart Hall (1997, 2006) whose work is also relevant for understanding semiotics, cultural identity and diasporas. I find also very accessible for undergraduate students Lutz & Collins' article on reading National Geographic (1993), as it help them decode photographic and media representations of difference through both visual depiction and the captions given to them.

Besides the concepts of power (in its many direct and indirect manifestations) and political economy, that I expose my students during the first weeks of class, one of the most important concepts is that of "intersecting identities" (a model to understand identity formation) first proposed by Black feminist scholars, was later retaken by legal scholars under Critical Race Theory (CRT), and now widely used across the social sciences (see Crenshaw 1991). This concept is used today outside of academia by Black Lives Matter, women, LGBTTQ, and other social movements, in particular, after the "Trump regime", seem to have reawaken white supremacist sentiments in many regions, not only in the US. As I teach my students, we have multiple roles and multiple identities, and any particular identity rest on a particular axis (be it race, gender or class, for example). These identities are social categories assigned without our consent, are contextual, hence, they become sites of constant self/community negotiations, a space of relations particular to specific places and historical times. Another way of to say this is that identity is a *by-product*, not a priory essence, but generated in a contextual frame intersected by multiple forms of social conditions, self-identification and group alliances. The less "natural" weight we assign to these ideological constructions, the more conflicts of intolerance could be avoided.

Basically, an intersectional model of identity, as explained most clearly by Crenshaw (1991), proposes that we all have multiple identities relational identities that combine to shape our experiences, and that these multiple axes of identities *place* us (by historical chance) within a spectrum between marginalization and privilege, according to the prevailing social categories and norms in a particular society and historical time. This way of examining identity formations as a *process* and *product* is very useful not only for research projects, but also to address in our college classrooms issues of diversity, discrimination, and ethnocentrism, that have, as well implications outside the classroom, as students are bound to encounter constant negotiations of differences in their everyday lives. More broadly, group identities are also not fixed, but negotiated, contextual, and historical, hence we use also the concept of "identity politics," to point to group alliances, belonging and conflicts which are negotiated in social life. To illustrate, Blackness or Whiteness by themselves can only mean something when we examine how it intersects with other axes. For example, the "American" experience of Michelle Obama is not the same as that of a Black transgender homeless woman in the streets of NYC. This might seem like an extreme contrast, but the idea is for students to become aware of how each axis could place a person at more risk of marginalization. A white male law student, who happens to be gay, gets attacked in a hate crime in Waco, Texas in 2003 (a real case I read about while living in Austin). This event puts in evidence how, in different contexts, one axis of class or race privilege cannot protect us, when we are perceived to offend the normativity standards of certain groups (in this case, what is considered "proper" masculine performance in public).

The concepts of "subjectivity" (Ortner 2005), the politics of "experience" (Mohanty 1995), and the politics of location or "situated knowledge" (Haraway 1988) are other theoretical ways to analyze the complexities of identity and group formation. Some of these fine-grained distinctions are best suited for more advanced seminars, however "situated knowledge" has proven so useful that I introduce it even in the most basic courses). Lastly the concept of "performativity" mostly developed by Queer theory (Sullivan 2003, Ahmed 2006) is useful when discussing gender/sexual identities, but also to destabilize heterosexual norms (I am noticing, for example, more and more "non-gender conforming" or gender-crossing students, a young man who wears earrings, make-up or paints his nails, yet self-identify as heterosexual). Finally, since auto-ethnography requires individual personal data, and a narrative in first person to create a coherent account, it was important to understand and question the concept of "experience." I have been using the article "On Experience" by Joan Scott (1991), a social historian, as a good source to understand the usefulness, yet the problematics of using individual experience as "evidence" and as "data," as all narratives and accounts that people offer about their lives are mediated by representation, hence by interpretation (not only at the moment of re-telling their stories but also at the moment when those events occurred). This fine-grained examination (which is understood by students through their project) is important to avoid assuming the existence of fixed, essentialized identities and communities, rather to focus on contextual, situational alliances and ruptures, and in the performance of belonging through practices and narratives, paying attention hence to environments, relations, interactions, and to material culture in daily life.

Critical Auto-ethnography, with the help from these concepts, becomes hence, truly critical, going beyond an academic exercise, it could be used as a tool for personal and collective liberations, grounds us in the embodied situated experience of our researching bodies. It helps us imagine holographic pieces of potential resources we have, to nurture the vision of our life projects. A Critical auto-ethnographic focus on everyday life, gives us the chance to appreciate and to document tiny details of our roots and routes, those public-private realms that have huge ripple effects in our understanding of our realities. There is also a kind of poetic justice in privileging the local, the personal miniature intimate spheres of relations and senses of home, in contrast to the already well documented wider cultural histories and huge time-space of global forces that frame our lives. There is power, pleasure and challenges in producing our own personal and community primary sources, to privilege our own partial perspectives and narratives, is a leaving of traces and creation of archives for our own histories. As I say to my students, and remind myself, if we don't research, document and celebrate the history of our families, their hopes and struggles, who will? Taking responsibility for our situated personal experience help us to become more tolerant and solidarious with other's differences, to practice new forms of non-exploitative interactions and to create spaces for healing for ourselves and for others.

Auto-ethnography is a powerful methodology, an obscure jewel, with great potential for personal and collective liberations. It has been neglected in anthropology, but thankfully it has been recognized and utilized effectively by other academic fields and in non-academic cultural productions. I predict a bright future for this approach, within and outside anthropology, a mainstreaming of sorts, that will allows us to further refine this tool and to push its limits, instead of wasting our energy defending its rightful place in research and writing.

References

Acosta, S., Goltz, H. H., & Goodson, P. (2015). Autoethnography in action research for health education practitioners. *Action Research*, *13*(4), 411–431.

Adams, T. E. (2012). *Narrating the closet: An autoethnography of same-sex attraction*. CA: Left Coast Press.

Ahmed, S. (2006). *Queer phenomenology: Orientations, objects, others*. Durkham: Duke University Press.

Alexander, M. J. (2005). *Pedagogies of crossing: Meditations on feminism, sexual politics, memory, and the sacred*. Durkham: Duke University Press.

Allen, J. S. (2011). *¡Venceremos?: The erotics of black self-making in Cuba*. Durham: Duke University Press.

Allen, J. S. (2009). For "the children" dancing the beloved community. *Souls*, *11*(3), 311–326.

Anderson, L. (2006). Analytic autoethnography. *Journal of Contemporary Ethnography*, *35*(4), 373–395.

Arrom, J. J. (1992). Fray Ramón Pané, Descubridor del Hombre Americano. *Thesaurus*. Tomo XLVII. Núm. 2.

Banks, S. P., & Banks, A. (2000). Reading "the critical life": Auto-ethnography as pedagogy. *Communication Education, 49*(3), 233–238.

Block, B. A., & Weatherford, G. M. (2013). Narrative research methodologies: Learning lessons from disabilities research. *Quest, 65*(4), 498–514.

Boylord, R., & Mark, O. (2014). *Critical auto-ethnography: Intersecting cultural identities in everyday life.* Walnut Creek, CA: Left Coast Press.

Boylorn, R. M. (2013, April) Blackgirl Blogs, Auto/ethnography, and Crunk Feminism. *Liminarities: A Journal of Performance Studies, 9*(2), 73–82.

Burawoy, M., Burton, A., Ferguson, A. A., & Fox, K. J. (1991). Ethnography unbound: Power and resistance in the modern metropolis. Los Angeles: University of California Press.

Camangian, P. (2010). Starting with self: Teaching autoethnography to foster critically caring literacies. *Research in the Teaching of English, 45*(2), 179–204.

Cattan, M. (2013). Ramón Pané y su Mundo Monológico. *Dialogía, 7*, 196–226.

Chang, H. (2008). *Autoethnography as method: Developing qualitative inquiry series.* Walnut Creek, CA: Left Coast Press.

Chavez, M. S. (2012). Autoethnography, a Chicana's methodological research tool: The role of storytelling for those who have no choice but to do critical race theory. *Equity & Excellence in Education, 45*(2), 334–348.

Clifford, J. (1988). *The predicament of culture.* Cambridge: Harvard University Press.

Clifford, J. (1997). *Routes: Travel and translation in the late twentieth century.* Cambridge: Harvard University Press.

Crenshaw, K. (1991). Mapping the margins: Intersectionality, identity politics, and violence against women of color. *Stanford Law Review, 43*(6), 1241–1299.

Dalton, M. M. (2003). Media studies and emancipatory praxis: An autoethnographic essay on critical pedagogy. *Journal of Film and Video, 55*(2), 88–97.

Danticat, E. (2011). *Create dangerously: The immigrant artist at work.* NJ: Princeton University Press.

Dorst, J. (1987). Rereading Mules and Men: Toward the death of the ethnographer. *Cultural Anthropology, 2*(3), 305–318.

Ellis, C., Adams, T., & Bochner, A. (2011). Autoethnography: An overview. Forum: *Qualitative Social Research/Forum Qualitaive Sozialforschung, 12*(1), art 10, January [retrieved from: http://www.qualitative-research.net].

Enns, C. Z. E., & Sinacore, A. L. (2005). *Teaching and social justice: Integrating multicultural and feminist theories in the classroom.* American Psychological Association.

Esteban, M. L. (2004). Antropología encarnada. Antropología desde una misma. *Papeles del CEIC. International Journal on Collective Identity Research, 2004*(12), 1–12.

Foster, K., McAllister, M., & O'brien, L. (2006). Extending the boundaries: Autoethnography as an emergent method in mental health nursing research. *International Journal of Mental Health Nursing, 15*(1), 44–53.

Foucault, M. (1980). *Power/knowledge: Selected interviews and other writings, 1972–1977.* NYC: Pantheon.

Gilroy, P. (1993). *The black Atlantic: Modernity and double consciousness.* Cambridge: Harvard University Press.

Gramsci, A. (1997). Hegemony, intellectuals and the state. *Cultural theory and popular culture: A reader*, 210–238. London: Routledge.

Gramsci, A. (2000). Hegemony, relations of force, historical bloc. In *The Antonio Gramsci reader: Selected writings, 1916–1935.* New York: Schocken Books.

Gruenewald, D. A. (2003). The best of both worlds: A critical pedagogy of place. *Educational Researcher, 32*(4), 3–12.

Gruenewald, D. A., & Smith, G. A. (Eds.). (2014). *Place-based education in the global age: Local diversity.* London: Routledge.

Hall, S. (Ed.). (1997). *Representation: Cultural representations and signifying practices* (Vol. 2). New York: Sage.

Hall, S. (Ed.). (2006). Cultural identity and diaspora. In *Diaspora and visual culture* (pp. 35–47). London: Routledge.

Hanson, S. S. (2004). Critical auto/ethnography. *Ethnography Unbound: From Theory Shock to Critical Praxis,* 183–217. Albany: SUNY Press.

Hao, R. N. (2014). Performing fortune cookie: An autoethnographic performance on diasporic hybridity. In Robin M. Boylorn, & Mark P. Orbe (eds.), *Critical autoethnography: Intersecting cultural identities in everyday life* (pp. 96–109). Walnut Creek, CA: Left Coast Press.

Haraway, D. (1988). Situated knowledges: The science question in feminism and the privilege of partial perspective. *Feminist Studies, 14*(3), 575–599.

Hayano, D. (1979). Auto-ethnography: Paradigms, problems, and prospects. *Human Organization, 38*(1), 99–104.

Hayden, D. (1997a). *The power of place: Urban landscapes as public history.* Boston: MIT press.

Hayden, D. (1997b). Urban landscape history: The sense of place and the politics of space. *Understanding ordinary landscapes, 133–158. The power of place: Urban landscapes as public history.* Dolores Hayden (Ed.), Boston: MIT press.

Hills-Collins, P. (1986). Learning from the outsider within: The sociological significance of Black feminist thought. *Social Problems, 33*(6), s14–s32.

hooks, b. (2000). *Feminism is for everybody: Passionate politics.* London: Pluto Press.

Hurston, Z. N. (1935). *Mules and men.* Florida: J. B. Lippincott Company

Kelley, R. D. (2001). *Yo'mama's disfunktional!: Fighting the culture wars in urban America.* Boston: Beacon Press.

Kelley, R. D. (1996). *Race rebels: Culture, politics, and the black working class.* NYC: Simon and Schuster.

Kondo, D. K. (1986). Dissolution and reconstitution of self: Implications for anthropological epistemology. *Cultural Anthropology, 1*(1), 74–88.

Lutz, C. A., & Collins, J. L. (1993). *Reading national geographic* (Vol. 59). Chicago: University of Chicago Press.

McClaurin, I. (2001). Theorizing a black feminist self in anthropology: Toward an autoethnographic approach. In Irma McClaurin (Ed.), *Black feminist anthropology: Theory, politics, praxis and poetics*. New Brunswick/London: Rutgers University Press.

Martin, B., & Mohanty, C. T. (1986). Feminist Politics: What's Home Got to Do with It? In: *Feminist studies/critical studies* (pp. 191–212). UK: Palgrave Macmillan.

McInerney, P., Smyth, J., & Down, B. (2011). Coming to a place near you? The politics and possibilities of a critical pedagogy of place-based education. *Asia-Pacific Journal of Teacher Education, 39*(1), 3–16.

Minh-Ha. T. T. (1982). Réassemblage. 40 mins. Color. Women Make Movies, Third World Newsreel.

Mintz, S. W. (1986). *Sweetness and power: The place of sugar in modern history*. New York: Penguin.

Mohanty, C. T. (2003). *Feminism without borders: Decolonizing theory, practicing solidarity*. Durham: Duke University Press.

Mohanty, C. T. (1995). *Feminist encounters: Locating the politics of experience* (pp. 68–86). New York: Cambridge University Press.

Moraga, C., & Anzaldúa, G. (Eds.). (2015). *This bridge called my back: Writings by radical women of color*. Albany: SUNY Press.

Morella-Pozzi, D. (2014). The (Ddis)aAbility Ddouble Llife: Exploring Llegitimacy, Iillegitimacy, and the Tterrible Ddichotomy of (Ddis)aAbility in Hhigher Eeducation. In Robin M. Boylorn, & Mark P. Orbe (eds.), *Critical autoethnography: Intersecting cultural identities in everyday life* (pp. 176–194). Walnut Creek, CA: Left Coast Press.

Narayan, K. (1993, September). How 'Native' is a 'Native Anthropologist'? *American Anthropologist*, New Series, *95*(3), 671–686.

Ortner, S. B. (2006). *Anthropology and social theory: Culture, power, and the acting subject*. Durham: Duke University Press.

Ortner, S. B. (2005). Subjectivity and cultural critique. *Anthropological Theory, 5*(1), 31–52.

Pané, F. R. (1999). *An account of the antiquities of the Indians: A new edition, with an introductory study, notes, and appendices by José Juan Arrom*. Durham: Duke University Press.

Powers, A. L. (2004). An evaluation of four place-based education programs. *The Journal of Environmental Education, 35*(4), 17–32.

Reed-Danahay, D. (2009). Anthropologists, education, and autoethnography. *Reviews in Anthropology, 38*(1), 28–47.

Reed-Danahay, D. (1997). *Auto/ethnography: Rewriting the self and the social*. New York: Berg.

Scott, J. C. (1990). *Domination and the arts of resistance: Hidden transcripts*. New Haven: Yale University Press.

Scott, J. W. (1991). The evidence of experience. *Critical Inquiry, 17*(4), 773–797.

Sobel, D. (2004). *Place-based education: Connecting classrooms & communities*. Great Barrington: The Orion Society.

Sturken, M. (1997). *Tangled memories: The Vietnam War, the AIDS epidemic, and the politics of remembering*. Los Angeles: University of California Press.

Sturken, M., & Cartwright, L. (2001). *Practices of looking*. Oxford: Oxford University Press.
Sullivan, N. (2003). *A critical introduction to queer theory*. NYC: New York University Press.
Trouillot, M. R. (1995). *Silencing the past: Power and the production of history*. Boston: Beacon Press.
Ulysse, G. A. (2006). Papa, patriarchy, and power: Snapshots of a good Haitian girl, feminism, & diasporic dreams. *Journal of Haitian Studies, 12*(1), 24–47.
Warren, J. T. (2011). Reflexive teaching: Toward critical autoethnographic practices of/in/on pedagogy. *Cultural Studies ↔ Critical Methodologies, 11*(2), 139–144.

CHAPTER THREE

Critical Auto-ethnography in the Classroom

Auto-ethnographic Projects, Toolkit for Critical analysis and Course Design

When I hear, I forget; when I see, I remember;

When I do, I understand

(Chinese saying)

In the sections that follow, I ground the academic discussions shared in the first two chapters through descriptions and analysis of how I use critical auto-ethnography methodology in my teaching, and what I have learned in the process of guiding students to design, develop, and implement an auto-ethnographic research project, to write a report of their findings, and to present their findings to their peers and university community. I discuss then the benefit that students' get from completing their final reports and evaluate the powerful significance of auto-ethnographic research and writings in students' lives. Going beyond college courses, I offer reflections about the use of an auto-ethnographic approach in other contexts. Additionally, to contextualize how to complete an auto-ethnographic research project that goes beyond a personal narrative, that is contextualized in a socio-cultural analysis. I include descriptions and vignettes of what I do in the classroom, how I train students to use of theoretical concepts (Toolkit for Critical Analysis), and the *how* and *why* of my choices for course design, teaching materials and classroom dynamics. I close this chapter with testimonial narrative passages;

a sort of grounding *in-place*, by describing the situations of the students I teach at UPR, and the adaptation of my approaches to such circumstances.

My intention in this chapter is to share a pedagogical testimony about the benefits of using a project-based approach and experiential assignments to understand specific semester's topics from local, regional, hemispheric, and global dimensions. The descriptions and reflections below are based on my college teaching experience in the US (Austin and New York City) as well as now in San Juan, Puerto Rico. The courses taught include not only Cultural Anthropology, but also general education courses such as Global Studies, The American Experience, Social Problems in the US, Comparative Contemporary Issues (Africa & the Caribbean), interdisciplinary Caribbean courses, and even Writing and Art trimester courses at a technical Institute in Austin, Texas.

I am offering my approach not as representative of best practice for college teaching, but rather as one perspective, taking responsibility for my specific cultural history, academic formation and situated praxis. Hence, this chapter, as the rest of the book, takes the shape of an auto-ethnographic testimonial narrative. I share these insights to inspire more experimental ways to create learning opportunities for adults, that rescue the pleasure, challenges, and excitement of learning beyond the classroom, and of teaching, as bell hooks recommends, for liberation, this is, teaching as a "practice of freedom" (1994), by giving students tools for their own self-empowerment.

Research-Centered Teaching: The Auto-ethnographic Project and Evaluations

> I didn't know I could be a primary source
>
> (student evaluation of using Auto-ethnography)

For each of my courses, I assign an auto-ethnographic research project, framed by a specific semester's theme, within which students choose topics of relevance to their personal-local lives, yet showing evidence of its collective socio-cultural significance for local, national and/or global spheres. The project's time-frame is one semester and is completed in assignments steps, to make it doable: free-writing proposal, workshops in class, report draft, peer review of drafts, final report, final presentation and poster. The main purpose is for students to learn how to design an original project, learn to collect data, answer a research question, and write a report about their findings. The project requires fieldwork and other kinds of data to answer the research question, interpreting critically the data gathered, and presenting findings in a scholarly way. The main outcomes of the project at the end of the semester are a written—or other media—final report and a poster for the oral presentation to the class and to display outside of class (the set of posters is called The Harvest—La Cosecha). Whenever possible, the final poster and the student's experiences of completing their projects are shared with the wider university community and beyond (some students have used a revised version of their final reports to present at conferences and/or to publish articles in student journals). It is important to clarify, that this is the core design for the auto-ethnographic project, however, the academic intensity of such projects can be simplified, according to the type of courses we teach and the educational levels of our students. Below I outline the "whole enchilada," to explain in detail how the project unfolds from brainstorming to final report, so readers can choose the modifications they wish to tailor according to they own needs.

Core Assignment: Project Design and Research Process

In the first few weeks of the semester we have in-class workshops to brainstorm students' ideas related to the theme of the semester, and to choose a topic for their projects. Once the students have identified a topic and formulated their research question, they begin their process of research. The most important part of this process is to generate an auto-ethnographic research question, that is answerable in the short term of a semester; this is indeed the main guide and the backbone of the project. To organize the research process, the project is completed in steps, for which I have created a template with guidelines, that also informs students how the assignment will be graded and the numeric value of each part (see sample rubric in Appendix). For the completion of the project students need to gather diverse sources of data to develop academic skills, such as gathering interdisciplinary references from databases, editing data, drafting, using concepts learned in class (to produce theoretically informed critical analysis), write their drafts creating a synthesis of their diverse data to answer their research questions, evaluating the practical or policy implications of their topics, completing a peer review, and revising drafts for their final reports and poster abstract.

To gather data and to complete the project, students: (a) Collect *memory-data*, using free-writing techniques, this is a kind of narrative about their relation to their chosen topic to examine past memories, and from these, identify at least five significant *landmark moments* of transformations; (b) Conduct *auto-ethnographic fieldwork* (participant-observation) to generate data from the present, this requires students to do "deep-hanging-out" with themselves, through their daily life (as related to their topics and research question), and to write fieldnotes to keep tab of their habits, routines and movements—or routes—in their neighborhood and areas between their home and the campus; (c) *Collect primary sources* this include one oral history, with a person well known to them, to obtain a different experiential perspective about their topics (requires signing a consent form), and searching family archives (to find records, documents, photos, etc. related to their topics); (d) *Collect secondary sources* (through library and online academic research and history related to their topics, to find out what has been published about their chosen topic and which theoretical interpretations might be useful for their analysis), these references serve to place their personal perspectives in socio-cultural present and ethno-historical contexts (considering implications at local, national, regional or global scales); (e) *Manage data* (organize, edit and analyze data) to find answers to the research question and to write their report of findings; (f) *Draft report*, finish a draft of report, exchange with peer to help each other improve their reports, before assignment is due to professor; (g) *Revise and correct draft* for final report—with feedback from peer and professor—format and upload a PDF copy of their final reports through the course management site; (h) *Create a basic poster* (81/2" × 11" page) with heading, image and a project abstract, to use in class presentation (see Appendix).

Through weekly classroom workshops, students share progress reports about their projects, get my 'live' feedback and their peers, bring to class their doubts about project management, rubrics, methods or any other aspect of their projects, as well as share examples of the kinds of data they are collecting (see example of workshops in Appendix). In these workshops, students get also training in ethnographic ethics, reflect in writing, orally and graphically (mapping exercises) about the project, about the process of research, about the "micro-politics" of fieldwork, about the logistical challenges of managing the completion of milestones, and about writing their final report (especially how to integrate references in their analysis). Our last workshop is about the poster and the significance and pleasure of choosing good titles. When a step or assignment is about to be due, we take the workshop meeting to read together the rubrics and to clarify students doubts about what to do about report contents and format. This systematic checking-in of the progress report is helpful to support the completion of the project and I have noticed that results in better written final reports. In-class workshops are useful also because they help create a collaborative spirit in the group; peers learn how to support each other through witnessing the successes and challenges of others, they offer feedback about projects' contents and form, such as asking questions when things seem confusing to them, or sharing references that they believe might help their peers. These *talleres* could be intimidating for some students at first, but gradually become a comfortable, fun and productive work-space, and many students report looking forward to these informal exchanges as a group. By the second month of the semester these exchanges become very lively and inspiring, as students get to know each other better through their projects, and this creates a cohesion that benefits all the rest of the coursework we need to complete, including the review for the final exam.

Once students narrow their topic, generate a research question that makes sense to them, and allow themselves to commit sincerely to their projects and to the process of research, they invariably get excited about their work and I know the final harvest will be great. The most confusing challenges for students come when trying to formulate an original, well-articulated and answerable auto-ethnographic research question. Some students begin recognizing then, that what they are doing is not a rehearsal, but *real* research, with the uncertainty of original creation, issues of data handling, emotional vulnerabilities, boundaries and roadblocks as well as competing priorities, but also full of insights and pleasures of hands-on learning. Those moments of confusion and crisis, I cherish, and students dislike. It is at those junctures, when what we call "rich points" of ethnographic practice happen, when unexpected productive insights are found. After the impasse of realizing that we and our projects want different things, that we could go in so many different directions, and that sometimes the "data" and our questions are in slight contradiction (the agonizing exciting loops of creativity and growth), then suddenly something happens through which we glimpse clarity and a new direction that was not there before. Sometimes the challenges are ethical and emotional; for example, a grandma who does not want to sign the consent form for the oral history, or memory-data free-writing discoveries, sadness or trauma related to their memory-data, which requires reframing intentions for the project, so the student can feel safe to proceed. Remaining as a soundboard, through the weekly workshops and through individual consultations during office hours, I allow students to reflect and evaluate their challenges and to find clarity about the direction they are going. I ask lots of questions and acknowledge their progress, struggles, and the courage they show in taking responsibility for the development of their work.

By the time the draft assignment and peer review are due, I can evaluate the quality of project design, the students' commitment to the research process itself, the skills they have gained in class to best integrate knowledge from multiple sources, and how prepared—or not—they are to create a critical argument in the discussion of their findings. At the beginning of the semester, I pair students with a peer (by roster order, to introduce chance encounters, as in "real" life) for them to complete the peer review assignment; students exchange emails addresses and work together during workshops, but the only requirement for grading is that they review each other's drafts in writing, to help each other improve their final reports.

The peer review assignment is very helpful; students get to evaluate each other's progress and read concrete examples of excellent draft parts and terrible ones (*partes chuecas*, as I call them, to lighten up the critiques). It is important to clarify that this is not "group work," which, although beneficial, can cause tensions and conflicts for some students. The main purpose of the peer review assignment initially, was to train student in this academic convention, and to make them conscious of the collective production of knowledge. Yet the benefits are many, as students have themselves expressed, when I ask them in class to share feedback about their experience with this assignment. Many coincide in three major benefits: they feel motivated to finish a better draft (since a peer will read it), they feel a sense of responsibility to complete their work, since otherwise their peers would not be able to complete the assignment and get a 0, and the most important, they feel inspired by what the peer is doing well, to revise their draft to make it up to standard with the example of their peer. One issue has been identified as a challenge: a sense of vulnerability, knowing that their peer will read their memory-data, the most personal part of the report. I remind students that they have always the choice of what to include or exclude for their reports, and that auto-ethnography is an academic genre, meant to be shared with an audience, which gives them the chance to negotiate, in a way that is comfortable to them, how to re-present themselves.

After the students make the revisions recommended by their peers, I read the drafts, and make group and individual recommendations for revisions, identifying those areas in which the majority seem to be having the most challenges. For seminar and smaller groups, I give direct feedback through track changes, for larger groups I give one overall comment, and ask those that need the most help to meet in person during office hours. The final reports do not contain all the data, nor all the fieldnotes, that the students collected and produced; they are rather edited versions of what is relevant to answer the students' research questions, and what they feel safe to share with me and with their peers. By this stage, some students are unable, unwilling or feel they do not have the time or skills to accept the auto-ethnographic nature of the project; some drop the course or never complete the final reports. I accept and understand this, and wish them well, telling them they are welcome to my courses if they decide to try it again in the future. If they express a desire to continue with the course, we work together to figure out how to complete their projects, and how to make this research experience and writing practice useful for their careers and lives, regardless if they don't wish to utilize auto-ethnography ever again.

The poster assignment for the final class presentation, has multiple purposes and productive outcomes. There is a simple guide-rubric to complete the poster (see Appendix), student are asked to create a small 8.5 × 11" poster in PDF (to upload to course management site) and two printed copies they bring to class for their oral presentations (one for them to read and one to pass to their peers in the class circle). The poster includes a title and heading, a photo, graphic or table (preferably created by the author) and an abstract of 500 words or less, summarizing the project and main findings (answers to research question). This assignment is very productive, as it helps students gain academic skills of writing an abstract of their work, a challenge, even for experienced scholars, this is common format to submit work for conferences and publications, that shows students how to present research findings. Many students have expressed that doing the poster give them new clarity about what their project is really about, is a last chance to revise their title to make it coherent with the actual contents, and the abstract serves as a checklist for the last revision of the final report. Besides the use of posters in presentations and as assignments to grade, the printed copies are also shared publicly, on a wall or area of exhibition (this is optional, students can choose not to show their work, without any penalty).

The Harvest: Final Reports and Students' Evaluations of Auto-ethnographic Projects

The project's completion process (data gathering, fieldwork, drafting, etc.) is not clear cut; basically I remind students when they need to stop, for data gathering at least three weeks before draft is due, in order to write the report of research findings (the auto-ethnographic narrative answering their research question). This report, although called final, it is only a draft; many more revisions could be needed if they wish to present it in a formal public forum or submit for publication. To create the harvest of posters for the final presentations, students need to complete a draft of report and exchange with their peer for the review. After receiving peer comments and my feedback on the draft they address the most urgent changes and are then ready to prepare the posters for class presentations. The revisions continue, however, to give them more time, but need to be completed before the final report is due at end of semester (after final exam for course).

As explained at the beginning of this chapter, I have created a template rubric to guide students in how to structure their auto-ethnographic narratives (see example in Appendix). This guide could seem, at first, a bit rigid, yet it is very useful; the flexibility is in the contents of students' essays and in the author's voice they express through their writing. I developed this rubric after the first semester of trying out this auto-ethnographic approach, as I noticed the terrible quality of final reports. I am pleased with the results, as I have seen the content quality and presentation of reports improve tremendously. Also, for the purpose of grading,

I needed to standardize the final report, to be fair to all students, as in the reporting of findings they show if they have done the research required, and if they were able to effectively answer their research questions. Through the imposition of a guide-rubric students are, ironically, liberated to produce their best writing, without the anxiety of how to do it and where to put what. I make clear to students that the *project* and the *report* are two different things; the project is the whole research design, process and gathering of data, which can continue the rest of their lives, the report is only one possible outcome, informing about how far they have gone in answering the research question they posed. There is one last workshop where we address the significance of titles, going from a broad "working title" for the project to a narrow title, specifically tailored for the final report, to best frame the essay that they have composed, but also to take advantage of this opportunity to teach them another academic skill. The discussion of the poster rubric (see Appendix) before this assignment is due, also helps the group understand how to use titles to gain clarity about what they are presenting, how they do so, and for whom (issues of audience and intentions).

Through an interactive exercise and the use of title examples from previous semester reports, I show students how titles work for the readers; it is a promise, gives hints of what is coming, points to an argument, entices and inspire curiosity, among other benefits. I also explain how titles function in online databases through keywords for searches. For authors titles have many benefits; it guides us as a checklist to see if we are delivering our promise, it helps us frame and structure our writing to make sure we address what the title announces, and, for many of us, is an inspiration to help us finish the plate of food that our menu is announcing. I am aware that I feel great pleasure in drafting versions of titles, and that I might be making too much of this part of the report; it is not necessary to refine titles for students to produce good contents in their essays. For the conclusion part of the final report rubric, I ask student to summarize their answers to their questions, discuss practical and public policy implications (if any) of their findings, and to close with an evaluation of their project, process of research, and to evaluate their experiences using the critical auto-ethnography methodology (skills gained, challenges or rich points, or anything else they wish to share). After the conclusion, and before the list of references, I ask students to write a short paragraph of acknowledgements and dedication. This requirement is an indirect way of teaching students about the collective production of all knowledge, the solidarity developed in the process of research, and the ethics of thanking oral history collaborators, librarians and others who have contributed to our projects. In my own research experience, I find that writing this paragraph, as soon as I am done with data gathering, inspires me to finish my publications, as I feel a debt of gratitude to those I name, and since I dedicate my work to loved ones—usually to my dead mother—I feel a stronger commitment to finish a good product (yes, I have done that for this book).

The students' final reports are narrative testimonies of the process itself of researching the topic and trying to answer their own question. This report gives students the chance to feel a sense of completion in the mist of so much uncertainty, making visible their local histories and their subjectivity, sometimes, for the first time in their lives. As we discussed our last day of class during the semester of the strike at UPR (one that we were not sure how it would end), students and I had a conversation about project logistics and their challenges with completions. I shared some of my experiences completing projects, and how, in spite of the challenges, respecting deadlines and guidelines for completing projects liberates energies to begin new projects, gives us the illusion of closure, which is very satisfying, helps us in letting go. Long-term perseverance also helps us to develop courage and keep us constantly revising our priorities. Locating ourselves at the least provocation can become part of the ritual strategies for self-management—especially during long project completions, these tricks help us enjoy the process, keep track of logistics, while being present, living fully our daily lives, which do not stop during the process of research.

Students' writings and research has brought me surprise, laughter and tears due to the powerful voice, originality and sincerity in the writings that students are able to produce with this tool. The harvest of papers and posters that students have, and are producing in my courses, have become one main criteria for continuing to use critical auto-ethnography. Writing the final auto-ethnographic essay gets the students' feet wet in taking responsibility for writing position papers and new kinds of academic narratives, paying attention to how to present with care tiny details of their everyday personal lives. Yet, the process of paying attention to these "trifles" (as Clifford Geertz would say), has monumental impact in our understanding of the huge realities we negotiate as humans. Below I share some passages extracted from students' final reports. These come from diverse years between 2008 and 2016, from diverse courses, and universities in Austin, New York City and San Juan. I have edited the paragraphs to show only parts related to project evaluations, research process challenges and experiences using auto-ethnography (see Appendix for more evaluations, with less editing):

> I didn't know that I could be a primary source! It took me a while to take myself and my daily life seriously [...] I also didn't know much about my family or community history, now I have become a memory-data junky ...
>
> [Student response about the auto-ethnographic project. *Course: Contemporary Societies: Africa and the Caribbean*]

... With this project I have cried more than Alice in Wonderland [...], it has shaken the fixed foundations of what I thought it was my life [...], growing up as a Mexican-American Mormon in a small town like Alice, Texas, this kind of learning has blown my head-off ... even though this has been the hardest research I have ever done in college, I would do it all over again, I want to keep using this method as part of my life's toolkit ...

[Student response about the auto-ethnographic project.
Course: Critical Ethnography Seminar]

Thanks to the auto-ethnographic methodology I have acquired skills for how to study in more depth the ingredients in the foods I consume and how these affect my health ... if the project had been a term paper it would have not made this impact in me.

[Student response about the auto-ethnographic project.
Course: The Poetics and Politics of Food]

This method brought me a lot of challenges, pushed me to get out of my comfort zone, to question my actions and interactions [...] Auto-ethnography make us analyze and reflect who we are as individuals, and to study the borders that exist between 'I' and 'we'.

[Student response about the auto-ethnographic project.
Course: Topics in Cultural Anthropology]

I never knew I could write an 8 single-spaced paper without suffering, but it is possible! It was hard work, but it didn't feel like it, I wanted to finish this paper for personal reasons and to share with my father with whom I have not being able to communicate well ...

[Student response about auto-ethnographic final report.
Course: Globalization]

I have never done anything like this, I have never had a homework, project or something that I need to be in the environment studying for a while, this was like a new leaf for me and my life. My experience with this auto-ethnographic exercise was great.

[Student response about the assignment *Being There*.
Course: Introduction Socio-cultural Anthropology]

This methodology helped me to reflect on a personal and macro levels (it was healing). I have learned about a topic I thought I was foreign to [salsa], but now I understand how it is so deeply linked to my culture, class, gender and race (in spite of being a Puerto Rican that doesn't dance salsa)... I believe this kind of writing has great potential to reach multiple people who could feel their experiences reflected or validated ... however, if one is not able to frame experiences at different levels of analysis along the personal, local and global, otherwise it is a collection of personal anecdotes ...

[Student response about the auto-ethnographic project.
Course: Caribbean Cultural Diversity]

As appear in these evaluations above, students have found many challenges and benefits of using auto-ethnography and express that it has been beneficial to them, even as a one-time experience. The *challenging* aspect of the process is key to understand the potential of the auto-ethnographic approach to develop a new kind of "common sense" beyond the classroom. As a way of researching, writing and disseminating knowledge, auto-ethnography becomes a useful tool for anyone eager to try an alternative approach to understand the huge issues of our times and how these affect our personal lives. Likewise, the intricacies of how people do what they do, including our own personal ways of doing, reveals what the *cultural* is. The constant jump between the personal poetics of our intimacy, in relation to the public messy spaces that we share with others, help students understand what the *social* is. This scaling up and down process helps students appreciate the accessibility and pleasure of qualitative research methodologies that initially they consider too subjective and messy.

Reading students drafts of final reports, and the revised versions, reveals that students can learn to truly care about producing excellent work, when they feel the project is *theirs*, not a mere assignment. Being a caring witness to students' projects, this is, becoming a collaborator for them to succeed (rather than a judging witness ready to pounce on them when they have challenges), helps me to be more understanding and persevering, in spite of challenges, in completing my own research and ethnographic writings. Students struggles and joyful discoveries in mastering basic research skills reminds me, regularly, of the potential of research as a tool for liberation, as a challenging *praxis* that can benefit, sometimes in unsuspected ways, our private and public lives. As stated at the opening of this section, students' final reports and the evaluations they make of using auto-ethnography have been one of the main reasons I continue using this methodology in my teaching, as I see the repercussions it has, not only in their academic formation but also in their personal lives.

Through the assignment of an auto-ethnographic project students learn not only how to research a topic of relevance to their lives, develop and learn to trust their writing "voice," but also become active agents in creating archives of their personal lives, their families', communities' and, more broadly, their local histories. Being the author and main "primary source" is a potent combination that seems to further good original writings, and we all need that; students for finding their voice, for empowerment, to pass the course with an A, for us teachers not to fall asleep, tired at 3 a.m. in the morning, due to the exhausting reading of boring, uninspired papers at the end of the semester. This approach is also useful for departments and colleges to meet the mission of their programs, that is, nurturing research initiatives and increasing graduation rates. The completion of the project and meeting the course's Student Learning Objectives (SLOs) are the main goals of my courses and sharing what students have produced is also part of the creative academic process or of any other knowledge and cultural production. In democratic discussions with students, and giving them the option of not participating, we share the final posters with the Department and wider university community. We have been doing these public activities physically through printed poster displayed on whatever walls we get permission to use, but I am in the process of creating a website dedicated to share the posters digitally as well. In the last two semesters at UPR, we had also the opportunity to record radio programs through the university radio station (in the program *Hasta las Piedras Hablan*), and we hope to be invited again. Thanks to the generosity of the producers, student got copies of the podcasts and were proudly sharing it with their family and friends. This public forum served also to feature the work of some of my more advanced students to share their multiple auto-ethnographic harvests (as they have taken many courses with me), and to talk about the graduate programs they were about to pursue, and ideas about the kinds of future projects they wanted to develop, which seeds came from their auto-ethnographic projects.

No amount of lecturing can get to the core of self-discovery as the practice of *doing* research; test-driving tools, gathering—creating actually—new sources of data, reflecting and writing, answering questions whose urgency we did not suspect, analyzing possible answers and their implications, evaluating their methods, the process of research and the new knowledge they have found. At first, guiding students into *accepting their wings* (their agency, their partial yet inherent freedom and intellectual capacities, their right to express what they already know, to find out what they don't and to imagine, with critical awareness of the present conditions, what still doesn't exist), it is hard work. The apparently simple poetics of the quote that opens this section (*"I didn't know that I could be a primary source!"*) made me cry when I first read it, and is doing now, as I write this paragraph. It taught me how aspects of auto-ethnographic research, that I was taking for granted have tremendous impact on a student empowerment. I have already been paid ten thousand times for the time and energy invested in helping students design and complete their projects. These first person writings are critical memory-work, seeds for a poetic archive, to hold a different kind of original knowledge, one that is not only about a social "problem," but rather is about the wider "I," the complexity of how our grounded cultural perspectives are shaped by others and by our relations to multiple intersecting institutions, from states to our homes. But is also about *positionality*; our agency to re-invent the "self," the kind of relations we want, the communities want to belong to, and to the kinds of new worlds that we envision.

Auto-ethnographic projects have a potential healing effect, as the process help generate spaces for critical memory-work (in the sense of going to the socio-cultural roots of our personal challenges). There are studies that are relevant because they give us new data, to best understand what is going on, evidence. Others give us new forms to understand old data or theories, in light of new refined tools. Others shake us out of our complacency, rip the veils in our internal or external realities. There are other works, beyond fiction, cinema or literature, that help us *feel* life, in our bones, those are the stories, old and new, of particular "someones" engaged in their culturally specific life journeys. These kinds of stories, of struggle, of beauty, and sometimes of horror—like auto-ethnographies—inspire an urgency in many to experiment for the first time with new methods, ways of archiving and narrating their own histories. Auto-ethnography is just a portal, a seed planted for future healing; later, the person can decide how to deal with diverse aspects of traumas and treatments for mental conditions; in the meantime, it clarifies basic foundations, to support further therapy or self-directed liberation paths.

In becoming a caring witness to students' challenges, struggles and hopes completing the projects, two memories, in particular, come to mind; a student, who was diagnosed with cancer, lost his hair and was so weak he could not continue attending class, decided to continue his auto-ethnographic project, re-focusing it around his health condition. A young woman who was raped at mid-semester in her dorm room; we arranged for her to continue working from home to complete the course, and she also re-framed her auto-ethnographic project to take into account her traumatic experience and her search for support and treatment. At the end of the semester, they both thanked me for "allowing" them to complete the course and to change the topic of their reports, to be able to examine their new traumatic experiences. But I did not give them "permission" as a favor, I wanted them to write about their tragedies, I encouraged them to do so. I wanted them to use the auto-ethnographic tools, just in case that helped unload their burden, and because I felt sad and impotent, for not being able to help them in their suffering, and I was angry at the social and health conditions that placed them under such challenges at such young age.

Modifying Auto-ethnographic Approaches According to Teaching Situations

My course design, teaching approaches, classrooms dynamics, and the assigned research project, vary according to particular institutions where I happen to be teaching. For example, I was not always able to assign the full critical auto-ethnography project; in such cases, I had to device shorter auto-ethnographic assignments tailored, for example, for general education courses. However, the auto-ethnographic *perspective* has remained the core of my teaching. Once I discovered the potential of the auto-ethnographic methodology to help students take charge of their learning, regardless of the particular course they were taking, I kept using it. I noticed that indeed any kind of auto-ethnographic assignment help students produce original works, of relevance to their lives beyond the classroom. For me as a teacher, auto-ethnographic-centered assignments mean more work, but also a gift worth the time investment and the emotional intensity. It helps me to develop more effective and enjoyable teaching strategies and to become a witness to the diversity, remarkable human resilience, and creativity of the students that pass through my classrooms. In this sense teaching has become for me the most appropriate way of engaging with a different kind of social justice activism; one that is not fixated on a particular ideology that I wish to promote, but rather contributing the best I can to a more compassionate human liberation from suffering, respecting the diversity that such liberation might take for each student.

The kinds of students I have exposed to auto-ethnography have varied also according to the type of college where I teach. At public research universities, such as the University of Texas at Austin (and in a different way and in a different language at UPR-Rio Piedras), I could assign a semester-long research project and use an online course management program, and sometimes a media-lab to help students develop more complex projects and acquire other transmedia skills. At liberal arts private colleges, such as St. Edwards University in Austin, Texas, I had the luxury of teaching small groups ranging from 12 to 20, which allowed me to conduct classes in the form of seminars, giving each student more individualized attention, and spending more time giving feedback to their final report drafts and other written assignments.

In my general education courses at CUNY-Brooklyn (NYC), I served a diverse student population. My classrooms were a United Nations metaphor, sometimes with 30 plus ethnic groups represented, whose first language was not English. Many Caribbean and African immigrants—or 2nd generation—students were part of these groups. For example, I taught students from African (from Kenya and Nigeria) and "west Indian" students (from Grenada and Jamaica), and other 2nd generation Caribbean immigrants in NYC. Invariably at the beginning of the assignment they believed that they knew their region of origin, or how "banking in Nigeria" works, however their auto-ethnographic projects became a powerful tool to discover the strangeness of the familiar and the silences in official narratives they were taught through national or ethnic group belonging. A Russian student, who initially thought that she did not have any connections to Africa or the Caribbean, did auto-ethnographic fieldwork in her kitchen and wrote an excellent final essay on Haiti and Russia relations. Through this research she discovered personal and collective implications of global consumption (sugar and bananas), and how ignorance and stereotypes of those regions was, in itself, another kind of relation.

At St. Edwards University (a liberal arts college in Austin, TX), I got the opportunity to work with mostly "white" students, many of whom considered themselves, the generic norm, non-ethnic Americans. However, through the research for their auto-ethnographic projects, they discovered their hidden cultural histories, through an exploration of the migration routes of their family ancestors, and others discovered how their sexual identities, disability challenges or even their ideologies, *placed* them in vulnerable positions of difference, in relation to the US and Texas social norms, regardless of their whiteness. Some of my Mexican-American students, who were also part of those courses, had the chance to examine the diversity among them and their peers, as is not the same being a Mexican-American, to whom the border crossed their ancestors in Arizona or California in the 19th century, that being a 2nd generation Mexican-American dreamer, whose parents have crossed the border before they were born, or when they were just babies. I remember also a powerful food-centered project, that a Mexican-American student produced about family, gender and her Vegan choice of diet; in the process of writing the final report she discovered that her choice, and the conflicts that apparently her diet caused with her family, went beyond food, implicating also religion, ideology and gendered oppression.

On the other extreme, at a vocational school, also in Austin (ITT Technical institute), the teaching challenges were considerable; ranging from gaps in students' functional literacy, the social context of their lives, their migration status, to classroom conduct and diverse kinds of learning disabilities. And yet, even in this case, many of my students produced excellent works, which became even more significant given the odds. For example, a Vietnam veteran student, who, after resisting the auto-ethnographic assignment, was able to complete a food-centered project about banana consumption that allowed him to explore traumatic military memory-history that had marked him, and was able to "locate" himself along three axes of his multiple intersecting identities as "a southern, white male imperialist." He cried in front of the class during his final presentation, and he made many of us cried. At the same institution, a student brought a box of boa constrictor snakes to his final presentation, to show us the informal business "products" he was distributed, an informal business venture that he researched for his auto-ethnographic project (yes, he taught us how to handle them and the class enjoyed that experience). Another student, a pregnant woman on probation, was able to finish her final oral presentation, while guards waited at the classroom door to take her back to jail, for having missed to report to court. Echoing Ruth Behar (whose work

I discussed in Chapter One), there is an "anthropology that breaks your heart," and there are also students and classrooms that squeeze our emotional beings to the core. Yet, they also amaze us, and inspire us to develop our own strength as humans.

Auto-ethnographic approaches can be used also outside of college classrooms, through more streamlined short workshops, to serve diverse kinds of individuals, in collaboration with cultural and community organizations. Two examples come to mind: creating a workshop with undocumented high school students (in Austin, Texas), as part of my collaboration with Suzy Seriff and Linda Ho at the Texas Museum. This experience resulted in beautiful hand-made books about their experiences of crossing the US-Mexico border (some with parents, others alone). A more recent example occurred while working at *Casa Dominicana* (in San Juan, PR) with adult Dominican immigrants (ages 50 and above), who have been able to learn to read and write through C-Migra literacy program. This initiative aims at helping Dominican immigrants to protect their civil rights and to integrate them more fully to the Puerto Rican society, while achieving their educational goals. We worked for few months to support them to practice writing and reading skills through diverse auto-ethnographic exercises. These activities were centered through their undocumented migrant experiences, the labor they perform to earn their living now in PR, and their local place and community-making in diverse neighborhoods in and outside of San Juan, through their food routes.

The first semester I began using an auto-ethnographic project as the backbone of course design, I noticed a shift in classroom dynamics, as both the students and I *felt*, a liberating energy of co-creating in collaboration rather than in tension with each other. Using an auto-ethnographic methodology to research place and experience has been so far the most effective way I have found to help produce critical work and liberation opportunities in the classroom, to nurture my commitment and, simultaneously, to maintain a joyful disposition in spite of the challenges of critical pedagogy. Yet, I acknowledge that this "teaching for liberation" (hooks 1994), using auto-ethnographic research projects, in a democratic classroom environment, requires a deep commitment to an intense process of learning, re-adapting our collaboration with diverse students, yet its rewards are many for teachers. From the fragile vulnerabilities of the *private* to the macro spheres of the *public*, auto-ethnographic work bridges the conceptual gaps between how the individual and the collective articulate in our daily realities. To produce any creative work help us to live purposefully, rather than only endure life. That is what resilience means to me, a form of "self-empowerment" that liberates space-time for us to trust our intuitions, to discover our value and how we could live our lives, with a sense of wellness, connection and joy. Auto-ethnographic methodologies *place* in evidence how "the personal is political" (and vice versa); when used in a democratic and inclusive classroom context, it helps students and teachers develop awareness to negotiate our response-ability to our local histories, to nurture our imaginative capacity to face—in solidarity—the crises of our times, and to celebrate our individual liberation paths.

Support for the Auto-ethnographic Project: Using a Toolkit for Critical Analysis

To help students make sense of their project data and to be able to write more critical auto-ethnographic narratives, that go beyond biographic testimonies or memory-data, I use a *Toolkit for Critical Analysis;* a set of interdisciplinary concepts (such as culture, power, identity, politics, poetics, etc.) in a version shaped by the most current critical analysis in the social sciences and among feminist cultural anthropologists in the US. I believe these concepts, once understood and applied to concrete events and experiences in students' lives, are beneficial beyond acquiring academic skills, as they serve also for students to make sense of their personal histories, to find out about their civil rights, to respect diversity, and to understand the differences and commonalities in our complex human experience. These concepts become very useful for diverse classrooms in which we need to learn how to work together. I find that an understanding of these concepts creates also opportunities for self-empowerment among students of color, for those who come from marginalized communities, sexual minorities, students that are functionally diverse (new term for disability), or those who confront prejudice due to other areas of difference. Providing a way to begin interpreting social realities and examine the relative positions of normativity and difference, these concepts help galvanize the cultural capital and sharpness about life "out there," that students already bring with them, as they offer a new vocabulary to continue researching ways to support their life projects and their educational goals.

As I explained in Chapter Two, the versions of these concepts that I use, come from social theory in more contemporary interpretations and have specific theoretical framework origins (I include citations to sources in Chapter Two). I gathered the *Toolkit* into separate written handouts, that undergo periodic revisions (and Spanish translation), to make it more accessible to students and to keep up with academic updates in their usage by cultural anthropologists (see example of handouts in Appendix). I refer readers to Chapter Two, if they need to understand my reasoning in choosing specific version of the concepts outlined below. I relocated that discussion there since it seemed to me that such theoretical details could become too distracting in a chapter that is centered on the *practical* uses of auto-ethnography and the supporting coursework to make it happen. Below I give a list of the concepts and define some of them, in "arró y habichuela" (this means in simple accessible terms, in "rice & beans"), showing the way that I introduce them in class.

I have created written handouts that contain definitions and examples of application of the chosen concepts, and assign some or all of them, depending on the course level. The handouts are assigned previously, as class readings, and discussed during the first three weeks of classes. I place this discussion after I introduce the course's topics, and before I give a general overview of the semester's theme, that serves as framing for the students to choose their specific topics for the auto-ethnographic project. The titles of the handouts are: At-Ease-Handout, Representation Redux, Material Culture & Power Redux, Intersecting Identities Redux, Multi-Feminisms Redux, Queer Theory Redux and Ethno-Semiotic Analysis Very Redux. The concepts are grouped in the handouts and are discussed in the order of this list: culture, ethnocentrism, prejudice, discrimination, stereotype, code-switching and code-mixing, the matrix of power (power for/power over, knowledge/power, force-control, hegemony-consensus, agency-resistance, micro-politics and infra-politics, spiritual power), political economy (economy, politics, materia prima, material culture, labor, geopolitics, colonization, globalization), normativity-difference, situated knowledge, intersecting Identities, performativity, gender-feminisms, representation (poetics and politics, representation as process and as product) and ethno-semiotics analysis (one page guide for how to "read" or decode cultural signs). To get an idea about how they are defined in context, I provided some of the handouts in the Appendix.

There is no way to define these concepts accurately, or to find the "correct" version to teach; as I clarify to students, what they mean and how we use them, changes with academic trends, according to where, geographically, we our located, and in the space-time period of history in which we live. I also make sure that students understand that these are not "realities," but "concepts," representations, arbitrary linguistic signs that we use to interpret our complex socio-cultural processes (like the Zen Buddhists say, "the finger is not the moon"). I like using also the metaphor of fruit trees; you cannot, for example, go out there and pluck "culture" from a setting, as if it were a concrete thing, nor can one point to them and say look at it!). From the concepts listed in the Toolkit, there are some that I dedicate more class-time to discuss.

The first four concepts that I discuss are: matrix of power, political economy, intersecting identities and representation, I find these become a good trampoline for discussion of the other concepts. For the concept of power, political economy and intersecting identities I use kinetic exercises in class where we need to physically move in the classroom, this approach has been very useful and students "get it" faster and in more lasting ways. For example, to begin the discussion of power I ask the group to stand up, look at them for no more than 3 minutes, in silence ... I then ask, why did you stand up? Their responses generate the discussion for defining the multiple forms of power, and for questioning our behaviors, motives and the influence of others in our lives, as well for how we give others power over us, consciously and unconsciously. Yes, students invariably say that they stand up due to peer pressure or "because you are the teacher and asked us to do it," but some are more candid giving unexpected reasons, for example, "because I needed to stretch," very few have ever decided to stay seated). I then go to any student seated at the front of the class and demand their chair, then ask the group, what choices do I have to get *that* chair; we proceed then to enumerate possible ways and their consequences. This approach allows me to expand on related aspects of power, such as control, force, hegemony and consensus.

For the concept of *power* the most important emphasis is for students to understand the positive and negative aspects of it (power *for* and power *over*), to understand the complexities of diverse forms of negotiations of power, to question the simplistic dichotomic assertions that there are "people with power" and "people without power" (besides the dialectics of agency, resistance and consensus, we *give* power to others over us in myriad forms). I do a brief stop also on hegemony/marginalization and the dialectics of this negotiation (we are always hegemonic and marginal, in relation to someone else). The discussion of micro-politics and infra-politics seem to be useful also for students, to understand the subtle negotiations of power in our most loving and intimate relations, but also in the exercise of power of those we name "powerless." For discussing *agency*, I use interactive concept map (on the blackboard); using as example a person in jail condemned to death penalty (this was poignant when I was teaching in Austin, Texas), I ask students to consider the choices that person has and its consequences. I end this exercise reminding students of slavery and marronage; how for centuries slaves did not give up their resistance and their hope for freedom, passing on that freedom dream project, generation after generation. One last aspect of power that I have introduced in the last few years is the concept of *potency* or spiritual power, a form of agency that goes beyond external conditions of power *over* or power *for,* since it resides internally, according to cosmologies of many indigenous peoples (*pueblos originarios*) of our Planet. It is an internal life force closer to shamanic spirituality, it is a power that develops from the inside out, based on our growth as cosmic beings. In the traditions of the Native Americans is also a form of power that is earned in the process of serving our communities, a legacy of respect, a sort of wisdom archive passed on from the elders. Similar conceptions of magical, imaginative or artistic power exist also in the western conceptions of charisma (*duende* in Spain).

The *political economy* concept lends itself well for interactive exchanges also that seem to have benefits for students understanding. Asking them how did the desk got into our classroom is the springboard for a chain of power actions and transformations, that go from how raw materials are converted into usable items to the political decisions taken by bureaucracies at our universities to provide educational materials, to the labor dimensions of the economic process and to the socially produced benefits or such labor (e.g., I remind students of the cleaning workers that make the classroom ready for us and of the others that remove the garbage and clean our bathrooms). To make sure students don't get an essentialized, deterministic idea about economy, I link this discussion to the discussion of power, with concrete examples, relevant to their lives and related to local issues in the area where the college is located.

The *intersecting identities* concept is of great relevance—as are the others—for the effective completion of an auto-ethnographic report that goes beyond a personal narrative of a generic human recounting how they feel about a particular topic. In the final report, I ask students to "locate yourself" using three axes from their multiple identities, since this specificity helps them produce a more in-depth critical analysis of the answer to their research question. The "intersecting identities" concept basically means that that we are complex social beings, located, labeled and treated across diverse social categories, assigned by our societies and historical times. These categories (or cultural identities) are historically specific, and have concrete and symbolic effects in our lives, placing us in situations of privilege and marginalization (according to context). This concept is useful to research and examine interlocking forms of oppression, but also interlocking senses of belonging, community-making and resistance struggles. During this discussion I take the chance to clarify definitions for major social categories (such as gender/sexuality, class, race, ethnicity, nationality, citizenship, etc.). It is important to take the time to clarify with students that we are not determined, bound fully by these categories, in spite of the undeniable weight they do have in our experiences. We can always claim (or at least try) some wiggle room for our own re-labeling, this is where I find it useful to include a discussion of *subjectivity*, or how we *position* ourselves in relation to these social categories, consent to them, resist or subvert them. I add to our discussion also the concept of *situated knowledge*, basically how our perspectives (this is, our ways of knowing, perceiving, experiencing and taking action) are shaped by *where* we are. This *where* implicate micro and macro scales of the local and global, the personal and the political, the individual and the collective, from geography to spirituality, from geopolitics to our household composition and the culturally specific neighborhoods we inhabit. The where is conditioned also by those intersecting identities, discussed above, and by the forms of power that we negotiate daily. Our "situated perspective" is, hence, not fixed, but historically specific, and again is not destiny, we always have choices, even if those options have a high price (as the migration process shows so clearly).

The concept of *representation* is one of my favorite concepts to discuss with students, and the most dangerous, since (as a visual artist) I tend to get so involved, that I could take up a whole class-time to explain the intricacies of the *poetic* and *political* aspects of this concept. I begin by showing students (again through interactive questioning and response) how we interact and communicate through mediations, and how these could become also invisible in our everyday life. I have learned few phrases in obscure languages; I begin speaking these to the class, as they, suddenly, wake up making wonderful faces of confusion; I explain then how we need a common code to communicate as a group. I address communication in general, animal, plants and human languages (including gestures and other non-verbal signs), as well as linguistic arbitrariness and the modified Sapir-Whorf hypothesis (how language *shapes* our perceptions, does not determine them), and issues of translation, and the important role of technologies, media and visual culture in our lives. An important distinction (explained at length in the handout) is of representation as *products, processes* and *practices*, including their cultural, legal and political implications.

Whenever possible, I use co-curricular events outside of campus to expose students, in a practical way, to the concept of *representation* (supplemented with other resources related to an event, for example the TED talk by Adichie on the *Danger of a Single Story*). A focus on art, popular culture and representation, serve, for example, in de-constructing and challenging stereotypes of Africa as the ultimate *otherness*. It floored me when a student made this comment: "I didn't know that Africans could be famous artists!" (in response to an extra-curricular event I assigned for an exhibition of the painter El-Anatsui's murals at the Brooklyn Museum). Representation, hence, became a necessary concept because students bring such strong racial prejudice of Africa, the Caribbean, and of diverse groups in US society, regardless if their own history is linked to these regions and groups, or not.

Course Design, Teaching Approaches and Classroom Dynamics

The course design, classroom-work and classroom interactions I have created over the last ten years, serve to train students in the basic foundations of interdisciplinary social science knowledge, through exploration of topics of current significance in our human experience. In addition, this approach helps me create an appropriate context for the development of the critical auto-ethnographic research project. The project, as well, besides serving as a tool to meet the SLOs of each course, becomes a good support for classroom-work, to create a more participatory classroom, especially through reading discussions, workshops for the project and through the harvest of final presentations.

Regardless of the course, I organize each semester around a specific *thematic frame* of a relevant issue in the region where I am teaching, or around an issue of global significance for our current times. This approach allows me to address more concretely the learning objectives and to help students acquire skills of democratic and engaged citizenship. One example that was particularly productive at UPR-Rio Piedras in 2015 was the theme of "Water and Ecology," which we explored during a period of drought and rationing of water in Puerto Rico, by which all of us in the classroom—in our homes and in the campus—were affected. This theme was also the framing required for students to design their auto-ethnographic research projects, as it helped us make academic knowledge relevant to the immediate conditions of students' local places, their society and global realities (water crisis being a global phenomenon). Students were able to research concrete aspects of their personal relationship with water, and how the water crisis in PR was affecting their lives in profound ways, and to link the topic comparatively to ecological challenges at a global scale.

It could appear that imposing a thematic frame would restrict students' research possibilities; yet, giving certain limits to the endless explorations of potential topics for their auto-ethnographic projects, liberates their creativity and grounds it in concrete ways of researching social issues. This was the case with the *water and ecology* theme within which students developed a diversity of topics about the roles of water in their lives, from access to water in their neighborhoods, water in the tourist industry in the Caribbean, to the symbolic religious uses of water in their faith community. The coursework, readings and other resources (including the soundtrack) were tailored to discover the wider ecological, geopolitical and cultural implications of a taken-for-granted resource such as water. Using multiple strategies for teaching around one particular framing theme contributes to develop scholarship, furthers classroom productivity, help students ground their intellectual engagement, foster collaboration and expands the walls of the classroom to reach the whole Planet.

Framed by the semester's theme, all the resources encountered in class are put to the service of the auto-ethnographic research project; the materials assigned help contextualize, problematize and critically decode the semester's theme and hence help students think critically about their project topics. As discussed earlier in this chapter, *Toolkit for Critical Analysis* is a key component of the project design, as it serve to train students to analyze and contextualize their personal experience within a wider geopolitical, socio-cultural and historical context, with attention to their place-specific experiences. The constant practice of applying these Toolkit's concepts in the Critical Responses (CRs) due at every class, is a rehearsal for students' data analysis and interpretation for their final reports, and the CRs help them also to develop their own writing "voices" and to express themselves with more confidence.

During my first two years of college teaching, I tried different ways of approaching the class meetings; I was frustrated with the nice, yet useless PowerPoints I spent so much time composing. I also kept running out of time, and students felt lost in the tropical exuberance of my approach. After reflecting and evaluating in writing my frustration with these approaches and experimenting with new strategies, I discovered that having a fixed structure created a more appropriate space for the *bricolage* of resources that I wanted to use, and for the kind of interactions and participatory exchanges I wanted to create with students. This fixed structure freed me to be engaged with the contents, rather than figuring out how to shuffle what I need to cover for each class; what varies now is the day's menu (which I print in one page, and write an outline on the board, so we all see what we need to do and where we are going). This choreography of a predictable sequence gave me a productive stability to get into an inspired trance, instead of getting students confused with the materials assigned, overextending myself, trying to share everything with them all at once. A fixed structure for class also created a nice flow of diverse activities that appeal to different learning styles, keeping the group awake and engaged with the day's topic, and giving choice of participation for each student, according to their abilities, interests and comfort zone.

With minor changes, according to the course, the characteristics of specific groups each semester, and the type of college where I am teaching, the sequence of my classes goes as follows: (a) *Greetings and logistics* (asking for a volunteer navigator—with audible alarm—to help us keep track of time for each part); announcements of events or updates made to course management website; and circulating roster for students to initialize their attendance; (b) *Now Playing soundtrack* or short video (related to the day's topic) and responses from students; (c) *Drawing of concept map* on the board for students to tease out the most important points of the assigned resources (mostly from PDF readings); (d) *Short interactive lecture* where I highlight or clarify concepts and points that students left out, and link the readings or media assigned to the topic of the week and to the overall theme of the semester (in this part we also keep a running list of concepts to be tested on the final exam); (e) *Questions and clarifications* about the contents of lecture; (f) *Workshop for auto-ethnographic project* (oral progress reports from students, exercises to develop project, discussion of rubrics for assignments before due date, etc.). We try to finish at least 5 minutes early, I thank navigator, and off we go.

In terms of how the dynamics unfolds, I give some examples to clarify. After playing a short video or soundtrack ("Now Playing") related to the topic of the week, the class is ready to discuss the resources I have assigned previously, for which students write informal reflections before that day's class (see Critical Responses in Appendix); we decode these sources through concept mapping (or branching diagrams) on the board for 15–20 minutes (by navigator's timer). This way-finding period allows students free-form participation to sort out the most significant points of the readings, videos or events assigned and their relevance for our understanding of the week's topics in our calendar, and the semester's theme. After this section we proceed to my short interactive lecture, and the last section are dedicated to the project workshop (again all of these are timed by the student navigator, according to my instructions). The class concludes with reminders for the next meeting, and students usually linger around to ask individual questions or exchange news about their project's progress. The role of the *student navigator* is voluntary, rotating, and carries participation points (students that are otherwise timid to participate in class, take advantage of these points). The navigator becomes a crucial help for a productive class, to help us keep a good rhythm, and it seems to help students feel energized, rather than tapping their fingers or glued to their cell phones waiting for the class to end. For seminars that have a smaller group, we re-arrange the chairs in semi-circle to create a more suitable space for dialogue and discussion; instead of concept mapping, students have more time to converse and debate about the materials, while I pass roster silently, marking on the roster each student attendance and participation for that day. The other parts of the basic class sequence are kept. For seminars, the workshops last longer; I get a chance to work with students in peer-pairs, while the rest share their project's progress with each other.

In relation to the resources that I use to support the course contents, I arrived at my current bricolage approach also out of frustration. For example, encompassing yet critical textbooks are rare to find for any topic, but especially for courses about the Caribbean. Likewise, textbooks covering wider areas of the Americas (such as Sanabria's Anthropology of Latin America and the Caribbean, 2007) discuss, only partially, complex aspects of the Hispanic Caribbean region. The simultaneous formations of race, class, gender/sexuality, national formations, and social movements are particularly absent from discussion in most anthropology or other textbooks about the Caribbean and Afro-Latin America. There are excellent histories of the region (see Martin 2011), yet those do not offer in-depth discussions or analysis of the socio-cultural process (Hillman and D' Agostino 2003). Excellent works exist also about specific historical periods or processes in the Americas (Knight 2011), but these texts miss important processes or present a fragmented view by language areas (naming the region *West Indies*, Caribbean or Circum-Caribbean are already revealing of this fragmentation). Given these limitations, I have developed the practice of choosing, for each kind of course (including the food courses), a mixture of chapters from different textbooks. These are however not enough, so I have been concocting my own mix of sources; using journal articles in PDF, videos, music, websites (such as.edu,. org and.gov), popular culture production, podcasts, radio programs and local events, related to the courses topic and semester's theme, as well keeping a list of co-curricular activities (museums, exhibitions, dance halls, films, local street food, etc.) to give students choices for this experiential assignment. I found that exposure to diverse voices and media help us engage "huge" global formations and ideologies, while recognizing unique historical experiences and remaining focused on more miniature details of local everyday life.

For each of the group of sources assigned (not more than 4 at once), the students need to upload one written Critical Response (CR) to the course management site (such as Blackboard, Moodle, etc.) due by class-time (see Appendix for rubric). In short informal essays, students reflect on what they have learned from these diverse media sources. The CRs have three main purposes: (1) to encourage students to read and prepare, since they need to respond to the materials before they are discussed in class; (2) to practice systematic free-writings, to improve their composition and to develop confidence in their writer's voice; and (3) to test-drive the critical use of theoretical concepts, that they will need for their final reports, but also to identify which two references from class could be useful for their projects. Some of the sources for CRs have remained regular, for example few chapters about auto-ethnography and short examples of auto-ethnographic writings (discussed in Chapter Two). The Critical Responses are also beneficial for me as a teacher, as I feel more inspired and pressured to keep up with current literature, but also to read with enjoyment and interest (even when revisiting sources that I have already read, or videos I that I have already watched), since I get to read with other eyes, trying to imagine what is felt from the perspective of the students when reading the articles, watching the videos or listening to a podcast. Reading students' responses to the assigning of a reggaeton song link and its lyrics, their amazement that we could learn something from popular culture, and how they recognize the validity of alternative archives, helps me realize we could do so much, with so little.

Some resources have also become regular fare because they have sparkled very productive discussions, seem to appeal to the majority of students and go well for almost any kind of courses that I teach: Three You Tube videos, in particular, *The Vision of Wangari* (PBS 2009), Chimamanda Adichie's *The Danger of a Single Story* (TED Talks 2009) and Ron Findley's *A Guerrilla Gardener in South Central LA* (TED Talks 2013), have been particularly productive. Thus, I use them as opening for the first CRs in courses such as Introduction to Cultural Anthropology, the Anthropology of Food and Cultural Diversity in the Caribbean. The use of a *Now Playing soundtrack* that I play in class for each course, is tailored to each semester's theme; I find that it helps me ground the discussion of topics and give students a taste of global human experiences through music (see example in Appendix for a Food course soundtrack). Depending on the type of course, I assign other cultural productions for CRs to give students a rest from readings (such as food, visual arts, primary sources, poems, songs, comics, radio, local archives, markets, fests, architecture, monuments, etc.), these are good ways to ground in localities whatever topic we are addressing and are good departure points to make wider connections visible. As I have read in their CRs, students welcome this diversity, they respond well to the use of multimedia and place explorations, which lure their interest in the contents (see example of students CRs in the Appendix).

The use of *transmedia* resources to explore the semester's theme is justified, in part, by the necessity of exposing students to diverse sources of knowledge and experience and to make learning accessible to students' diverse learning styles (auditory, visual, tactile-movement, verbal, etc.). These strategies also help meeting learning objectives, as they support integrative learning, especially through assignments that are also diverse (formal and informal writing—by hand and computer—drawings and mappings, co-curricular events off campus that are experiential, such as eating at a restaurant, attending a public event outdoors—such as a concert or a march). Part of these resources include bringing into the classroom guests—such as professionals, artists, writers and interdisciplinary professors from campus—to offer their expertise and perspectives about the semester's theme. Making emphasis on representation for teaching is helpful, to distance ourselves enough from the weight of tensions that the discussion of heavy social issues creates, yet that we need to discuss in the courses. It also allows us to recognize the constant *mediations* through which we encounter reality, and how these imaginaries play a significant role in shaping our perception of our survival conditions (and vice versa). However, without showing students how to critically decode any kind of representation (through the Ethno-semiotics handout), this teaching strategy could fail. For example, student can miss the global racial logics through consumption and advertising, the problematic representations of difference in social media, and will not be able to identify representation in the political sense; the legal system, issues of migration, legal documents and citizenship.

The transmedia class strategies explained above are limited to the kinds of classrooms I have access to, in the colleges where I teach, and even when available (as at UPR in Puerto Rico), technical issues and old equipment not always allow me to make use of media resources. Yet, it is not the technology that is important, but how we use it; we can create lively participatory environments with very simple tools such as a blackboard (not always black), chalk, paper and pencils, and even without them, under a tree. We decide—as teachers and researchers—what are the boundaries of what "teaching materials" are, through our choices and communication strategies. For example, it was by chance, and not in my best spirit for teaching, that I brought one day—from my walk to campus—a Trinitaria flower (*Bougainvillea spectabilis*) into a classroom in my first semester at UPR-Rio Piedras. Then, I asked students questions that ranged from immediate details of the plant itself to the Columbian Exchange, western taxonomies, colonial global social formations, and Caribbean religious practices, and back to local experiences in their daily life. I remember a palpable sensation of understanding and comprehension happening, an energy of learning through the simultaneous firing up of dendrites among multiple beings, yet each resonating with their own unique experiences, histories and desires. We took an exciting and unsuspected tour through ecological, socio-cultural and ethno-historical interconnections through that plant. It surprised me because it was an improvisation; I had prepared the topic of the day, but I was not sure what would be the best way to begin the discussion. I share this example, to show that it is not necessary to create a full media production—as that shown above in my course choreography—to have an engaging class, or for learning to happen; we not always we have access to facilities and equipment to use digital resources in our classrooms.

Not all forms of engaged pedagogy require following a formula, for the teacher to be media-heavy or to create interactive busy-work; even a quiet lecture can be powerful enough to awaken. Even if only the teacher speaks, if she/he leaves cracks for the students to test-drive the tools and untangle their own confusion themselves, it achieves similar liberation results. Teaching moments of pleasure and caring for what we are doing are where learning happens for all, including the teacher. As a scholar-artist, I appreciate the privilege that some of us have in our teaching to enjoy paying attention to the *poetics* as much as to the *politics*, to magnify the subtleties, and to be present, in spite of the vulnerability we risk when being sincere. Such risks have produced ongoing discoveries, and shown me how collaborative-interactive learning happens, this is also part of what keeps me coming back to the classroom.

A "democratic" classroom requires, from my perspective, the co-creation of a kind of learning community based on solidarity, collaboration, respect and appreciation of diversity, but also fun, pleasure and celebration of our weird and beautiful humanity. This combo helps us all, to commit to returning to our "safe-space" classroom one more day, no matter what challenges we are confronting in our personal lives outside of campus. These are desperate times for students, as part of families and local communities (economic hardships, over-employment, underemployment, unemployment now and later, food insecurity, housing crisis, student loan crisis, migration crisis, etc.), in their struggling for access to affordable quality education, while dealing with their concrete survival and maintaining their health. To meet students where they are, with their concerns and their human experiences, seems to me the only way to make higher education matter at a more fundamental level than job training. In the case of students in San Juan, this is a time of profound national crisis of the ELA (Estado Libre Asociado, legal framework status for the Commonwealth of Puerto Rico), which is severely affecting the University of Puerto Rico's ability to do its job as a public education institution. I have witnessed the repercussions in my students' lives, but also their interest in understanding their locations, what is happening around them nationally and globally, through the diverse semester themes we have explored and through their auto-ethnographic projects. Their *locations* are, however, *particular* not only a generality at the broad national level, they live their challenges and offer their contributions from the specificity of their micro-histories, from their grounded localities. Hence, paying attention to place-memory, embodiment and community gives us a wider portrait of the diversity of student's human experiences and life challenges, and reveals the necessity to recognize and name socio-cultural and other differences to be more inclusive and equitable in our work.

It is important to remind the readers (and especially to those of you who are teachers), that the learning and revision of our teaching approaches has no end. I continue evaluating, revising and updating my approach to using auto-ethnography, to my course design and to kind of classroom work that I have developed. For example, after hurricane Maria, I realized that I needed to simplify the research project, and through that experience, I have become more interested in modifying the semester's theme to focus on solutions, not only on examining a social issue critically, but also explore potential solutions that students can propose, as a blueprint for future actions. There are always challenges and frustrations, but I don't believe in "mistakes," as miles Davis would put it for jazz, "there are no wrong notes." Being open to experimental approaches to teaching is precisely that, continuous growth and learning from what our students do with the tools we share with them.

Teaching and Learning from *Where* We Are and *with* the Students that We Have

"As I completed the draft for this chapter, all the entrances to the campus where I teach are closed with barricades and signs due to the break down in dialogue and negotiations; most activities are paralyzed or on stand-by; groups of students hold teach-ins and workshops inside the campus, and the surrounding community of ordinary citizens and grassroots organizations, and we, the professors, periodically bring donated food and other supplies to support them. The University of Puerto Rico (UPR) is on a system-wide student strike in reaction to the proposed $450 million dollars cuts to the UPR budget. A Federal Commission ("la Junta"), a team of overseers, is in charge of implementing the Promesa law, approved by the US congress to deal with PR debt crisis, imposing a major neoliberal re-structuring of the country's economy. Accordingly, public education, health, government employment and retirement funds have been targeted as areas of budget cuts to pay for mostly corporate bonds. It is necessary to situate this narrative from the grounds of my current local experience, from Puerto Rico, from the Caribbean, in a colonial crisis of centuries in the making, on a teaching stand-by during this semester, as my Rio Piedras campus is, at the moment, immersed in fragmented tensions, uncertainty, and high stress levels from all the sectors affected by the strike …

As the strike kept going on, we instructors had to evaluate if we respected or not the strike (since it was decided democratically in students' assembly, and hence legitimate). Since all my assignments are posted in the course management site, I decided to let my students decide if they engaged or not with the assignments, and I did not punish any of those that did not completed them in advance, once we resumed classes. Since some of my students were active part of the strike, and others disagreed with the strike, I had to create assignments that allowed this diversity of perspectives to express themselves safely … There were diverse perspective and tensions among each of the groups, unskillful actions took place and opportunities for dialogue missed. Yet, regardless of the outcomes, I believe the students nos han dado cátedra, this is, they have been teaching us in so many ways. In a sense they are right that this process has opened the doors of campus while closing the gates. The demands of a coming of age generation of engaged citizens is a valid response to the country's crisis, regardless of the multiple ego-trip motives that participants in this diverse student movement could have as individuals …

Feeling frustrated myself, disappointed with some of the faculty responses (with the lack of unity, and with some outright hostilities between groups), I didn't want to break strike, but I also had reservations about the amorphous leadership of the student movement. I decided then to do what I usually do, which is to focus on what is going on with food. I began to monitor the food practices and food security in campus through the comité de la comida (through the mediation of one of my students). Entering the campus was not an issue, especially when escorted by a student camping there or if one was a researcher with an active project. For few weeks I had the chance to observe, collaborate and document the organization of food preparation, consumption and production through the kitchen and the garden (huerto agro-ecológico). The bulk of donated foods and cooking tools have been provided by local communities, parents, churches, professors, and neighbors to the Rio Piedras campus. I also listened to the narratives of diverse students volunteering there, their perspectives about the strike process and why they chose these food tasks in particular. Through conversations with cooks and novice farmers, and through their Facebook page, I learned about the history of the garden, El Huerto Semilla, was a project started by a previous generation of UPR students during the 2010 strike. That was apparently the first time this 'strategy of resistance' was used in the long tradition of UPR strikes since the 1970s. The UPR administration did not continue to support the agricultural experiment after the 2010 strike, yet, volunteers have kept the grounds fertile and growing minor herbs and produce, and they were able now to revive the space (the cook, a sociology major, told me that they did so because for them that is 'the deeper revolution', food justice).

I realized also how important food is within the logistics of social movements, as I became a witness of this strategy of struggle of these new generations of UPR students. This trend is hugely relevant for planting tiny seeds of autonomy in PR, where nearly 85% of its food is imported which make the country vulnerable to food insecurity, especially among the near 46% of the population who live under the poverty level ... I gained respect for these compañerxs, who expressed that their commitment to food autonomy and social justice, and their engagement with communities, did not begin and will not end with the strike. I also liked how the food committee decided to remain in the shadows of the student movement who were at the gates getting the media coverage; they kept feeding, cleaning and supporting at the most concrete level what they believe is possible for their society. As I noticed the divisions, tensions and conflicts also within the very student movement conducting the strike, it became clear to me that the present and future of PR needs to be negotiated, not in spite, but precisely through diversity and difference, welcoming any interest and abilities to care. In this critical juncture inclusion is not a mere choice; we need everyone. I left the campus that afternoon hopeful for PR and its present, and slightly ashamed that my generation have left so much work for these new humans to do ..."

The passages above (chosen from longer fieldnotes I took) locate where I was in my last revision of this chapter in late 2016, since then much else has happened; hurricane Maria hit Puerto Rico, we were without electricity, water and other services for nearly six months, and some rural regions of the country are still in recovery mode. All my students were affected by Maria, in one way or another, some have left the country, others were left alone, as all their relatives moved to the US, others have been further affected by the political and economic hurricanes that continue to plague PR, some have quit their studies at UPR due to the doubling of tuition ... Many interruptions to our teaching at UPR happened also; in a campus devastated with fallen trees, without electricity and water, with mold in the buildings, and un-useable bathrooms, we formed brigades to help with clean up. Eventually we were all anxious to return to some degree of normality and began holding classes under statues, in the clearings we could find, writing assignments by hand, and creating lists of needs to serve and resources available in our communities. For some courses I lost half of the class, some could not find a way to come to campus or to communicate. Thankfully I found out eventually that all my students have survived, but many lost family and neighbors, death as direct or indirect consequences of the hurricane or lack of access to health services. Many of my students were food insecure or malnourished from the canned and military foods they have been eating, but we were alive, and eager to gather and to find hope and reasons to go on.

Once we resumed classes officially at UPR our work continued; we held conversations to pay attention to where we were, to our challenges, we cried and laughed at the stories told, and took care of each other the best we could. I modified the course and research project considerably to make it easier for students to complete the semester and begin the new one shortly, almost without vacation in between. For their final report I created an emergency rubric, for students to reflect in writing about their experiences post-Maria (see rubric and examples of posters in Appendix). The rubric include questions about the situation in their households, few days before, during and after the hurricane, their food security and access to basic services, identifying three major challenges, three lessons of resilience, the networks of solidarity and community discovered or missed, the role of the Puerto Rican diaspora in their recuperation, the role of media, municipal and national government, their new vision about the country after seeing the poverty and social inequality that this natural disaster revealed, and to share three personal unexpected gifts of the hurricane. For this last part I also did my homework; I wrote and drew auto-ethnographic comix at home, discovering the gifts of Maria in my own life. The students wrote moving testimonies from the heart tearing challenges of their lives, but also full of lessons of kindness, solidarity and self-empowerment that the conditions created in their families, communities and in their personal lives ...

As of today, in 2019, the budget cuts proposed for the university and other public and social services for the country have also gone through, in spite of hurricane Maria devastation, affecting our livelihoods and well-being. We had—before and after Maria—many social actions and demonstrations full of hope and solidarity, that ended however, with tear gas, police repression or indifference by the government and mainstream media who misreported our intentions, to scare the rest of the people into quiet compliance. Yet we remain hopeful, as the whole country has discovered, not only the social conditions of this US colony, but also the grassroots resilience of their communities, their creative capacity to find solutions, and the necessity of *auto-gestion*, of not waiting to create the just society we want, but to begin at micro levels, right now. I am pleased to report that the students from the strike's Food Committee, the ones that cooked and revived the garden, have continue their work at Huerto Semilla at UPR campus, and are helping create options for food autonomy in sustainable ways. They are part of a nation-wide nascent food movement concerned with food security in the country. Part of this movement is an organization called *Comedores Sociales de Puerto Rico* who offer affordable meals at UPR campuses and in the surrounding communities (it is similar to a soup kitchen, but is not charity, they make available "pay as you can" meals, open to everyone, in exchange for few dollars, work at the comedor or with donation of one food item). As many other grassroots organizations they got financial support from the Puerto Rican diaspora in the US post-Maria since these mutual-aid groups became the first responders after the disaster. This CSPR was initially a student organization serving meals at UPR campuses. They have also started recently a for-profit venture to be able to fund their projects is called *Cocina Revelde* [Rebel Kitchen], a small restaurant in the urban decayed area of Rio Piedras, closed to campus. They have a healthy menu of choices, vegan food and affordable prices, the place is beautiful and uplifting with empowerment and memory of resistance slogans. Other students and ex-students opened *La Olla Común*, a soup kitchen now serving mostly the homeless population in Rio Piedras, but which, during the first few months after the hurricane, were serving all of us in this area of San Juan.

These auto-ethnographic grounding passages are ethically necessary to write and to share with readers, as this is *exactly* what I ask my students to do: to situate themselves in their *ethnographic present*, from the local grounds of their experience, from where the auto-ethnographic project and our coursework are approached. In a sense, this whole chapter is a homage to my students, for having the open mind and disposition to test-drive the critical auto-ethnography methodology that I share with them, for becoming vulnerable with themselves, with class-peers, and with me as a caring witness, yet also as a task-master. This chapter is also an homage to all my teachers and mentors, for what I learned, with all of them and through them, about how I wanted to teach and how I prefer learning. This chapter is the heart of this book, and its reason to be; the testimony presented in this chapter was the seed that inspired me want to share my teaching experiences.

References

Hillman, R. S., & D'Agostino, T. J. (Eds.). (2003). *Understanding the contemporary Caribbean*. Boulder: Lynne Rienner.

Knight, F. W. (2011). *The Caribbean: The genesis of a fragmented nationalism*. Oxford: Oxford University Press.

Martin, T. (2011). *Caribbean history: From pre-colonial origins to the present*. New York: Routledge.

PBS. (2009, April 10). Taking root: The vision of Wangari Maathai. *Trailer*. [Video File]. Retrieved from https://www.youtube.com/watch?v=gzp_GYVv7y0

Sanabria, H. (2007). *Anthropology of Latin America and the Caribbean*. New York: Routledge.

TED Talks. Chimamanda Ngozi Adichie. (2009, October 7). The danger of a single story. [Video File]. Retrieved from https://www.youtube.com/watch?v=D9Ihs241zeg

TED Talks. Ron Finley. (2013, March 6). A guerilla gardener in South Central LA. [Video File]. Retrieved: https://www.youtube.com/watch?v=EzZzZ_qpZ4w

CHAPTER FOUR

Cimarrón Pedagogies

Marronage, Critical Education and Liberation Paths

Decolonizing minds, one at a time ...

L. Marte

What Is *"Cimarrón"* and What Does It Have to Do with Education?

Is there a "*Cimarrón*" pedagogy? if so, which are its sources, its characteristics, its usefulness? Even though Afro-diasporic pedagogical history is diverse and has not being fully documented, I envision a *cimarrón pedagogy* inspired in the long-term struggles, creative resistance and legacies of Afro-diasporic communities in the Caribbean, and Afro-Latin America more broadly. This kind of pedagogy takes *cimarronaje* (marronage), consistent liberation strategies developed under colonial regimes, as a metaphoric narrative that goes beyond a historical moment, and that has implications for education.

Cimarrón was a term first used by Spanish colonizers in Hispaniola, to name run-away goats and pigs that escaped to the mountains, became wild and multiplied. Not much later, the colonizers used the term to name indigenous groups and African slaves in the Caribbean, and their descendants, who ran-away to the mountains escaping from slavery bondage, violence, and labor exploitation, in search of their human right to a dignified existence. This term also became the name given to the formation of autonomous communities, created by runaway groups who were the successful ones (others were re-captured and punished, in many cases with amputations of limbs, and brought back to the plantations). This word was also used to name any "unlawful" or "criminal acts" of resistance by enslaved individuals and groups, for any suspicious activities that were considered to undermine the colonial regime. In the Caribbean slavery experience, the complexity of this project included acts of *grand* marronage (escape and organization of *kilombos* or *manieles* as autonomous communities in the mountains) and *petit* maroonage, that is, every day acts of resistance to fulfill basic needs, to avoid violence, exploitation and to claim spaces of pleasure and creativity. The term can be used as a verb (see Bonilla 2015) in the sense of "running away" to create spaces of partial autonomy, which requires re-inventing and imagining new ways of producing resources to meet basic needs, community institutions and cultural productions to make sense of the world. *Cimarronaje* or *maroonage* refers, hence, more to a condition of survival and a life project rather than to an identity, more to a resistance movement than to a struggle for full independence given conditions of harsh violence and exploitation. *Cimarrón* can be used, hence, to point to the concrete ethno-historical experiences of enslaved populations in the Caribbean, Brazil and, in a more reduced scale, among Afro-communities in Latin America. Also, the term refers to "*Cimarrón* actions" as part of social movements (sometimes spontaneous, sometimes fully organized) in the present.

The *Cimarrón* strategy was focused on challenging and resisting slavery, on creating opportunities for marronage *as verb*—be it grand, petit or leger (see Price 1979, Bonilla 2015, for a full discussion of these terms). These acts of marronage were everyday maneuvers, in the micro-politics spheres of those enslaved lives. Later these "everyday forms of resistance" (Scott 1990) became full rebellions and social movements, and eventually formed alternative autonomous communities, through the process and experience of survival (trying to create a sense of "home" in such a hostile environment). The run-aways first had to convince their fellow slaves and, one by one, in their consciousness or loyalties, woke up to their realities and possibilities of change that rendered their enslavement unacceptable. I image that in the process many negotiations, alliances, and ruptures of relations and sentiments occurred, as well as strong focus and organization of the logistics needed. Cimarrones had to produce their food, defend their *manieles* o *quilombos*, set up bases for their (if not democratic, at least inclusive) deliberations and social rules, division of labor, etc. They had to learn how to trust themselves and how to trust *others*, for some of them maybe, for the first time.

Cimarrón communities in the Caribbean and Brazil represented, besides a palpable example that political resistance was not futile, a concrete experiment in food sovereignty, before the concept for this movement even existed, a veritable alter-native project of nationhood. This daring way of life did not wait for the "revolution" or independence, to begin implementing their visions of becoming self-sufficient, free, joyful and dignified. As a historical process of dis-placement and re-placement, Afro-diasporic populations have been re-making and re-imagining such possible communities until today. In his discussion of marronage and queerness as transnational "identity politics" strategy of resistance, Cummins proposed the term "crossroad identities" as a way of understanding the project and legacy of marronage as a "tradition of sustained subversion" (2010: 171). The author proposes that diasporas, marronage and queerness have had to engage the guerilla tactics of "visibility/invisibility" and had to build communities of struggles outside of nations and empires crossing diverse boundaries, nurturing whatever marginal sites are left, to build counter-memory archives to pass on to others. The visions and daring of past *cimarrón* communities in the Caribbean and Brazil, their legacy of creative resistance and the leaders who helped organize them were teachers; in the resonance to conditions in the present, and as a form of productive memory-work, they are still teaching us now.

The concept of marronage could serve as a way to agglutinate dispersed, yet common, paths of "bricolage" in pedagogies of the oppressed, feminist and critical pedagogy experiments (see Kincheloe 2004 for relation among these kinds of approaches). In teaching from within institutional and bureaucratic disciplining, from within neoliberal visions, one is, in a way, declaring one's classroom a *cimarrón* space, *breve territorio liberado* (brief liberated space), at least for a few hours. It is in this sense that I propose that a critical pedagogy classroom could become a space of *petit* marronage, temporal and micro, yet with huge lasting effects. This kind of "maroonaging" from the classroom requires a grounding on place-specific histories, integrative strategies, fringe knowledge, improvisation and "radical" imagination, not as teaching techniques, but as essential aspects of a *Cimarrón* vision and logic, which values bricolage and diversity, the wise willingness to pay attention to *any* source of learning. *Cimarrón* ways, empowering ways of learning and teaching, could be developed from the vantage point of diverse teaching methods, that are aware and concerned with maintaining the delicate negotiations, respectful communication, creating common codes, sharing tools, strategies, and skills for learning, that go beyond "imparting" knowledge, as we recognize that we are also learning and engaging with our own liberation paths. These ways of teaching-learning require also to be aware of the situated conditions from *where* and *when* we are teaching, and whom are we sharing the classroom with. We need hence to become attentive to the ethno-historical specificity of our students, and to our own personal trajectory, to the place-memory relation we have with the neighborhoods we inhabit, and with the institutions and country where we are teaching.

This teaching=learning *with*, requires the risk and trust in the creative capacities, both personal and communal, poetic and political, from where we humans re-invent ourselves, to create dignified conditions for our lives, even under desperate circumstances (for this metaphoric usage see Robinson 2007).

Marronage can also be productive as a metaphor for current visions of communal projects engaged in the reclamation of dignified and healthy ways of living, ecological justice and food autonomy. Such projects require simultaneous awakened consciousness at individual and collective scales, differences and boundaries, need to be acknowledged, respected and negotiated in the process. Human rights should include access to land and resources, but also our inalienable right to experiment with diverse ways of life, to create parallel communities utilizing diverse solutions to the same challenges, and to create and enjoy sustainable worlds that make cultural sense to each community, including how to learn and to teach in diverse way, beyond a wester education regime. "Marronaging" goes beyond mere resistance or demand; it is not waiting for the "ideal" conditions for a different world to arrive, but it begins to be created by our everyday actions and solidarity, from civil spaces, from below; it is also a non-violent strategy (historically, the Cimarron guerrillas engaged in self-defense only when attacked) just going away and "making salt" (like Gandhi and his people in India). It is productive to think of labor migration (and their diasporic formations) from Latin America to the USA (as women, men and children, alone or together, almost by any means and transport) as post-colonial also (and in the case of Puerto Rico, colonial) forms of marronage, running away (or faking documents) to find other local homes under better life conditions. The migration of these demographics represents to me *grand* marronage in the sense of the drastic movements, dangers, border crossings and cultural transformations, but *petit* in the sense that the struggle for basic survival continues, and a wider project of autonomy not always prevails. Yet, through grassroots networks and organizations, some communal foundations are created to continue struggling for their human rights in the new society.

Gilmore suggests three ways to continue threading, what she calls the "backroads" of research and teaching: (a) *expose* (what is going on and what it means to those participating), (b) *confront* (self and others' use of taken-for-granted filters that blinds us to exploitative common sense; and (c) *transform* (e.g., using "local ethnographic perspectives to achieve small acts of transformation in the way we relate to each other beginning in the classroom" (2008: 110)). Documenting how local narratives and grounds are imbued in global predicaments entails "dialogic learning" to understand how to listen to the many voices that emerge from this space-time negotiation. *Transformation* (trying to avoid the almost inevitable ideological directionalities of what teachers feel students should do with such knowledge) is the recognition that we will die before completing our work or achieving the just and democratic societies we envision. Hence, contributing to passing on the tools as well as helping refine our toolkits seems the only way to keep archiving our proposals for future generations to take apart and question. A heterodox way of knowing and teaching—Gilmore's "picaresque pedagogy"— (or my *cimarrón* version), requires the teacher-student-researcher as protagonists and narrators (in a similar way, Kincheloe (2004) proposes *bricolage* in our choices of research methods). Only then can we hope to transform the palpable contradictions of domination, to help us—with as much pleasure and political seal—to critically dismantle old stories as much as to unveil and re-imagine new multiply situated stories.

The testimonial vignettes about my use of critical auto-ethnography methodology in the classroom shared in Chapter Three, are not isolated instances of making college teaching relevant, fun and useful or trying best strategies to meet institutional goals. My intention is not to propose a formula that teachers interested in critical pedagogy should follow. The descriptions and reflections about the process and products of the auto-ethnographic research project, my approaches to course design, choice of teaching materials, and democratic classroom interactions are rather practices and conceptions within my wider "life project" (Mohanty 2003), this is, a wider purpose to live our lives and to work with others for the kinds of just societies we want. My commitment to critical consciousness, radical imagination, and social justice as well as the recognition, understanding, and protection of diversity are at the core of my feminist life praxis. Within this life-project—and since I decided to earn my plantains as an academic—I have the goal to teach the best I can, whatever I need to teach, and to *anyone* who walks into my classroom (or into a workshop). Hence, "*cimarrón* pedagogy" is more a goal than a description of what I do in the classroom.

Pedagogical Genealogies: Critical Education Routes and Radical Imagination

> Radical simply means grasping things at the root.
>
> Angela Davis

By critical education in the title of this book, I refer to more than applying critical pedagogy strategies, for instance, I refer to contextual conditions of policy that guarantee the access to quality, critical education as a civil right and as pre-condition for democratic citizenship. For example, students from marginalized communities—or from working-class households—should be able to get access to complex critical teaching, regardless of the perceived gaps that others identify in them, and for which they are usually taught with an emphasis on technical learning, preparing them only to join the workforce. Part of a good critical education is exposure to a diversity of approaches, resources and interdisciplinary fields, as this could inspire diverse students in their choice of professional paths and sometimes to find passionate vocational choices from which they could make great contributions to future generations. Below I discuss some genealogical routes through which I came to create the *cimarrón*-bricolage approach in my college teaching. Rather than a literature review, this is a discussion of how these resources became significant in my own educational routes and what I took from them to nurture my teaching strategies.

Grounded Genealogies for Critical Education

A *Cimarrón* strategy is a good metaphor to name my teaching vision, but it could also be used to refer to a wider "community of practice" (Wenger 2000) of teachers all over the planet who have similar visions, goals, and life projects. My teaching approach is not unique; it is rather a *bricolage* nurtured by diverse sources where I found echoes of my concerns. I have found many online communities of teachers—by accident, as most good things—and feel I am part of them, at least virtually. But before the internet was our public sphere, through diverse publications and authors, I learned—and continue learning—about critical education. My teaching practice and vision exist within a wider life project, which is centered on creativity, awareness, joyful solidarity, and caring.

My teacher training has been in the making even before I became a college instructor. Below I pay my debts of gratitude to some authors-teachers-mentors, for the cultural capital and legacy they have shared and for the vulnerable risk they have taken in disseminating their tools and what they have learned. I believe that these works nurture empowerment and healing, they help us transform our colonial Post Traumatic Stress Disorder (PTSD) into critical knowledge/power and into an ongoing liberating and creative praxis. I wish I could write about many more authors-teachers, but there is only room to acknowledge some of the ones who have been the most crucial in my critical feminist pedagogy approach. I offer below some landmark moments in the way I became interested in pedagogy, and I discuss briefly which aspects of these sources were the most appealing to incorporate into my teaching. I discuss the works in the order that I found them; many of these have become mentors to me, even if I have never met them, and have made the greatest impact in my way of learning and teaching.

Critical Pedagogies

I first encountered the term "critical pedagogies" in the preface to the Paulo Freire's book *Pedagogy of the oppressed* (see Shor and Freire 1987, Freire 2000), this was in the 1980s, when I was a college student at the University of Puerto Rico-Rio Piedras campus (UPR). At that time, I still experienced the classroom—and life—as a student, from the other side. When I read that short book it opened a hole in my skull, as I realized I was not receiving—with rare exceptions—a critical education, and that the "banking system" of teaching has been the norm in all my educational life from Dominican Republic to Puerto Rico. This was the first realization, the social context part of the critique I already had it since I have been heavily politicized since my childhood about the struggles for justice in DR and the references to the whole history of Latin America. I was also an avid reader already of Latin American history and literature.

It was, however, one particular book, that showed me what a critical pedagogical style feels like, and how it could help me learn and teach in a different way. Aníbal Ponce's book *Educación y Lucha de Clases* (*Education and Class Struggles*, first published in Mexico in 1937), has become, since I first read in 1987, a constant companion, which I re-read, at least once a year (see Bonus Track for details about how I found this work). Ponce's book showed me how much I had still to learn, the many tools I had yet to discover, and the power of critical teaching to open the potential of our minds and hearts. In my non-expert opinion, this book is the best analysis of European "western" education development from the middle ages until the beginning of the 20th century, discussed in political economic context of transformations that led to Capitalism. It is also a sharp critique of the hegemonic discourses that have shrouded the actual practices of teaching and learning, and of the many working class struggles to gain access to quality public education. I appreciate not only the contents and his fine-grained humorous analysis, for his ethnographic and gender sensibility (he was doing ethnography in the historical archives), and for *how* it is written. Ponce's writing style is a marvelous example of sharp prose, full of poetic irreverence and lack of intellectual sentimentality. I have today the complete works of Aníbal Ponce (published in Cuba, he is not well known in his country of origin), and return to his essays periodically, many of which are directly or indirectly related to his vison for critical education. In the preface to the complete works volume I learned that his work was compiled posthumously and the material for *Education and Class Struggles* book were his teaching notes for his seminars. I also learned about his commitment to education, not only as a topic of research and scholarship, but also as a civil right—within a wider Marxist praxis—that he was contributing through his dedicated teachings in México (to where he migrated and where he died).

To get and to give a critical education is necessary that we gain some understanding of the ethno-historical context of the societies where we are learning and teaching. In relation to my experience the greatest frame of relevance is the colonization of the Americas by European nations, all of which were represented in the colonization of the Caribbean. In this sense a post-colonial perspective and a project was born early in the Caribbean, with the marron communities and later this long historical burden filtered through into theorizations, historical analysis and other works by public intellectuals. I like to mention, yet will not discuss in depth, just few of those that were relevant in my undergraduate formation in the 1980s at UPR. Aimée Cesaire *Discourse on Colonialism* (2001) and Franz Fanon *Black Faces, White Masks*, were not only crucial in my formation, and painful to read, but I assign—at least some passages—today in my Caribbean courses. Eduardo Galeano's Open veins of Latin America (1997), another landmark work about the atrocities of the colonial and imperial interventions in Latin America, gets balanced by the more poetic and hopeful trilogy *Memorias del Fuego* (Memories of Fire), both are a tour of the terror and beauty of this region's ethno-history. The works of Betances (1986) and Hostos (1873), I found early on in mentions from history books before I got to college, yet it was reading their own words that I got a sense of their visionary work on behalf not only of the Puerto Rican nation but of educating for freedom, through their actions and their writings, and through their common project for regional unity to create more just nations (la federación antillana).

Fast-forwarding many years to Austin, Texas (and skipping my years in New York City) *Auto-ethnography* became my main tool for teaching, but I found it later in my life, when I was an anthropology graduate student at the University of Texas at Austin. Once I began designing and teaching my own courses in 2008, I began utilizing this methodology to create a research-based, project-focused approach to teaching, and I have seen the tremendous benefits of auto-ethnographic projects to nurture a critical education (see Chapters Two and Three, for a full discussion of Auto-ethnography). Yet before I got to this decision, I had a long, intense, and at many points, joyful journey to fill up other gaps in my basic intellectual foundation, while I was gathering the toolkit for my dissertation's ethnographic research (see Chapter One for a genealogy of those sources).

Feminist Pedagogies

I encountered news and examples of something called "feminist pedagogies" (see Weiler 1991, Mohanty 2003, Luke & Gore 2014) indirectly first, also during those years as a graduate student at UT-Austin, specifically through courses on feminist anthropology, African Diaspora and the research methodologies seminar. However, I also found feminist pedagogies as a necessity. When one has the commitment to ending gender discrimination and inequity, one needs to know also how to teach new generations to continue creating knowledge and policies to end inequality. Feminist pedagogies, as critical pedagogies, aim at teaching students how to learn critically, and how to take responsibility for their own education and for defending their civil rights. Going beyond these basic skills, feminist teacher-scholars focus specifically on gender and its multiple intersections, and they prefer certain methodologies, such as oral histories, life histories, and personal narratives. Central to this approach is also creating "safe spaces" and consciousness growth in the classroom (risky, yet necessary, and a focus of many critiques aimed at feminist pedagogy).

Before I could understand this teaching approach, however, I had to fill up—mostly on my own time, outside of graduate courses—my huge gaps on what "feminism" was, and to trace it through some of the classic texts, just to be able to understand the more updated versions, beyond the second and third wave. I found out that feminism was plural and complex, more than social movements or women movements, included centuries of intellectual, philosophical and academic genealogies of women all over the world, claiming a right to their full creative humanity, not only to their civil rights. Through this learning spree I found the works of bell hooks (yes, in lower case, as she spells her name, to honor her grandmother) her essays on feminism (see 2000) were very accessible to me and from them I learned a great deal. And through her more classic cultural studies articles and video interviews I leaned about the intersections of representation, feminism, race and gender. Through her writings I also learned how to be a scholar that is not afraid to be accessible to wider audiences. It was more recently that I discovered her books about pedagogy (see 1994, 2003), where she described some of the classroom dynamics, her reasons for her teaching style and her wider hopes for college education in general, not only for Black students. I found in those pages, echoes of my own concerns and visions, and I felt that I was also part of a new vibrant way of teaching, in an old and venerable feminist tradition of critical pedagogy.

I had excellent anthropology professors at UT-Austin, and some, like Polly Strong had a very effective feminist critical pedagogy teaching style, that I wanted to emulate. Another professor and mentor, Jafari Allen (see 2011), through his course readings and through his powerful writings, exposed us to queer Black feminist scholars, who helped me fill in some important gaps in my intellectual formation. Two of the most significant for me, again because of the power and fierceness of their writings, were Robin Kelley, from whom I learned about the long history of "radical Black imagination" (see 2002) through which

I recognized the legacy I have also received of this tradition coming from the Afro-Diasporas in the Caribbean. I found also Audre Lorde (see 1971), a poet and teacher who was for me more significant than any anthropologist. I found out years later, in 2012, while reading her autobiography, that her parents were from Barbados, she was a 2nd generation Caribbean immigrant in the US. This small detail of her personal history meant a lot to me, as she had become a teacher and empowering scholar to so many "women of color" in the US, regardless of their origins.

The works of Lorde through her essays and poetry, and in particular through her book *Sister Outsider* (1984), showed me the power of the personal when contextualized within wider social realities and, watching videos of her conference presentations, I realized what an effective teacher she was, as these were de facto teach-ins experiences for the audience, as were also any of her written essays. Through her work, Lorde generates a space for radical pedagogy, born from her struggles to survive as a working class, single mother and a Black lesbian woman intellectual (intersecting differences that placed her in marginalization, in the US of her life context between the 1930s and 1980s). As important and productive as her reflections and de-construction of her differences and struggles, was her discovery of her own power to reclaim a life of dignity, creativity and joy, in the mist of all those challenges. Other scholars kept coming into my life, in the trail that Allen, and my new relation to African-American peers and mentors at UT-Austin (such as *Omi* Osun Joni L. Jones and the other artist-scholars who gave us mentoring through The Austin Project, a workshop for "queer women of color and their allies"). These new experiences of working with women across our differences, and using those as assets to create together, opened for me other spaces of growth and learning that have greatly benefited my teaching. It was through the Austin Project, in 2005, that I first heard of "jazz aesthetics" and found the poetic "revolution" that June Jordan was creating through her teaching, by making the writing of poetry accessible to underserved students and creating community networks to explore critical issues beyond literature.

As I was writing these passages, I realized that the works and teachings of these Black feminist and queer mentor-scholars discussed above, were, in an indirect way, auto-ethnographic, even if they had never heard about ethnography, or if they did, they were not claiming to be using it in their works and writings. Many of these scholars coincide also on the necessity of "de-centering the west" through post-structural and post-colonial feminist pedagogies (see Tisdell 1998, for details of this, by now old proposal).

As a bridge between feminist-queer pedagogies and place-based education is the use of oral history in education, not only as a method to gather data in students research projects but also as way to include and document the perspectives of surrounding communities, of students' families and to create dialogue across generations and other forms of diversity. As explained in Chapter Three, oral history is one of the kinds of field data that I request that my students gather for the completion of their auto-ethnographic projects, to contrast other perspectives in local histories. An oral history is *not* an interview in the standard sense, but rather a life history that includes more than answers to researchers' questions; it is a testimony that should contain the flavors and vivid contents of the ways of speaking and narrating of those that agree to collaborate. These ways of speaking are to be respected in the exact way in which people pronounce (the dialects), the specificity of their non-verbal communication, as well as a description of the context through which the interaction and recording of the oral history took place. To make sure this is the case the best way is to do short fieldwork with the person (or "deep hanging-out," even if only for few hours in three consecutive meetings). There are excellent oral history readers, many of which come from the explosion of interest in this method during the 1970s–1980s (the rescue of *herstory* and other subaltern subjects). From these I found repeatedly the work of Shopes (2002), as one of the most relevant for the study of communities through auto-ethnography. Her own work documenting working-class lesbian women herstories in NYC, evidences how oral history methods help us create classrooms out of communities, and in the process rescue from silence and erasure social groups that have been excluded from official histories.

Place-Based Education

I discovered place-based education indirectly, during the design and completion of my dissertation project, but also through exposure to the work that teachers with a commitment to ecology—mostly from the natural sciences—were doing, particularly for primary grades in public schools. This interest in place/space (was first an appealing geographic notion to me, yet a vague abstraction, until I bumped into Dolores Hayden's remarkable work about the "power of place" (1997), specifically through her focus on workers' landscapes in the USA after WW II. The concepts of *place-making* and *place-memory*, as well as feminist political ecology frameworks, that I found through her work became crucial for my research and, hence, for my teaching. Although not quite related to literature about pedagogies, I discovered cultural geographers' contribution to mapping methods and I also fell in love with their potential for my research and teaching (see Christie 200?). It was from Hayden and Christie that I discovered also feminist political ecology (see Fraser 1990, Duncan 1996, Massey 2001) which helped me to develop an ethno-semiotic thematic mapping method that I called *foodmaps* (see Marte 2007 and examples of students' hand-drawn foodmaps in Appendix). I later found texts that explained the pedagogical strategies of bioregionalism and "place-based education" (see Gruenewald 2003, Sobel 2004), to open the classrooms to the surrounding communities and ecological regions (see a more detailed discussion of this in Chapter Two).

Political ecology helped me to become aware that another dimension of place is ecological awareness. We are witnessing new forms of planetary consciousness never seen before; new generations, at least since the 1980s, have been able to grow up seeing gorgeous images of our Earth from outer space. This new view of our planet as a common "home" is to me as monumental as I imagine it was when the first news circulated in the European renaissance, about the roundness of an earth that was no longer the center of their known universe. To help further a respect for this unity in diversity, as suggested by place-based education and eco-feminist practice, and to push the limits of radical imagination, I expose my students to the ecological dimensions of the human experience. Beyond the basic survival needs for food and water, dealing with natural disasters and climate change, or the effects of housing and air pollution on health, an environmental justice framing also help us develop a multispecies sensibility (the very boundary of our "humanity" is defined by the existence of other life forms). I try to make students aware of our shared grounds with all forms of life in the planet, how we use them, eat them, invade their habitats and destroy them, put them in zoos, but also how they have become pet companions through domestication and how many humans are invested in helping preserve endangered species (animals and plants). In a way, I became an anthropologist because I have serious challenges with accepting my own humanity, and tend to communicate better with plants and animals, forms of consciousness as complex as ours, yet whose difference I find strangely more familiar.

Part of a place-based critical education is the aspect of geopolitics; to teach paying attention not only to localities, but also to national and regional context where we are located, and in relation to diasporic networks present in our classrooms through the cultural histories of both students and teachers. In relation to this, I am looking forward to research projects that could help me fill other gaps in my learning and teaching, about the history and currents state of college education, in relation to the Caribbean as region and of Africa, because of the diasporic relation to Afro-Americas. Two sources I found as I was closing the revisions for this book (but did not have time to read), seem very promising, How (2000) on higher education in the Caribbean, Bristol (2012) on plantation pedagogy, Ladson-Billings and Henry (1990) about African liberation pedagogy,

Lavia (2006) on post-colonial pedagogies of hope, and Lather (1995) on post-critical pedagogies. I include these in the references for readers who are interested.

Informal Education

One major source of critical education, not only for me, but for any human (as the use of auto-ethnography in the classroom shows) is daily life, the places we inhabit and the social relations through our families, networks and communities. Yet this formal education is never separate from daily life, hence, I acquired my informal education through the past and present intersecting communities of practice and sentiment, that I encountered through the diverse localities I have inhabited, and these became important sources in my learning and teaching (see Bonus Track for more details). These rich sources of informal education were key to survival and for my liberation paths, and similarly are helpful for any human, since these contrasts help us to appreciate the wider classrooms of life. From the women in my family who taught me the power, beauty and dangers of being a woman, to diverse neighbors, workers, street vendors and other ordinary folks (through their practical consciousness and sharp-witty proverbs), I discovered an everyday powerful poetics, that made me question how little I knew about the complexities of life and helped me to develop a sense of humbleness, teaching me, as Milton Mayeroff (1971) would say, that "no source is beneath me."

There are ways to bring the ease of our informal learning elements into our classrooms. Through my own experience and through my years of teaching, I have discovered that we learn better when we are relaxed and having fun. Joyful learning is an investment in "*pachanga* mode" or *relajo*. Both words point, in the Hispanic Caribbean, to an irreverent *cimarrón* attitude, a disposition to humor, and a willingness to *celebrate at the least provocation*. Hence, I use any resource I find could help students learn. For example, besides helping to promote learning, I use music, comics and stand-up comedy videos in my classroom to lighten up the heavy topics we need to discuss, at times traumatic and violent negotiations, in the American experience and in our shared global human condition. A food course for example, can become quite depressing (as my students have expressed after some heavy readings). This moment is when it is urgent to balance out with an exposure to the poetics of the human experience, the weirdness, beauty, pleasure and creativity of food production, consumption, how food is represented and used as a metaphor (from sex to national identity), the role of food in helping us ground our deepest emotional connections, our culturally specific ways of speaking about food (which feeds our aesthetical needs), and the place-memory grounding that invest food with symbolic meanings beyond a basic nutritional need.

Conceptual Frameworks: Intersections of Diaspora, Race and Representation

> For the master's tools will never dismantle the master's house
>
> Audre Lorde

Lorde's quote above, to which I will return at the end of this section, is a good framing to discuss some theoretical frameworks (encountered through African-American scholars, during my graduate training) that have been very productive to develop the kind of *cimarrón* critical pedagogy approaches that I discussed in the previous section of this chapter.

African Diaspora paradigms frameworks have many currents; the ones that have been the most useful in my classroom and in my own research are taken from diverse fields, including, Critical Race Theory (Delgado & Stefandic 2001), cultural studies (Hall 1997, 2006), Post-colonial, Black, feminist and queer theory (Scott, Mohanty, Allen), and racial formations scholars (Omi & Winant 1986). CRT, for example, has become the most relevant framework for research in higher education and proposals for public policy changes in the US public school system (Nisbett 2013). Another critical intervention of African Diaspora frameworks is the focus on racialization processes, rather than race (a problematic concept, debunked scientifically, yet deadly real), and to question "Blackness" as political project with diverse and contested versions, yet allowing for a contingent use of race ("strategic essentializing") from a "standpoint" position, when people need to create alliances to defend their political and cultural rights. CRT is defined as "complex legal and intellectual tools for making sense of all forms of human inequality" (Ladson-Billings 2004: 57). This framework has become an interdisciplinary community of scholars, interested in advancing a new kind of common sense, in that coincides with feminist and social justice frameworks who seek to end all forms of discrimination, not only those based on gender and race. To me, the first hook to use Diaspora as a framing concept to understand diverse group transformations was its anti-essentialist conception of identity.

In which way do African Diaspora paradigms help us understand the significance of migration trajectories old and new, boundaries, borders and mobility of all sorts? and why is this focus necessary in education? African Diaspora, as a wider frame of cimarronaje in the Americas, is conceptual toolkit, that could help us develop teaching resources tailored to global conditions that all our students encounter, regardless of the communities where they come from. These frameworks serve also to find concrete and metaphoric spaces to re-image *cimarrón* projects within alternative visions of post-development. A diasporic framing allows us to interrogate fixed boundaries and bounded belongings, be their identities, nations or communities (Sleeter 2004). Beyond migration, across nation-states, focusing on routes is more productive than searching for roots/origins. Diaspora as "dispersal across space and time" (Lukose 2007: 412) also includes imaginative and cultural productions, what *those people in movement* archive and tell themselves and others about their experiences. These narrative memories matter as much as the concrete history of slavery and plantation system. A focus on *private* memory and how this is negotiated under particular contexts help us pay attention to *public* narratives, to notice how they generate each other beginning, if we wish, with the recycled nature of the colonial images of "its others."

Social Darwinism conceptions of race in college classrooms, are the norm. Students bring racial prejudices with them, not only about others, but even internalized inferiority complex and stereotypes about themselves, their families and communities. Beginning then with a decoding of images of Africa and of the Caribbean opened a path for students to question any other familiar images of otherness that they bring to class. I recognized that I needed to first address these representational filters to move on to understanding the topic at hand, but also for students to be able to analyze their auto-ethnographic data, using a critical race lens. Addressing regional stereotypes and prejudices could help us to interrupt other forms of intolerance to differences. Taking time to develop in students a "racial formations" literacy seemed then imperative and unavoidable in my classrooms in TX, NYC and now in Puerto Rico, where racism is present (although disguised in euphemisms) and internalized in the way students perceive race in everyday life, shaped by family narratives, institutions and by popular culture and media.

As a case in point, Africa has the greatest genetic variety in the planet and, yet, it has been used as a "boogie-man" continent, a perpetual case of underdevelopment, revealing the punishments due to those daring to resist western progress. These pervasive stereotypes reveal great ignorance of Africa's significance in human history, the existence of a vibrant complex African continent in the present, representing the population as millions of starving poor dark people—born underdeveloped—rather than the most ancient and diverse indigenous societies of the Planet and the first "origins" in the endless diasporas of our humanity. The Caribbean region is another case in point. The region is usually represented as a touristic free-zone of exotic and illicit bodies, landscapes and pleasures, political revolts and cultural extravagance. The Caribbean as portal to our current globalization's first experiments with industrial production has been a crossroads of empires and of significant historical events. Ironically it is also the birth-place of remarkable intellectual works of liberation and artistic expression, and one of the most diverse regions of the Planet. There are obvious connections between Africa and the Caribbean in historical terms and through the present echoes of racial colonial legacies. The stereotypical images of the Caribbean resonate quite closely with those very sources that helped generate the images of Africa. The tasks of teaching how to un-think and re-imagine the Caribbean and their diasporas as well as other colonized subjects (as suggested for example, by Trouillot) is harder without exploring wider ethno-historical contexts, otherwise, we risk reproducing the usual stereotypes, tropes, and silences in colonized people cultural histories.

The challenges of teaching *about* the Caribbean *from* the Caribbean and *for* Caribbean students at UPR in Puerto Rico (where I currently teach), has taught me how much more needed is teaching *with*, rather than teaching to, which is a must within most feminist pedagogy approaches. Reclaiming a safe space to directly address race, diaspora, and blackness in the Hispanic Caribbean matters right now and is socially significant because of my relations to PR and DR through my own cultural history and because of the delight and burden of understanding the closest communities we inherit and keep making. Puerto Rico, as other Caribbean countries, is indeed a diverse society, and one could think that cultural nationalism, class, and citizenship are the most significant identity politics areas of contentions, given the colonial relation of PR to the US. However, the subtle erasure of race and ethnicity seems a perpetual elephant in the room that not many teachers and students wish to acknowledge. For example, Dominican immigrants of first and second generations—as some of my students at UPR—are marked as black, a way of otherizing in relation to race, yet this is also the case for visibly black Puerto Ricans students, who are "confused" with Dominicans, revealing a questioning of their national belonging, which is very damaging to these students. It is then easier to understand why both Dominico-Boricuas and Puerto Rican students who are visibly dark-skinned distance themselves from a reclamation of blackness. Teaching about racialization, although still risky, for those of us who dare teaching it, is a productive way of creating safe spaces for these students to learn and express themselves, and for opening alter-native views that value difference, as resource and as challenge, to re-imagine and to create truly de-colonized ways of relating. I teach racialization (and the ethno-historical conditions from which the colonial concept of race emerged) in an intersectional way, this is, racial as one of the many intersecting axes of difference that condition how we are located in our societies (the other major ones being gender/sexuality and class).

My choice to use African Diaspora paradigms, Critical Race Theory and to address racialization as central to teach about difference, represents additional challenges in my teaching. I am still grasping with finding a balance to engage—"with loving care" as suggested by W. E. B. Du Bois (1996)—with the poetic immediacy of local communities, while putting spotlights on the global racial dimensions that are at the origins and current predicaments of African and Caribbean countries, in their fierce national specificities and in their shared regional struggles and hopes. Another challenge has been the accusation on the part of some Latin American and Latinx colleagues, that those of us focusing on race, are reproducing US cultural imperialism. Many a times I had to clarify that in focusing on race and afro-diasporas, my intention is not to impose a category that I am well aware people in the Hispanic Caribbean, and their diasporas in the US, do not use in their daily life. I also clarify that, although is well known in academia by now, that the category of "race" has no biological validity, openly discussing this concept is a way to denounce this social construction, and to help transform the discriminatory practices and social inequalities that it continues creating. We could pretend that race does not matter socially, (that might be convenient for those "Hispanic" or Latinx who could pass as "whites," and who are not objects of daily racial micro-aggressions), but if we need a different approach, if we want our teaching to be relevant to the realities that our students (and our own families, in their many shades of blackness) are facing, and if we wish to become allies for social justice in and outside of our classrooms.

To address this critique, usually directed to those of us trained in the US, using theoretical frameworks of diverse origins and publishing in English, I return to the quote of Audre Lorde's that opens this section: "For the master's tools will never dismantle the master's house" (1984 and 2003). I first read her article, titled likewise, in 2003, but it took me a while to realize that this quote had resonances with my graduate education and with my Caribbean experience. This phrase kept coming to my mind in different periods of my life ever since, as I keep questioning my own academic training and my teaching approaches. My interpretation of this quote is given in the form of a question: Can one liberate oneself with the same knowledge that created the bonded conditions? This question is one of the ways that I understood the above quote from Lorde, which refers to the actual slavery regime within which African-American communities in the United States had to reclaim their lives, but also refers to the oppressions she experienced in her own life, as a working class, lesbian Black woman in the US during the 1940s–1980s.

Although I agree with the most obvious historical referent of this quote, I have also another perspective, about what the *tools* the *house* and the *masters* mean. Afro-diasporic peoples in the Americas, and Caribbean people in particular, are the direct syncretic by-products of the process of colonization: only 60 years after 1492, most of the indigenous groups that inhabited the Islands had disappeared through direct violence, mass suicides, illnesses for which they had no immunity, and the rest had mixed with both African slaves and Europeans (it is referred to as the process of ethnogenesis). The colonial sciences, resources and education in the Americas, and the global hegemony of most of the European nation-empires were obtained with pillage, genocide, forced labor and forced acculturation of indigenous and African people. Hence, to me those *tools* have already been paid for, with blood and continue through structural inequalities and in the repercussions of colonial traumas. Those tools also continue transforming and are still developed and produced collectively today, with voluntary and force exploitations (such as the extraction of *coltran* from Congo, to make the technological marvels of smartphones). The masters' *house* was built by the workers, not by the masters (slaves even cooked for them and raised their children) and economic production rested on enslaved and later proletarian masses. Beginning in the 19th century with nation-states, building and entering other "houses" (institutions such as schools) have also been claimed and obtained with long struggles for civil and human rights that continues today (Brown vs Board of education, is one of the most widely known in the US, but is only one of those many struggles' landmarks). In colonial times, the *masters* were not homogeneous (just as they are not today), and they did not remain unchanged by the whole colonial process, since, as Fanon and Memmi have so powerfully argued, the colonizer/colonized are tied in an inseparable dialectics of de-humanization.

I know that Lorde's quote is complex and contains many questions with many possible answers, according to who is implicated, I propose here an answer to my own question: I believe that what are called western master's tools do not belong to the masters. Instead, communities and generations for centuries labored to build, with sweat and blood, those "technologies" and continue paying today a deadly price for their resistance to give up their human dignity and joie de vivre, and their right to celebrate themselves, even in the mist of unspeakable conditions. In summary, we have paid already for the advances in western sciences, for democratic rights, and for the right to a western education, and we do not have a choice but to acquire one today, if we want to have a dignified life. I agree that we need to continue questioning how to "dismantle" oppressions, and to be critical of our acquisition and usage of knowledge with questionable colonial and imperialistic origins. It is important to ask from where and from whom, we get our *tools*, to which *houses* do we have access, and under which roles, and who are the *masters*, but is also imperative that we become aware of our complicity in the reproduction of master ideologies that justified these tools, houses and masters' powers.

To dismantle and rebuilt *our* houses, our senses of home, is to create, as the Zapatistas suggest, "un mundo en el que quepan muchos mundos" (a world within which many diverse worlds can coexist). I do trust that we can, indeed, *modify* whichever colonial master's tools we choose, to use them for our liberation, as the cimarrones of the slavery period did, as many communities and teachers do today, and as many alter-native and minority scholars do in the US academy. If we were to discard what we use today (or even what we eat today), based on boundaries of pollution and purity, we would be paralyzed; when it comes to humans, bricolage of horrors and beauty is the norm. Hence, I will continue using racialization literacy and Afro-diasporic frameworks integrated into my critical pedagogy praxis, as these resources serve me well to engage with and to acknowledge the place-memory experiences and micro-political negotiations of differences that my students deal with inside and outside the classroom. As a complement to this approach, I will also continue using critical auto-ethnography; when this methodology is used as a long-term approach for projects, it becomes also a "perspective," one more strategy in the toolkit of our liberation paths; a way to re-invent, re-imagine and re-mold "the masters' tools."

"The Personal Is Political": Engaged Research as Tool for Multiple Liberations

> For we are the ones we have been waiting for
>
> Elders of the Hopi Nation

Why is *cimarrón* pedagogy (as a form of "engaged pedagogy" aimed at sharing strategies for liberation, of all sorts), so important to me and to my "communities of sentiment," that is, to those who hold similar teaching visions? Taking responsibility for my situated perspective (as I constantly ask my students to do), I remind the readers that self-locating always reveal the *partial perspective* that we embody and the kinds of narratives we inhabit, our taken-for-granted signifying frames. I offer below testimonial reflections of how I interpret the benefits of an experiential critical education approach for students and teachers, outside the classroom, as a way of wrapping up the discussions in previous sections and in the other chapters. I have shared a testimonial tour with this book, to spark hope in the value and potential of our students, and to share insights about the challenges and potential of *Cimarrón* ways of teaching, that are willing to engage not only critical and feminist pedagogy methods, but also vernacular knowledges and experiences of the students we are teaching, of the places where we are teaching and with a commitment to the communities that surround our classrooms.

Learning (like eating, loving, going to the bathroom, like healing and liberation), is something that no one can do for us. Others can support us and cheer us in our journey, but they cannot take our place. It was the meteoric clarity of this realization, during my first year of teaching at UT-Austin, what convinced me of the necessity to use personal experience as a landing pad from where *embodied learning* could happen ("if we don't feel it, we don't understand it"). A mind is not a thing, or an isolated process; we learn with all our senses, from the concrete embodied experiences in specific places and in a particular historical space-time. The concept of "mindful-body" (Scheper-Hugues & Lock 1987) is helpful in this sense, as it points even further to the communicative tensions with others, that affect so deeply our health and quality of life. Educational spaces are like any other sites of social interaction and intercultural communication, not a sanitized rehearsal, but real life happening as we produce learning moments from common grounds. The classroom is also a space of unique cultural encounters; as the poet Tagore said in one of his books "we might never pass each other in this road again," nor in the same company of this *exact* group, as we are at that time (river echoes of Heraclitus). This accidental or chance encounter, is a precious opportunity for growth and collaboration across our differences. As I tell my students, if you find each other again in the future, the memory of this first encounter will open or close portals of communication and potential solidarity among old peers.

As we develop socio-cultural awareness of contexts, relations and histories, of how we as individuals are mapped in and out of societies, we reclaim our agency to re-invent our lives and to more effectively negotiate diverse circumstances. Learning strategies for copying with survival and health challenges could be a significant variable to consider in our curriculum. Mental health gets placed in the spotlight in our classrooms; in that sense, schools are public health sites. We influence through any teaching that we do, the physical, mental and emotional health of our students, their state of "wellness," and we can also contribute to the best integration of these dimensions to compensate for the uncertainty of our times, when we cannot even guarantee for them financial stability or even a job when they graduate, even with a PhD. Through a critical education, students can take time to find out first, where they *are*, and which cultural histories have shaped their survival, their sense of belonging and their present life projects, before they tackle possible solutions to their most pressing health challenges. Understanding needs to come first, before any changes are attempted, we cannot transform what we don't understand (and when we do, we risk creating more damage).

I teach other people's children, after they have been already domesticated, giving them a second chance to find other options to question and—maybe—remove the "tight dresses" (Hurston 1935) of their early enculturation. Emotional and social suffering, although less obvious wounds, are just as traumatic as physical ones, and can be recycled in families throughout life cycles for generations, unless someone awakens to the existence of certain tensions, which might give us an insight, sometimes by accident, to change our perspective and to produce a different kind of empowering narrative shift. Yet, when healing is approached only from an internal psychological dimension, the context of emergence of wounds and traumas within situations, cultural practices and power negotiations are not accounted for (institutional responsibility). Auto-ethnographic research goes even further, as students get to choose a topic of challenge or relevance to their current life experience, and the writing process needed to complete the project promotes integrative learning through narrative memory-data, but also, through critical examination that goes beyond the personal, as it requires contextualizing the personal in the wider political frames of socio-cultural relations. The auto-ethnographic writing process have been found by educational scholars (see Kwon 2016) serve undergraduate students as a healing strategy (especially those coming from marginalized communities).

Resilience can be nurtured in our classrooms through our teaching approaches, for example, research-centered learning is a tool for self-reliance, as it requires perseverance, persistence in the face of challenges, trust in our capacity to do, and learning to question and to contrast diverse perspectives. Yet, without a collective contextualization of our individual experiences, we de-claw our agency and capacity to create profound transformations. For dealing with these macro-aspects of liberating our minds and bodies, one of the benefits of auto-ethnographies is that it helps students to question how we learn, how we come to "know," and how we came to perceive particular issues the way we do in the present, to examine taken for granted collective narratives that seemed "normal" and "natural." As Gramsci has taught us, "common sense" is not so common, when claiming to be the only one is already false, since it is based on *one* particular dominant ideology in a specific place and historical time, even if some—like the positivist paradigm in sciences—linger for centuries. For example, the patriarchal western common sense that only conceives exercising and expressing power as force and exploitation, or the commonsense logic of colonization and slavery, that have justified so many genocides, were also part of an accepted commonsense narrative, and sadly its legacies have still repercussions in our times. We need not one, but many parallel forms of "common senses" and, for that, we need to recognize, respect, and celebrate diversity, as a resource and an asset, not as a problem.

I hope throughout this work I have shown the multiple and long-lasting benefits of using critical auto-ethnography methodologies in the classroom. These benefits are mutual; as a teacher, and as a person, I have expanded, far further, than I could have anticipated. How, then, have I benefited as a teacher from my investment in critical education? In so many ways; (a) to care for my own research and projects and to keep up to date in the interdisciplinary fields I teach through my courses and global news on current events, but also to focus on hopeful moments of solidarity and creative sustainable experiments, to balance out the bad news and historical traumas I need to expose them to during the semester, to remain joyfully committed to my job, in spite of institutional challenges, to witness new generations' coming of age, to feel in my bones, respect and appreciation for our common human experience, through the diversity of my students lives and through their wonderful projects; (b) on a personal level: to get out of my chronic solitude, to have weekly human contact, to care for my wellness (inspiration to care for my health so I could have the energy to give my classes); practice mindfulness, to take a *tregua* (pause-break) to be present with and for others, suspending briefly my self-concerns, getting out of my own way, to allow for magical thinking, even if only for the duration of the class; (c) to develop a flexible moral and a firm ethics; to accept and to work with anyone, as a dignified valuable human, who deserves my respect, regardless of their ideology, religiosity or how they might act outside of my classroom; in this sense, when I am in *teaching mode*, I become the best, kindest, human that I could be, even if only for the duration of the course.

The diversity of the students I have encountered taught me to practice awareness of my own ethnocentrism and prejudices, to be not only tolerant, but also compassionate and patient with the negotiation of our differences. For example, anyone in a military uniform was suspicious to me and I thought I could not possible have anything in common with them. Yet, many of my students in Texas, came from military families or were themselves enrolled in service or were veterans. I discovered their human qualities and the complexities of the live paths that shaped their decision to join the military. In spite of their ideological challenges they encounter in accepting some of the materials I presented, they engaged fully with their auto-ethnographic assignments, and some produced excellent final reports (a young Irak veteran woman, who researched US army policies, gender and the double standards of women claiming a right to serve in armed forces, yet were not willing to do battle in the front lines, through hers and two of her sisters' experiences). Another example was becoming a "Queer ally," at UT-Austin when I was a graduate student, through a chance encounter with an undergraduate native Hawaiian a transitioning male to female trans student; I was amazed at her beautiful human spirit, her kindness and the fierce commitment to her life project in spite of all the violence and obstacles she had experienced. I began mentoring her, since professors seemed not to take her seriously, and she was about to flunk her studies. Today, she is a promising scholar, finishing her PhD in anthropology at Washington State University. Even though I have been open minded since early in my life, for example to have friends from LGBTTQ communities, and as a teacher had the chance to work with many gay and lesbian students (many of whom came "out of the closet" while taking my courses), this transgender student was the one who taught me the most, about how to respect sexual identities and how to use the right pronouns. She also taught me, indirectly, to question and to understand my own sexuality spectrum, as a heterosexual woman by choice, but open to shifts in my desires, who resisted my family's gendered socialization, refused to reproduce, and as a being, capable of falling in love platonically with any human, plant, animal or stone.

Teaching has become for me a commitment to help in the healing of others, maybe as an indirect way to heal myself. During the revisions of the final draft of the manuscript for this book, I realized, after re-visiting in my mind so many entangled routes, that I wanted to share critical auto-ethnographic tools in my classroom, because I was once a lost student (secretly suspecting that there must be other ways), in search of strategies to re-invent my life, to understand what was going on around me. Discovering research as a liberation path and as a site of healing work gave me a life-line, which I can now share with my students, as something no one can take away from them, because it is "cultural capital" that they have created themselves. In becoming a compassionate witness to student hopes and struggles, I have also furthered my own liberation paths, which are, in a sense a form of spiritual and political praxis. I teach for liberation (despite the unfinished and contradictory nature of this aim), in part, because there are young people in my family who I wish I could help in finding healing paths. However, these young people in my family will end up in other schools, in other teachers' classrooms, and I want those teachers to treat them with the dignity and respect they deserve and to give them tools for creating the life they envision, as I try to practice in my classroom with my students. This is my gift of solidarity for those *accidental others* that I encounter in the classroom, to support their breaking of imaginary and tangible chains. I offer this testimony of what I have learned from teaching with the auto-ethnographic methodology, in case these tools might be helpful for others individual and collective liberation strategies.

My learning roots and routes began in the Caribbean, continue in Puerto Rico and solidified in The US (NYC and Texas); these places and my life projects, left me no choice but to struggle to obtain a Western education, without which I could not have become a college professor. Yet, it is not only Caribbean subjects who are compelled, even a Zotzil Maya girl in Chiapas, or an !Kung girl in the Kalahari desert of Namibia, if they want more choices for their liberation projects, need to become literate in the ways of the West, as the whole Planet has already been colonized. I wrote this book as a gift for others to find, by chance or search, in the same way that I found the works of others, whom I don't know, and they have benefited my learning, teaching and the constant revision of my own liberation strategies.

It is also a way of paying many overdue homages; to my intersecting learning communities and to my Caribbean experience, a humble homage to Cesaire's work on colonialism, and a contemporary echo to Aníbal Ponce's 1930s critique of Western education. I pay also homage briefly to virtual mentors and their pedagogical approaches, as well as conceptual framings that inform my practice of grounding my teaching (and my research) in the inescapable embodied geopolitics and poetics of localities, ethno-histories, and subjectivities.

This book is an invitation to other teachers to share their experiences of working with critical and feminist pedagogies in the 21st century, and to not take critical education so seriously as to kill its radical, yet playful imagination potential, its liberation capital. Transformations will happen regardless of our doing, however, focused intentional transformation—the ones that reduce suffering and give space-time for joy and creativity, for loving and building—are only possible if we take conscious risks and go with the flow of our intuition, trusting our value, to further our well-being in our everyday, from the grounds of our local lives (entangled in the global, as any corner of the planet). Rather than focusing only on oppositional politics—needed, yet not sufficient—we can balance our attention and caring energies to focus on solutions, on what works in and outside of classrooms, to create more spaces of non-violent collaboration and solidarity. We are not going to see the "end of the movie," nor see the full completion of the kind of social justice that we envision; we only have this present to do what we can, and to pass on the tools to others, so they can continue nurturing our radical hopes.

References

Allen, J. S. (2011). *¡Venceremos?: The erotics of black self-making in Cuba*. Durham: Duke University Press.

Annamma, S. A., Connor, D., & Ferri, B. (2013). Dis/ability critical race studies (DisCrit): Theorizing at the intersections of race and dis/ability. *Race Ethnicity and Education*, 16(1), 1–31.

Bonilla, Y. (2015). *Non-sovereign futures: French Caribbean politics in the wake of disenchantment* (299pp). Chicago: University of Chicago Press. ISBN-13: 978-0-226- 28378-4

Bristol, L. S. (2012). *Plantation pedagogy: A postcolonial and global perspective. Global studies in education* (Vol. 16). New York: Peter Lang.

Caldwell, P. (2013). A hair piece: Perspective on the intersections of race and gender. In Richard Delgado & Jean Stefancic (Eds.), *Critical race theory: The cutting edge* (3rd ed., pp. 360–369). Philadelphia: Temple University Press.

Césaire, A. (2001). *Discourse on colonialism*. NYC: New York University Press.

Crenshaw, K. (1995). *Critical race theory: The key writings that formed the movement.* NYC: The New Press.

Cummins, R. (2010). (Trans) Nationalisms, marronage, and queer Caribbean subjectivities. *Transforming Anthropology, 18*(2), 169–180.

De Hostos, E. M. (1873). *La peregrinación de Bayoán: diario.* Imprenta del Sud-America: Argentina.

Delgado, R. (2013). Storytelling, counter-storytelling and naming one's own reality: Oppositionists and others plea for narrative. In Richard Delgado & Jean Stefancic (Eds.), *Critical race theory: The cutting edge* (3rd ed., pp. 71–80). Philadelphia: Temple University Press.

Delgado, R., & Stefancic, J. (2001). *Critical race theory.* New York: New York University Press.

Du Bois, W. E. B. (1968). *The autobiography of WEB Du Bois: A soliloquy on viewing my life from the last decade of its first century.* Oxford: Oxford University Press.

Du Bois, W. E. B. (1996). *The Oxford WEB Du Bois reader.* New York: Oxford University Press.

Du Bois, W. E. B. (1999). *Darkwater: Voices from within the Veil.* MA: Courier Corporation.

Duncan, N. (Ed.). (1996). *BodySpace: Destabilizing geographies of gender and sexuality.* London: Psychology Press.

Estrade, P. (1986). El Abolicionismo Radical de Ramón E. Betances. *Anuario de Estudios Americanos, 43,* 275–294.

Fanon, F. (1967). *Black faces, white masks* (Trans. Charles Lam Markmann). New York: Grove.

Fraser, N. (1990). Rethinking the public sphere: A contribution to the critique of actually existing democracy. *Social Text, 25/26,* 56–80.

Freire, P. (2000). *Pedagogy of the oppressed.* New York: Bloomsbury.

Galeano, E. H. (1997). *Open veins of Latin America: Five centuries of the pillage of a continent.* NYC: New York University Press.

Galeano, E. H. (2010). *Memoria del Fuego*: El siglo del viento (Vol. 3). Madrid: Siglo XXI de España Editores.

Gilmore, P. (2008). Engagement on the Backroads: Insights for Anthropology and Education. *Anthropology and Education Quarterly, 39*(2), 109–116.

Hall, S. (Ed.). (1997). *Representation: Cultural representations and signifying practices* (Vol. 2). New York: Sage.

Hall, S. (Ed.). (2006). Cultural identity and diaspora. In *Diaspora and visual culture* (pp. 35–47). London: Routledge.

Harrison, F. V. (1997). Anthropology as an agent of transformation: Introductory comments and queries. In *Decolonizing Anthropology: Moving Further toward an anthropology of liberation.* Arlington, VA: Association of Black Anthropologists, American Anthropological Association.

Hayden, D. (1997). *The power of place: Urban landscapes as public history.* Cambridge, MA: MIT Press.

Hooks, B. (1994). Engaged pedagogy. In *Teaching to transgress: Education as the practice of freedom* (pp. 13–22). New York: Routledge (Taylor & Francis).

Hooks, B. (2000). *Feminism is for everybody: Passionate politics*. London: Pluto Press.
Hooks, B. (2003). *Teaching community: A pedagogy of hope* (Vol. 36). UK: Psychology Press.
Howe, G. D. (Ed.). (2000). *Higher education in the Caribbean: Past, present and future directions*. NYC: WW Norton & Company.
Hurston, Z. N. (1935). *Mules and men*. Florida: J. B. Lippincott Company.
Jordan, J. (1974). On Richard Wright and Zora Neale Hurston: Notes toward a balancing of love and hatred. *Black World*, *23*(5), 4–8.
Jordan, J. (1989). *Moving towards home: Political essays*. London: Virago.
Jordan, J. (1998). *Affirmative acts: Political essays*. NYC: Anchor.
Kelley, R. D. (2002). *Freedom dreams: The black radical imagination*. Boston: Beacon Press.
Kincheloe, J. L. (2004). Introduction: The power of the bricolage: Expanding research methods. In J. Kincheloe & K. Berry (Eds.), *Rigour and complexity in educational research: Conceptualizing the Bricolage* (pp. 1–22). New York: Open University Press.
Kwon, H. (2016). Writing witnessing, witnessing writing: Working through Trauma using performative autoethnography. *Visual Culture & Gender*, *11*, 8–17.
Ladson-Billings, G. (2004). New directions in multicultural education: Complexities, boundaries and critical race theory. In James A. Banks and Cherry A. McGee Banks (Eds.), *Handbook of research on Multicultural Education* (2nd ed., pp. 50–65). San Francisco: Jossey Bass.
Ladson-Billings, G., & Henry, A. (1990). Blurring the borders: Voices of African liberatory pedagogy in the United States and Canada. *The Journal of Education*, *172*(2), 72–88.
Lather, P. (1995). Post-critical pedagogies: A feminist reading. In *Postmodernism, postcolonialism and pedagogy* (pp. 167–186).
Lavia, J. (2006). The practice of postcoloniality: A pedagogy of hope. *Pedagogy, Culture & Society*, *14*(3), 279–293.
Lorde, A. (1984). *Sister outsider: Essays and speeches*. New York: Crossing Press.
Lorde, A. (2003). The master's tools will never dismantle the master's house. In *Feminist postcolonial theory: A reader* (pp. 25–27).
Luke, C., & Gore, J. (2014). *Feminisms and critical pedagogy*. London: Routledge.
Lukose, R. A. (2007). The difference that diaspora makes: Thinking through the anthropology of immigrant education in the United States. *Anthropology & Education Quarterly*, *38*(4), 405–418.
Marable, M. (2013). Beyond racial identity politics: Towards a liberation theory for multicultural democracy. In Richard Delgado & Jean Stefancic (Eds.), *Critical race theory: The cutting edge*. (3rd ed., pp. 580–585). Philadelphia: Temple University Press.
Marte, L. (2007). Foodmaps: Tracing boundaries of 'Home' through food relations. *Food & Foodways Journal*, *15*(3 & 4), 261–289.
Massey, D. (2001). *Space, place and gender*. Minneapolis: University of Minnesota Press.
Mayeroff, M. (1971). *On caring*. New York: Perennial Library.
Mohanty, C. T. (2003). *Feminism without borders: Decolonizing theory, practicing solidarity*. Durham: Duke University Press.

Muller, L., & Jordan, J. (1995). *June Jordan's poetry for the people: A revolutionary blueprint.* London: Taylor & Francis.

Nisbett, R. (2013, spring). Schooling makes you smarter: What Teachers need to know about IQ. *American Educator.* Retrieved from http://www.aft.org//newspubs/periodicals/ae/spring2013/nisbett.cfm

Omi, M., & Winant, H. (1986). *Racial formation in the United States.* London: Routledge.

Ponce, A. (1986). *Educación y Lucha de Clases.* Santo Domingo: Editorial Universitaria-Uinversidad Autonoma de Santo Domingo UASD (first published in 1937, in Mexico).

Price, R. (1979). *Maroon societies: Rebel communities in the Americas.* Baltimore: John Hopkins University Press.

Robinson, T. (2007). A loving freedom: A Caribbean feminist ethic. *Small Axe, 11*(3), 118–129.

Scott, J. C. (1990). *Domination and the arts of resistance: Hidden transcripts.* New Haven: Yale University Press.

Scheper-Hughes, N., & Lock, M. M. (1987). The mindful body: A prolegomenon to future work in medical anthropology. *Medical Anthropology Quarterly, 1*(1), 6–41.

Shopes, L. (2002). Oral history and the study of communities: Problems, paradoxes, and possibilities. *The Journal of American History, 89*(2), 588–598.

Shor, I., & Freire, P. (1987). *A pedagogy for liberation: Dialogues on transforming education.* Westport: Greenwood Publishing Group.

Sleeter, C., & Delgado Bernal, D. (2004). Critical pedagogy, critical race theory, and ant-racist education. In James A. Banks & Cherry A. McGee Banks (Eds.), *Handbook of research on multicultural education* (2nd ed., pp. 50–65). San Francisco: Jossey Bass.

Tanaka, G. (2002). Higher education's self-reflexive turn: Toward an intercultural theory of student development. *Journal of Higher Education, 73*(2), 263–296.

Tisdell, E. J. (1998). Post-structural feminist pedagogies: The possibilities and limitations of feminist emancipatory adult learning theory and practice. *Adult Education Quarterly, 48*(3), 139–156.

Weiler, K. (1991). Freire and a feminist pedagogy of difference. *Harvard Educational Review, 61*(4), 449–475.

Wenger E. (2000). Communities of practice and social learning systems. *Organization Articles,* 7(2): 225–246.

Yosso, T. (2005, March). Whose culture has capital? A critical race theory discussion of community cultural wealth. *Race, Ethnicity and Education, 8*(1), 69–91.

Bonus Track: Mapping the Calendars of My Educational Roots and Routes

> The scientific observation, that appears to only require clear looking, is impregnated, fatally, at each historical moment, with the dominant ideas of its time, to such an extent that the observer –be it aware or not- interprets the phenomenon in the same moment it perceives it
>
> Anibal Ponce
>
> [Pero la observación científica que parece no exigir más que el claro mirar, está impregnada, faltalmente, en cada momento histórico, con las ideas dominantes de su tiempo, a punto tal que el observador –lo sepa o no- interpreta el fenómeno en el mismo momento en que lo registra]
>
> Anibal Ponce
>
> (*Educación y Lucha de Clases*)

In the era of eight-tracks and music records (vinyl), many eight-track tapes, LPs and 45s used to bring an extra song, called a bonus track, a special gift for the customers, that was unexpected. Using that term as a metaphor, I consider this Bonus Track within this *Cimarrón Pedagogies* book an optional reading, not needed to complete the book, yet a nice gift. I wrote this piece for readers who know me, yet do not understand how I became who I am today; it is also for other readers whom I don't know, who might be missing a more direct personal grounding of my authorial voice. I am aware that I am making myself vulnerable, with this direct personal narrative (that might be unpalatable to some readers), yet isn't this exactly what I am challenging my students to do? to engage sincerely (not "honestly," which is different), to take responsibility for their perspectives ... to appreciate the ironic process of becoming vulnerable, precisely to discover our strength, our right to narrate the poetics and politics of one aspect of our lives, from our grounded "ethnographic present." This self-locating of my own educational trajectories and experiences, is also a way to show an example of cultural *cimarronaje* (marronage), in the ways that I have claimed my right to a higher education. This testimony shows some of the educational roots and routes that marked my life and through which I became a college teacher. This is also an example of the critical auto-ethnography *perspective* that I discussed in Chapters Two and Three.

OJO: What I am sharing below is not an auto-ethnography. I am sharing what is called "memory-data," which is one of the first steps to develop an auto-ethnographic project, and I am also sharing interpretations and reflections about those experiences. It is important to clarify, that all memory-data is not a faithful remembering of what happened, but a form of interpretation; anything we remember is done from our present life. Hence, we don't retrieve, but rather *create* a narrative that is filtered through our current experiences. In this sense, there is not such thing as "raw data," in auto-ethnographic, or any other form of writing, as stated so sharply by Ponce's quote above. The genealogies of my teaching-learning have been marked by different region and nations, but especially by the localities and neighborhoods from where I have tried to find a sense of "home." These routes show my discovery of diverse ways of knowing and of being in my multiple intersecting worlds, that I acquired since my earlier socialization and which continue transforming until today. These routes are not traceable lineally and chronologically; it is from the vantage point of my present examination of those experiences that I am creating now connecting points in retrospect, from a vantage point of my 50s.

The testimonial auto-ethnographic narratives in this Bonus (and the other fragments shared throughout the book) are imbued with three main axes of my multiple identities, which have been the most relevant in my own education paths: Class, gender, and migration. These locations have marked my informal and formal education since I first learned how to read in the Dominican Republic, migrated to Puerto Rico 1979, to New York City in 1988, went to Austin Texas in 1999 to get my PhD, and then returned to teach in NYC in 2012. In 2013, I came back to teach at UPR my *alma matter*, from the vantage point of a college professor, trained to research and to teach in US universities ... I returned to PR, in a magic-realist poetic turn, to teach, but also to continue learning, *from* the Caribbean ...

Educational Roots: Food, Gender and Violence in DR

As many children who grow up in Latin American and other colonized regions of the Global South, I became politicized very early on in my life, through my family's struggles for survival and through local environments soiled with social injustice and poverty. My grandmother Rosa Angélica died when she was 100 years old; she saw a whole century of transformation in Dominican Republic (DR), born in 1904, she was a child during the US invasions of DR and Haiti in 1906 and again in 1916–1924, the environment of violence, repression and social inequality continued until 2004 when she died. My parents grew up during the Trujillo dictatorships in their rural localities in the provinces of Montecristi and Santiago, respectively, after they met, they lived in working-class urban neighborhoods in Santo Domingo, the Capital of DR and later moved to Monte Plata. I was born in 1965, during the civil war when constitucionalistas were trying to restore Juan Bosch to power (the first democratic elected president), and I got baptized by another US invasion of DR that same year. My siblings and I grew up during the 12 bloody repressive years of Balaguer (the right-hand man of Trujillo). Political prisoners, harassment of farmers to take their lands and police murders of journalists and left-wing activist were in radio and daily newspapers. These historical contexts had tremendous effects in DR society past and present, in our neighborhoods, households and family mentalities where repressive, violent and restrictive gendered norms prevailed.

My informal education in DR was as significant—or more—than my formal education, as glimpsed from context of the neighborhoods where schools were located and the family's experiences through the diverse local places we inhabited. Even before I learned how to read, I was learning through signs in the landscape that linked my local Dominican experience to the global context of the Caribbean: signs against the IMF, calling to strike for a national minimum wage, and against US imperialism, such as "yanki go home" among many others, written on sidewalks and public walls. In our household, we were lucky to have a working-class mother taking time to help us memorize and recite the abbreviations of major international organizations (UN, NATO, etc.) that during the "cold war" and until recently were household names in Latin America. Likewise, Latin American news, popular culture, Nueva Trova (protest music) and popular literature (such as Mafalda and Rius comics) were present in our everyday life, as were storytelling programs and literacy lesson in local radios. Lessons on resistance and active engagement to claim civil rights and access to education were also taught to me through constant high school and college student strikes and street demonstrations. In our neighborhoods in Santo Domingo strikes and students demonstrations were also frequent. Many awful memories were etched in my child mind, two of those especially; the murder of the student Sagrario Diaz, very close to the school where we attended, and the eviction and murder of the farmer and campesina leader Mamá Tingó. This and other events had so many effects on me, that I am still processing their significance in my life. But there are also other memories, of brave and empowering actions that also left a legacy of hope in me; although as a Pentecostal Christian, my mother was conservative in some aspects, she was also a courageous feminist in other aspects; she worked as a carpenter and helped my father in his construction work (a hammer in her hand was a prodigious tool). During the Trujillo era, being also an excellent seamstress, she made her own clothing, creating ample skirts under which she used to hide her pants with nice pockets for scissors and other useful tools (pants were prohibited for women during the dictatorship). During students' strikes in our barrio, she and other mothers had what now seems to me a "ring of solidarity" with an unspoken slogan ("each student is my son or daughter"), as they were willing to protect and hide in their homes any student running from the police, even if they did not know who they were. They also cooked *bollos* (maize flour with sesame seed, boiled as dumplings) with hot chocolate to feed the students through a back door, showing solidarity, even with the risk of being beaten by the police. During Balaguer repressive years, to appease the hungry masses and to buy their votes, he distributed bags of rice, beans and powdered milk (the *funditas*), thrown to them from huge wagons. Although we were food insecure, my mother refused to go get funditas, because of the violent and undignified way of their distribution, snatching of food from a hungry crowd. This refusal showed us to claim our dignity and to recognize the duplicity of politicians.

As for formal education, the public education system during that era, in particular the one available to working-class and marginalized communities was underfunded, inefficient and repressive (there was still an image of Trujillo in some of the schools that I attended) and a banking education of rote memorization was the norm. We studied from obsolete textbooks, memorized lessons, had exams and no one expected us to amount to anything. The Dominican history textbooks were centered around great events and próceres (famous men) usually upper class and whitened, even though many were mulattos, reproducing racial stereotypes of Haitians as enemies and "others." This is indeed a complex issue, expressed in part by a distance and denial of Blackness, yet also by real historical wounds between the two nations, that left an open prejudice and discriminations against Haitians that lasts until today (yes, I was told as a child that if I didn't go to sleep a Haitian would eat me, "*te va a comé un haitiano*"), but also left a similar resentment of Dominicans by Haitians (only in the Diasporas in NYC have I experienced and witnessed a healing intention and new alliances among these groups). Throughout my elementary school, it was also puzzling that Dominican history was also taught amputated from the Caribbean region and wider global realities, and that we were never properly exposed to the history of the African Diaspora in the Americas, nor addressing the complex effects of plantation slavery in the region, without which our Dominican and Caribbean experience (and our internalized inferiority complexes) were much more difficult to understand and to transcend. After my father migrated out of DR after 1969, we lost our rural home in Sabana Grande de Boyá, and began a peregrination of diverse urban neighborhoods in Santo Domingo (*Capotillo* and *Vietnam*, among others) as my mother kept searching for the lowest rental housing and for any job she could find to support her seven children (mostly as seamstress and maid). Hence, I attended different elementary public schools those years, ranging from one room school for all grades to a repurposed wooden church. Later there was more stability when we moved to Los Minas, (a former *cimarrón* land-enclave from the 16th–18th centuries), a working-class sector of Santo Domingo, far away from the colonial center of the City.

By an unexpected lottery, my sister Arelis and won a scholarship to study for three years at a private catholic school opportunity. The St. Vincent de Paul, which was located in our neglected Katanga (Los Minas) neighborhood (they needed cheap land I guess), but their students were middle and upper-class kids not resident on our barrio, whose parents dropped and picked them up in cars during the week. The St. Vincent de Paul was initially a *parroquia* (catholic church) well attended by local residents with a mission to serve the poor neighborhoods where it was located, most of the priests and nuns were Spaniards and Colombians. The college grew up around this building to include many blocks of open land that have been abandoned sugar cane fields. Due to some critiques of their elitism, they made available five scholarships for "poor" children of our barrio every three years, after which full tuition needed to be paid if they wished to continue in this colegio. The experience of attending this new school gave me the opportunity to compare educational curricula and experiences in public and private schools, in class composition of Dominican society and in racial segregation and whitening ideals of Dominican elites. This educational shift was significant in my learning; the contrast was obvious; the pedagogical resources, the teachers preparation, the teacher-student interactions, the expectation of excellence, the environment, including gyms and outdoor sports, gardens and manicured landscapes, a school lunch program with plenty warm food, among many others. Such quality of education I now knew existed, and I took full advantage of it to become the best student I could, without effort, just out of the sheer pleasure of this plenty.

This environment also opened up for me many other avenues of engagement and creativity; I joined the theater group, took my first art classes, became part of the church choir, and became a pet child of the nuns, helping them with special projects (such as recording voice-over for pedagogical slides and silent films shown in many classes and conducting catechism workshops for students in elementary). These extra-curricular activities gave me a great sense of freedom and experience volunteering, not possible otherwise, as my mother would only let me stay after school with the nuns special permission (they wrote letters every week to assure my mother that I was only doing these exact activities, not hanging-out with friends). This extra time away from home also put me in contact with something I didn't know existed: libraries … there were three libraries!! full of books, on so many diverse subjects, that I could read as I pleased, and sometimes the nuns even let me take some home. Although I had classes now in many subjects (even geography!), in terms of the critical aspects of the curriculum, there was no much difference with public school, and this one had the added religious ideology, that although emphasizing being good to others, left intact issues of history in DR, the racial maps of this society, didn't give us tools to examine gender and class inequalities, to further social justice nor to pursue our empowerment and to create our own path of personal liberation. It was only in my last few months at St. Vincent de Paul, in 1978, that a new priest was transferred from Colombia to this church, who taught us—in small ad hoc classes—about theology of liberation and read to us poems of Ernesto Cardenal, León Felipe and R. Tagore. In Jan 1979, all students at St. Vincent de Paul chanted for the pope Juan Pablo II, a song in Polish—after rehearsing for months—during his visit to DR, I think it was the first time that the national media transmitted news from our Katanga barrio, that were not about street demonstrations, burning tires or police shooting students.

Educational Routes: Diaspora and College Education in PR

After my father migrated out of DR (to the ABC islands and eventually to US) he disappeared from our lives; my mother struggled to make a living in any jobs she could find (including as a maid for elite families in Santo Domingo) while also trying to get a visa to migrate. After more than 10 years she was able to travel to PR and eventually to bring her seven children, most of whom were already over 18th (I was the youngest). Once my family migrated to Puerto Rico in 1979, new educational routes opened for me; the first few years were challenging, confusing and lonely for me, but eventually I learned to adjust the best I could to the new environments in San Juan (from our Hato Rey neighborhood and that school district). My siblings and I lost our grade sequence due to migration, and some of my sisters and my brother were able to complete their GED.

This was still a decade of legal Dominican migration to PR, so the later racism, xenophobia and discrimination against Dominican was yet not felt. I completed my last year of middle school at the Pachín Marín school, not far from where we lived in Hato Rey. Fast-forwarding to 2013, a chance encounter with a former middle school teacher from that school, Elba Paoli, 30 plus years later, reminded me of those middle school years. When we greeted each other, there was joy, surprise, memories, and recognition of the powerful mutual effects we had in each other's learning. In her history courses, I learned to practice paying attention to details, the kind of attention that makes a difference in people's lives, even if that difference is not acceptable or familiar to us at first. Doña Elba (as I used to call her, before I became myself an old lady), was challenging with the quality of the work she expected from her students, but she also had respect for us, using a velvet hand with our emotional insecurities. Her trust in my capacity to learn, and her appreciation of my efforts, rescued me from the trauma effects of migration from DR to PR, a huge and sudden life shift in which I had no saying. She also taught me that if I did not "feel" the human suffering implications of those historical accounts that she was showing us, I would not understand them. I recognize now, that she was a powerful mentor for my future teaching. Meeting her again, now in her advanced age, revealed to me the urgency of expressing my gratitude to my teachers in PR, and to all my mentors everywhere.

The public education system in PR was still in good shape during the 1980s, schools were adequately funded, teachers had better pay, benefits and working conditions that allowed them to become dedicated to their work. I was fortunate, as a migrant child to find supportive teachers who cared about their students' learning and appreciated my disposition and interest in every subject. Although the curriculum was tinted with religious undertones, and not quite critical, teachers made sure we learned the courses topic well and mentored those students who showed enthusiasm for their learning. In spite of feeling strange and distant from peer socialization, I was able to do well in my courses and take refuge in my studies, to deal with the challenging situation in our household, which was, again, unstable economically and volatile, with constant conflicts between my mother and my sisters, as they tried to gain some degree of independence to do their lives and my mother wanted to make sure we were safe. I also felt repressed and unable to study well at home, and I began seriously considering an accelerated track or taking my GED, so I could leave home sooner. As I needed my mother to sign up the paperwork the confrontation was inevitable, and yet it was an important, if not crucial crossroads for my next paths. My mother refused to help me do that; she *begged* me to stay in school and to continue my studies. I was in shock, I expected her to impose her will as I thought her refusal was a repressive way to keep me at home. I realized, years later, that she gave me a huge gift of forward vision and love, for which I will be forever grateful. I decided to continue my high school and committed to learn the process for how to enter college, but also began planning how I could at the same time move out of home, when the time came.

I attended the Ponce de León high school in Hato Rey, from which I graduated with the highest honors and plenty of medals to decorate a wall, although I had no clear idea of what that meant at the time. At this high school I continue developing a parallel practice of reading and writing to complement what I was learning in my courses, became involve in the student's newspaper publishing, theater and oratory club. I had excellent teachers there, who became important mentors. Consuelo Sáez Burgos showed me the importance of women in Puerto Rican history, the usefulness of interdisciplinary foundations (she gave us theater workshops), and the powerful effect that extra-curricular local activities have in students. For example, I will never forget how she took us to the cemetery, to visit the tomb of the poet Julia de Burgos (her aunt); we brought flowers, and five of us read each, one of most well-known poems, while she was listening and crying. The other teacher, César Cruz, who taught Spanish, went beyond language and literature to expose, at least those of us hungry for more, to many other obscure sources, on radical politics, literature and history. Realizing I didn't have a library at home, he lent me twenty books, ranging from Alejo Carpentier to Bakunin (when I tried to return them, after my graduation, he told me they were gifts). Being first generation I had to figure out the whole process of applying to college, but the trust that my teachers had in my capacity to get a higher education, inspired me to complete the paperwork. I was accepted at the University of Puerto Rico, Rio Piedras campus and got a Pell Grant to pay for tuition and books. In search of my independence and a better environment to study, I moved into student housing and began working in whatever jobs I could find in campus (mostly work-study at the main library and research assistant) and in local non-profits.

Despite some butterflies in my stomach, I began my college life wide-eyed and excited to learn in a new way, and to experience the freedom of living away from my family. My first year, I didn't have yet a clear understanding of what I was learning, besides the required materials for courses, my reading choices were wildly diverse and fragmented, but I sensed the significance of some of those works and I was open to continue acquiring the skills I needed. In my second year at UPR, after completing the general education courses, I was able to access new courses at the School of Communication and through the honors program; in the honor's seminars I discovered the poetry and post-colonial work of Aimée Cesaire, and two powerful books that blew my mind, Eduardo Galeano The Open Veins of Latin America (in Spanish), and Franz Fanon Black Faces, White Masks (in an Spanish translation first, then I took French to read the original). These were painful, yet necessary readings, that broke my heart yet expanded my mind and desire for social justice. I had many other seminars at the honors program that helped me create an interdisciplinary academic foundation (ranging from Lacanian psychoanalysis, and semiotics to Caribbean and Puerto Rican literature).

At the end of that second year, I became involved in student and independence activism in campus, yet I was still not as interested in my cultural specificity as a Dominican immigrant. The closest I came to this was becoming a founding member, with other seven students of ASESDO, the first, and only since, association of Dominican students at UPR. This engagement made sense to me, in part, because of what I read in Freire about the need to address our own history. Our vision was still narrow, being all of first generation, we focused on issues of Dominican history and literature, rather than in our experiences as Dominicans in PR. Yet we organized good events in collaboration with Dominican historians in conferences we organized at UPR. We also helped each other expand our learning; a t the instance of the most politically mature of the members, we began a series of workshops on historical materialism and dialectical logic. With the ambitious arrogance of youth, I took German to read *Das Kapital* and other Marx works in the original, to discover that such a project could take decades, so I kept reading Marx in Spanish, and used my basic German to get a little taste of Rainer Maria Rilke's poetry. I share this experience because finding Marxism (not only as politics, but as intellectual current) was as important for me, as later finding semiotics and feminism; these *isms* were productive portals for me to encounter other works, many of which criticized and de-constructed these very frameworks.

An important moment in my formation as a teacher was through the work of an Argentinian educator and scholar, Aníbal Ponce, my best friend and member of the ASESDO gave me a copy of his *Educación y Lucha de Clases* (*Education and Class Struggles*). I had to take that Humanities II course the following semester, which was fine with me, as I realized that I still had enough Pell Grant funds for another semester, and they renewed the contract for my part/time job at the UPR main library. I had many other readings lined up, so I put that book aside, planning to read it at some point. In the summer of 1987, while I was preparing to take a Humanities II exam (Western Civilization: Middle Ages and Renaissance to the 18th century) to substitute for 3 credits of general education requirements, because I wanted to accelerate my graduation date. For some reason I began then reading Ponce's book and could not stop! in two days, in the mist of preparation for the exam, all I could do was read the book and go to the library to check some of the historical landmarks he was discussing, about education in European history. Despite having taken the exam at a small office, full of staff doing their chores, I was sharply focused, and I remember writing with pleasure, as in a trance, pages and pages. But ... I failed that exam (the grader's comments were that there was too much analysis and not enough data, and the grader was probably right). I didn't care, however; because of what I learned in that book, I was able to write the best critical essay of my undergraduate years, since I *felt*, for the first time, that I understood what I was writing about. All the information I had stuffed in my head for two weeks (from the assigned textbook for that exam) meant nothing, until I learned how to make sense of all that "data" and interpret it my own way.

Before I graduated from my BA at UPR, I had the opportunity to take honor's seminars and sociolinguistics courses with excellent teachers. Two of those wonderful teacher-mentors, showed me a teaching style that I wanted to emulate, even before I realized I was on my way to become a college teacher. Mercedes López-Baralt and Héctor Sepúlveda (two important Puerto Rican Scholars in literature and communication studies, respectively), assigned exciting readings, asked us to produce original work, to support it with good data, and cared about our critical learning. Their courses were packed, they become admired and dear among students, not only for the fun performance and enjoyment of their lectures, but also because we *felt* that were learning, and because we could see the passion they had for their work and for their teaching.

How I Found Ethnography and How I Became a College Professor ...

I became an anthropologist relatively late in my life, beginning in 2002 (after training and earning my living for decades as a photographer and as a visual artist in New York City). However, I realize now that since childhood I had a *para-ethnographic* eye, paying attention to everything around me and fascinated with collecting traces of images and documents. My anthropological work revolves around the thematic areas of food, place-memory and the Dominican diaspora in the US and Puerto Rico, and it is through these kinds of academic projects and publications that I have indirectly offered self-reflections about my own experiences, usually under the methodological and ethical discussions, mostly as a form of feminist accountability for our positions as researchers (as example, see 2007). My journey to ethnography and to using auto-ethnographic methodology in my classroom, and hence to becoming a college professor, came about through a series of detours and accidents, and an intense period of informal education through which I tried to make sense of the many fragmented forms of knowledge I had encountered.

After I graduated from UPR, I moved to New York City, where my informal and formal learning continued. Formally I began a doctoral program in linguistic at CUNY, and soon found out that was not my calling, nor was I any good at the skills required, so I dropped out I centered my live around my art and social justice engagement, supporting myself through graphic arts and photography jobs both full time and freelancing. I have been early in my childhood politicized in DR, later in PR I became engaged in activism, but also acquire basic Marxist critical tools to understand and explain social processes, or at least to ask better questions. In NYC I plunged myself into informal learning (occasionally taking free political workshops at *The Brecht Forum* in downtown Manhattan), focused in becoming fully bilingual and in understanding what this new country was and how to navigate it. I got up to date with US history and popular culture, directly reading and indirectly through documentaries, films, art, music and friendship with a diverse multicolored range of "Americans." I understood for the first time, now from the inside, that USA was as much a multi-dimensional complex nation as well as the empire I learned to despise from the outside. I found with amazement how the democratic development did not belong to the state, but rather had been—and continue being—an unfolding journey of constant struggles, organizing and reclamations from diverse social groups, in a context of as much violence as of alliances and solidarity. I also realized the diversity among "white" Americans, the odd alliances and sad ruptures among diverse "ethnic" groups, and how all were, after all immigrants, the Native Americans—despised, marginalized and invisible—were the true natives.

I absorbed like a sponge information and insights not only about US society—as lived *from* NYC, a very narrow view—but also global forces and global history. Although I was interested in the Dominican diaspora in NYC, and became a founding member of a photo-group name *Tragaluz* with four excellent Dominican photographers, I gave up a more direct political engagement, as it was frustrating the apathy and lack of interest in creating a community organization (I was part of that first attempt at creating a *Congreso Dominicano*). I turned my interest then to wider issues. Two films that I watched on the big screen, both on Dec 25th, 1988 and 1989, had a great a huge emotional impact on me and expanded my horizons, *A Dried White Season* and *Baraka*. I was in a daze for months after these experiences, not knowing how to make sense of this Planet and of my life ... It was fortunate, however that I saw them in that exact order, as the beauty of, and its more meditative and open-ended gorgeous cinematography left me a whiff of hope (even now when I know the story of its problematic production, it is still moving and well done). These films and many other experiences became a seed for a search to understand and to continue learning, not only through books or representations, but through social action. I contacted Dominican and Puerto Rican organizations, also I attended cultural events of other national organizations and was a regular at *Casa Las Americas*, at the time a Cuban cultural center in Union Square, at the *Museo del Barrio* and *Neuyorican Poets Cafe*. I also became a volunteer with labor, housing and non-profits organizations, in particular the women chapter of the International Garment Workers Union [IGWU], local 1199 (where I taught Spanish to union leaders and ESL-English to sanitary workers), Women for Racial and Economic Equality (WREE), whose director at the time I met at a Washington D.C. march (and ended up representing at the UN and visiting Eastern Europe an international women conference), and various solidarity committees for Nicaragua, El Salvador and to end Apartheid in South Africa. In 1990 I got the pleasure to join a Harlem crowd to welcome the visit of Nelson Mandela; we shouted over and over "Amandla!" and he stood there, his hand raised, and all of our eyes full of tears of joy …

Personally, those years in NYC became for me a huge life-school and an intense space of transformations and empowerment. In this city developed a "sense of home" that I had never experience before, nor in any other place after I moved out. In NYC I learned through my whole body, as I got to know all the boroughs, through the train and my extensive photo-walking routes. I used my photography and art practice as strategies of survival, to make sense of my life and my surroundings; from panoramic long shots to extreme close-ups, I learned how to pay attention, to the obvious, but also to details that no one cared about (like abandoned shoes and garbage piles), and this form of being present o deeply focusing, trained me for my future ethnographic research. The independence and freedom that I have searched for my whole life came into fruition in this city, and I internalized a powerful emotional map of its diverse neighborhoods, peoples and urban experiences. A new geography of possibilities opened in my life, as these new external mappings, helped me also re-create my internal maps; although engaged with art and labor and housing activism, I had personal challenges with depression and burn-out. I realized that external circumstances and intellectual engagement were not enough, that there were other areas of growth and self-care that I was neglecting. I began examining critically my life, inside and outside, gathering a toolkit of western and Asian psychology, music-sound and spiritual practices, that allowed me to integrate so many aspects of creative vision for the kind of life that I wanted to live. That survival and thriving toolkit is still the center of my empowerment, as I continue revising it and updating it, as I continue learning and finding new liberation paths. However, my understanding of my human experience, although informed by a social justice commitment, that I developed in the Caribbean, was still euro-centric and generic. Since I was not yet an anthropologist, I did not recognize myself as having a specific cultural history nor the personal marks left by my family history and the process of migration.

It was not until my mother died in 1996 (she was living in Miami, Florida), when my cultural specificity hit me and when I realized how lost I was; I needed to examine my lived experiences in the Dominican Republic and what happened after we migrated. A burning desire for understanding my family and communities who shaped my personal life, and finding an archive, or any traces to research that history acquired urgency. The realization of my mother's loss (not having any longer the chance to understand who she was as a Dominican woman, as an immigrant, as my mother), and therefore, also missing pieces of who I was, created a new kind of existential crisis. This sadness and heart break became, simultaneously, a huge gift, as it opened for me multiple portals for caring about my cultural specificity, loving more my family and wanting to understand my country of origin. Although I had a good job as a photographer and printer in NYC, I applied to graduate school in fine arts (since art and media were my BA previous training), and moved to Austin, Texas in 1999. I needed to re-invent myself, to find the tools I thought then, that were needed to understand and process, not only the emotional grief of my mother's death, but also the "social pain" I was feeling. This suffering was also guilt and shame, for not having value her history, enough to document it and to ask her about her experiences (I was so involved until then with my activism, documenting and understanding wider labor and world issues).

My dedication and commitment to auto-ethnographic methodologies is central to my life, and I have an archive on multiple projects that I have been researching and gathering fragmented data (mostly since 1996), yet I have not published any "proper" auto-ethnographic accounts of these research projects. I did publish an auto-ethnographic testimony about my health challenges while conducting fieldwork food research with Dominican communities in New York City (see 2010). During my MFA graduate program at UT-Austin, I produced photographic book-arts projects (see 2002), through which I explored my personal roots and routes as a Dominican woman immigrant in the US. Yet, since I was not yet an anthropologist at the time, these works are graphic memories, interpreted from my adult life in a symbolic or abstract way, and without texts, hence they need the outside presence of a story-teller to anchor them in what they refer to, and to interpret their culturally specific meanings. I wrote also a thesis, as requirement of the program, where I described my creative process behind each of the projects and gave an interpretation of how I learned how to *focus* on my surroundings (2002). This writing was very theoretical and poetically cryptic, as I was still hiding behind my intellect, and I didn't have the necessary knowledge to analyze my cultural specificity.

It was during my last semester of the MFA, that another "rich point" crisis hit me again; I felt, that, although I was pleased with the photo-books I had produced, and the intense crying process and cleansing they helped me go through, I realized that Art didn't have the tools I needed ... I enrolled in an ethnobotany course then at the UT-Austin Anthropology department, looking for other tools to help me finish the series of plant-memory books that I was making. In a sense, I could say now, that I got a PhD in anthropology, to finish an art-project. When I found ethnography in 2001 (through this ethnobotany course), I *felt* in my stomach the jolt of significance of such a methodology for the kind of work and life I wanted. Poetically and politically, I fell in love with the potential of this methodology; ethnography was the tool I needed to understand my mother, and family's history! Anthropology also had the resources I have been missing to do the kind of *bricolage* research and teaching that I wanted to do and to produce the kinds of outcomes I wanted to share with others. Without realizing it, I had changed in the process of completing the MFA, and I was not interested in dealing with the art market to earn my living, nor to be a photo-art professor, in a digital era that was becoming saturated with photo-images. This realization gave me permission to continue studying anthropology, regardless if I didn't have any clear plans for what that would mean for employment.

Even after I graduated from my MFA (and although I began, in 2002, my doctorate in anthropology), I couldn't stop making graphic books of all sorts, mostly based on my family memories in DR, once that watershed was open, I was hungry to continue revisiting and learning from my cultural history, and about my family's memories and migrant experiences (in particular, the gendered experiences of women in my family). My dissertation also began shaping up to focus not on food plants in the Caribbean, but on Dominican food, memory and migration to the US. Between 2002 and 2009, I made many other books, that no one has ever seen (nearly a 100 of all sizes, shapes and contents), related in one way or another to the memory of my mother and other women in my family (see 2005a, 2005b, for two examples of "video books" that I did get to show in public). As I have been taking notes, finding any traces of documents from my family archives (through my sisters), and remembering so many experiences in DR, I began writing memory vignettes inspired by the memory of my mother. These memory notes came to me in Spanish; the style of these essays were a mix of auto-ethnographic vignettes and cultural journalism, with topics ranging from food, my photographic practice and my Dominican and Puerto Rican experiences of place. In 2003, I shared one of these pieces with a Dominican friend in Puerto Rico (at the time the editor of the UPR university paper called *Diálogo*); to my surprise he wanted to publish it and invited me to continue contributing more pieces to the paper. Eventually I published a compilation of these vignettes in book form (see 2008).

It was not until 2008, after I graduated from Anthropology, when I got to teach the first college course of my own design (I created a *Seminar in Critical Ethnography*). Choosing the readings for this course, I felt the other jolt of joyful recognition, when I discovered in the book *Critical Ethnography* by Soyini Madison, where she mentioned the auto-ethnography methodology. Before this moment, I had only encountered it mentions of this methodology indirectly, through the reflexivity passages in the works of Zora N. Hurston, through the essays of Audre Lorde, and through position papers by other feminist scholars. The indirect way that I came to find ethnography and auto-ethnography, was also part of the indirect way in which I became a college professor. If I had not stumbled on Anthropology, I would have not become invested in an academic career, and if I had considered what an academic career would entail, I would have probably run in the opposite direction. Finding the auto-ethnographic methodology, testing its usefulness and realizing how students were benefitting from this experiment, allowed me to find a justification for my very presence in a college classroom; it allowed me to hold a job, since I am sure I would have quit academic jobs, if I had to continue using a standard teaching approach. Choosing an auto-ethnographic project as the core of my teaching, inspired me to find the other strategies I needed, to develop a critical pedagogy approach that made sense to me, and that it was of value for undergraduate students. In making this commitment to not only "earn my plantains," but to do so through engaged teaching that brought me joy, I found a way to connect my past roots to my diverse routes, and in the process, I found a way to make sense of my life.

Notes on Researching Educational Routes with Auto-ethnography

The passages of memory-data shared above are just that, preliminary explorations, they were not produced within an auto-ethnography project. They are, however, a good example of the genesis or seed for a critical auto-ethnographic project. If I were to start such a project, I would need to create a structure for a proper research process. This kind of seed data is so broad, that many different topics could be chosen to frame a particular project, for example, a good topic could be: *Diaspora, Gender and Educational Routes*; an examination of these 3 areas of my educational experiences, for which I would have to pick only some landmarks (from my childhood in the Dominican Republic to my present routes in PR). A topic is not enough to structure a project, hence I would also have to generate a basic research question, for example: Which experiences have marked most deeply my ways of learning and teaching today? These two framings would be enough to begin designing the data collection, which would include memory-data of place and school landmarks, experiences with formal and informal education, through teachers, mentors, my family and the multiple communities (like the one shared above).

I would also need to collect memory-data (written reflections about pasts landmark moments that shaped the way education has become central in my life). For example, one important landmark moment for me was making the choice to attend school, even when I was hungry. My mother used to give us the choice, that if we felt too weak to walk to our public school (a small run-down, yet brightly painted building, miles from home) when there was no food at home, nor hope of when we will get some, that we could stay home. My desire to attend school went beyond wanting to learn, I associated school with freedom (as my mother didn't let us play out of the house). This project would also require primary sources, any trace of documents, images, letters, institutional IDs, from family archives, as evidence of the era and the context of my education in Sabana Grande de Boyá and later in the capital Santo Domingo, in different barrios where we lived, such as Katanga, in Los Minas (a former *cimarrón* enclave from colonial times). Other forms of primary sources would be recording oral histories with my older sisters and brother, to get other perspectives to compare with my educational experiences.

My ethnographic present would supply other sources of data, as I would have to do fieldwork (or "deep hanging-out") in my current daily life, observing, documenting and reflecting about how I learn, research and teach now. For example, through material culture, I could trace a huge transformation in my life; coming from a home where the only book was a bible, my current apartment is now full of books, artworks and music from all over the planet, and artistic and academic works that I have created. Other data needed would be secondary sources; academic and historical references about my topic, in particular educational experiences in the Dominican diaspora, references about DR, PR and US educational systems (to contextualize my formal education), and references about the historical periods that I lived in these countries (to contextualize my informal education through my neighborhoods and communities).

As could be appreciated from this example, it would be a complex project, and too big to finish in one semester ... I would recommend myself, as I do to my students, to narrow it down, take it by phases, beginning with the most urgent questions that I need to answer to myself, and to clarify the purpose I have in mind for how, with whom and why to share my findings. For example, some narrower questions that could be explored could be: Which educational experiences marked the most my gendered identity? Is there any relation between my educational experiences and the thematic focus of my current research? (for this one, although a resounding yes immediately arises, I still would have to do research to gather data and show evidence). If I were to check my archives, I would probably find data that I have collected, to undertake an educational auto-ethnographic project in its multiple phases, and maybe it would be possible someday, but it will have to wait on line for now, as there are many other projects that need completion. For now, I feel that this Bonus Track, and this book (peppered as it is, with my auto-ethnographic voice) is also a testimony of the calendars and mappings in my educational roots and routes.

From examining the roots and routes of my desire for an education, since my childhood in DR (through which I searched for a sense of freedom from the gender constrains in my home), to my present life, pervaded with academic traces, I recognize a consistent commitment to learning in new ways, that have become echoes in my teaching. This exercise made me question, if I have failed to contribute to my mother (and my family)'s class mobility projects. I didn't become a lawyer, a doctor or a business woman, to "lift" them out of poverty, but chose, without conscious intention, two of the less likely careers to render financial wealth (Art and Anthropology). I have not, however, failed myself, as my search for freedom and independence have given the fruits that I most needed.

Closing Remarks ...

The personal roots and routes in my educational experience, that I have shared above, have shaped profoundly my present teaching practice, my research and my life. Any auto-ethnographic writing, regardless if it is part or not of an academic project, gives us the opportunity to discover the trajectories that shape our present lives, the collective context that have made possible our individual lives. In taking the time to explore this micro experience, we gain clarity for where we are and where we want to go next, and to value and to celebrate the people, places and communities that supported our survival and our thriving. Through my formal and informal education, through Art and Anthropology, I have gathered the toolkits I needed to navigate my life, with less suffering, taking responsibility for my own creative power to discover (and invent, if necessary) strategies of liberation and empowerment.

Working on this book has unleashed a watershed of insights, one of them is to give myself permission to design my next research projects as auto-ethnographies, instead of hiding behind "native" anthropology research, in timid self-reflexive personal narratives sprinkled over the methodological discussion of my academic publications. As I wrote in a recent "report from the field" (see Marte 2018), I think that I am "coming out of the close as an auto-ethnographer"; unapologetically I declare now my preference for projects grounded in the diasporic politics and personal poetics of my own roots and routes. I have many auto-ethnographic projects in seeds, others marinating, and others are ready to analyze the data and write about my findings. The work-load and urgency of academic labor has taken priority, it is only in the last few years (in part due to challenges with my ethnographic food research in PR), that I am considering making auto-ethnographic projects the center of my work.

As I write this last paragraph, I realize that calling this testimony a "Bonus Track" is very appropriate, as I consider my life after my 50s, just that, an extra gift of time-space, way beyond the years I thought I was going to live. Maybe for the first time, I can say, and mean it, that I appreciate my human life, exactly as it is. I am no longer disappointed that I am not a cat; I am finally at peace in this beautiful and weird unfolding. I no longer have anything to prove, to myself or to anyone else; I am just here, in this becoming, *deeply hanging-out*, until life recycles me. I am grateful for the remarkable people, places and experiences that I have encountered, for the wonderful teachers and students with whom I have collaborated, to continue expanding new *cimarrón* ways of knowing, and more joyful ways of being in our multiple intersecting worlds.

References

Marte, L. (2018). 'Rich Points' and 'Deep hanging-Out.' *Anthropology News*, April 5, 2018. DOI: 10.1111/AN.815. Access at: http://www.anthropologynews.org/index.php/2018/04/05/rich-points-and-deep-hanging-out/

Marte, L. (2010). MSG and sugar: Dilemmas and tribulations of a 'native' ethnographer. In H. Haines & C. Sammells (Eds.), *Adventures in eating: Anthropological experiences in dining from around the world* (pp. 145–163). Boulder: University Press of Colorado.

Marte, L. (2008). *El Reino de la imagen: Memoria, Comida y Representación* [The Kingdom of the Image: Memory, Food and Representation]. San Juan-Santo Domingo: Editorial Isla Negra.

Marte, L. (2007). Foodmaps: Tracing boundaries of 'home' through food relations. *Food & Foodways Journal*, *15*(3 & 4), 261–289.

Marte, L. (2005a). *Breathings* (DVD, experimental documentary). Produced as a reflection about the lessons gained in the 2005 workshop with *The Austin Project*. Screened at the Final Show for TAP, Women & Their Works Gallery, Austin, TX (January 14, 2007).

Marte, L. (2005b). *Memory Maps for Silvia Angélica* (Interactive DVD, experimental documentary, about Dominican history, gender and migration, *in Memoriam* of my mother). Produced at the University of Texas at Austin, Dept. of Media Studies. Screened at *Student Documentary Show* at the Blanton Museum UT-Austin (May 2005) and at the conference *Visual presentation of Self*, Nordic Network for Visual Studies, University of Iceland, Reykjavik—Iceland (Nov 26, 2009).

Marte, L. (2002a). *Hija de la Semilla* (series of 10 photographic artist's books, about migration, family memory and food plants). Produced for MFA Final Exhibition. Department of Art & Art History, University of Texas at Austin. The Creative Research Lab (Austin, Texas, May-June).

Marte, L. (2002b). *Alice in a Pool of Mirrors*. MFA thesis. Department of Art & Art History, University of Texas at Austin. (May).

Appendix: Teaching Resources

Framing Remarks for the Appendix Contents

This Appendix is included to support the discussion in Chapter Three and as examples of teaching materials. These resources were created specifically to be used in college classrooms, however, they could be tailored and test-driven according to readers particular needs and interests. These materials are also an example of concrete ways to measure how the research-centered, place-based approach, auto-ethnographic approach is used to meet and evaluate Student Learning Objectives—SLOs—for college courses, especially for courses that have as main goal furthering critical thinking, undergraduate research and experiential engagement of diverse students with their immediate communities. The rubrics show the blueprint that I offer, and students' works show from the perspectives of the students what they do with those and how they respond. This double vision helps us appreciate the limits and challenges of using auto-ethnographic research in a college setting, in the limited time of one semester. The few handouts included, are part of the set of readings that I call the *Toolkit for Critical Analysis*, the reasons and way that I use these concepts is explained in detail in Chapter Three, and I discuss the theoretical frameworks that inform them in Chapter Two.

For those who are not college level teachers or formal education teachers, these resources could be easily simplified and streamlined with less "academic" emphasis to be used in K–12 and other grades and outside school settings (e.g., by grassroots organizations, cultural workers and artists, among others) by anyone who wants to collect experiential place-based data, as the assignments could be tailored to function within short informal workshops. The mapping exercises are also suitable to adapt to diverse topics and training needs. Food mappings, health mappings and educational mappings work well with children and adult groups alike and serve to explore personal trajectories and local experiences. For example, (a) *Food Mappings* can help us find out about food security and food allergies, as well as foodways and particular food habits—such as ones related to obesity and dieting; (b) *Health Mappings* are adaptable to make discoveries about the onset and development of particular physical or mental health conditions, allergies, addictions and health access histories; and (c) *Educational Mappings* are useful to identify career paths, educational goals, educational access histories as well as learning about challenges and disabilities. These three types of mapping exercises are examples of the ones I have used; many other possibilities exist to map, *auto-ethnographically*, almost any aspect of our lives and human experiences. Here I only include food and racialization experiences maps.

I hope these teaching materials and sample of students works serve to illustrate, in more concrete ways, the teaching experiences that I shared in Chapter Three. As examples of pedagogical resources, these could help those interested to consider their own approaches, for how to nurture aspects of critical, feminist and *cimarrón* pedagogies. If you wish to share feedback and comments about your experiences tailoring and using any of these resources, or to share some of your own pedagogical tools, you can send communication to the author at: cimarronpedagogies@gmail.com

Contents for Appendix

The contents of this section are organized thusly: (1) Teaching materials related to the auto-ethnographic research project, (2) Materials related to coursework and in-class exercises and (3) Examples of students' responses to assignments; for the project I can only include here, examples of final posters and fragments of students' evaluations of their projects). The materials for the auto-ethnographic project are used regularly in colleges with BA, these are adapted and simplified for community colleges or technical schools. The course materials included are regularly used in all my college undergraduate courses, but the topic of the assignments varies according to the semester's theme and to the specific course I teach.

1) Auto-ethnographic Research Project

The sample materials selected for this category refer to the auto-ethnographic project assigned to students in college courses that last roughly 5 months (semester), considering days off for holidays and weekends. The topic of the project is open, as long as students justify its relevance in relation to that semester's framing theme. These are examples of rubrics and guides for assignments to complete the project in steps, which helps with the management of logistics and ease anxieties about what to do next. The rubrics contain numeric values for each section, so students know the criteria for evaluation. These guidelines are available to students digitally early on during the semester in a course management system (such as Moodle or Blackboard). Before each due date, we have a workshop in class to read the rubric out loud, to clarify doubts and to ask for progress report to help with challenges for specific areas of the project.

THE MATERIALS APPEAR IN THE FOLLOWING PAGES

ANTHO AUTO-ETHNOGRAPHIC PROJECT: FINAL REPORT RUBRIC

[Use is a template to structure you DRAFT and FINAL REPORT; remove instructions!]

HEADING [5 PTS]
[HERE GOES YOUR NICE 2 PART TITLE IN BOLD]

Your full name
Your Affiliation here
Socio-Cultural Anthropology/Prof. Marte

[USE SUBTITLES IN BOLD TO SEPARATE SECTIONS OR I WILL DEDUCT—10 PTS]

Introduction [keep subtitle in bold/15 pts]
[find a nice compelling way to open your report (anecdote, quote, personal resonance example, etc.); proceed to describe what your project and this report are about—your topic, relevance to the semester's theme, research question, personal motivations, social significance (one reference needed here), scope and limitations (what you will include and why), which audience are you speaking to in this report, what do you wish to contribute with this project?]

Methodology: Field Community & Fieldwork Approaches [keep subtitle in bold/25 pts]
[Delineate which were the boundaries of your "field"—physical and virtual—where, when, how long and with whom did you do fieldwork or "deep-hanging-out"?; discuss methods you used—how did you gather your data and which tech tools you used to document—and oral history collaborator; brief evaluation of success and challenges in finding good references (how your topic been researched); evaluate any ethical issues confronted during fieldwork, with writing "memory-data," with self-documentation and "deep hanging-out," oral history, etc.; explain how the project has changed from brainstorming to completion; if it change drastically, explain that "rich point" moment.

Personal Situated Experience of mobility & Transformation [subtitle in bold/25 pts]
[give a summary of the history and current status of your transformations or mobility, based on the area or practice that you have been researching (the personal experiences before-during-after, choose no more than 5 landmark moments

to describe, using the "memory-data" you collected early on); proceed to locate yourself along 3 axes of your current identities, which are the most relevant for the question that you are trying to answer; introduce your oral history collaborator with a brief bio, then proceed to site some passages from the narratives you recorded, analyzing the perspective of this person; compare yours and theirs POV, in relation to your topic; close this part with a brief evaluation of the micro-politics of fieldwork—discoveries, challenges and power negotiations-, how these identities made it easier or harder to gather your data, to relate to others and to write this report?]

Research Findings: The Poetics & Politics of Mobilities [answer to Question/50 pts]
[Introduce this section, re-state your research question and give a summary of your answers [1–2 paragraphs]; explain next from where you got those answers by discussing in more depth 3 sub-themes—give to each an underlined subtitle to separate—using passages of data fragments (from your auto-ethnographic fieldnotes + from deep hanging-out + from your collaborator's narratives), analyze critically what this data means, and place it in wider, collective social context using the academic references you have gathered related to your topic (short quotes or paraphrasing—*citation heavy area*). To close this section, analyze briefly the *poetics* and *politics* of your topic, in your society, in your locality and in your family history.

Conclusions & Project Evaluation [Keep the bold subtitle/20 pts]
[Re-state a summary of answers to your research question and discuss its implications for the course's thematic framing of mobilities/transformations [not in general, but from the geopolitical and culturally specific grounds of your life]; which practical uses or social implications for policy do you findings have?; in relation to your research question, how well do you feel you have answered it?; Evaluate your research process completing this project and your experience using critical auto-ethnography as a methodology of research and as a writing style; which academic and other kinds of skills have you developed through this project?]

Acknowledgments & Dedication [keep subtitle in bold /5 pts]
[recognizing that all knowledge production is a collective process; give thanks here—use names only if you have permission—your oral history collaborator, and any person, librarian, institutions/organizations, etc.—who helped you—at any stage—to complete your project; dedicate this work to someone special to you—dead or alive—could be human, animal, plant or non-physical beings].

References or Works Cited [keep subtitle in bold/20 PTS]
[Include here a list of 7–10 references—in alphabetic order—that you have used in your written report, only what read and mentioned above, not everything that you have found. References should look the same, clean and nice, no CAPS or mix of different fonts and sizes; loose links are no acceptable]. In-text citations for references should look like this: (Fu-Tuang 2008: 38). Use *APA style* or *this example*: Martinez, Luis. 2008. Urban Change and re-structuring of transportation in Los Angeles. In *Urban Anthropology Journal*, vol 2, No.3 July. NY: Blackwell Publishers. PP. 34–45.

BELOW THREE EXAMPLES OF CLASS WORKSHOPS TO DEVELOP THE PROJECT

WORKSHOP 1: Project Brainstorming Maps
[Exercise of 15 min or less/points for participation]

WORKSHOP GOALS: The purpose of this exercise is to explore potential topics for your project, related to the theme of the semester (Mobilities/Transformations), and to generate an auto-ethnographic research question to guide your data gathering process. The topic can continue to change until the date of the first assignment (an informal, free-writing proposal). The question will continue to evolve also, yet it should be clear to you before the draft is due, so you have time to do fieldwork to gather the data to answer it in your report. For this exercise you can use graphic elements and keywords, or short phrases, this concept map you can use later to develop into a brainstorm writing.

THEME OF SEMESTER & TOPICS: Mobility/transformations is a flexible broad theme that could be interpreted in many different ways, be concretely or symbolically. Her are some examples: Body mobility (such as dance or sports that you practice regularly), modes of transportation (by foot, car, public transport, etc.), transformations in your neighborhood or locality or in your family, change of residence, migration, social mobility (class mobility, be it up or down), birth, sickness or death, change of legal status (EX: getting married, or in migration status), getting out of closets (sexuality or of any kind), ideological or spiritual transformations (change in political or philosophical ideologies, religious conversion or loss of faith). And a long etc ...

1) *Where to begin? (Brainstorming):* Briefly describe 3 movements or transformations in your past or present that had a great emotional or other impact in your way

of life, that affected you personally (through family, neighborhood, or your place of work or study).

2) *Potential Topics for your project:* Considering the experiences described above, select a possible topic for each, that best describe the underlying social implications of those transformations. Brainstorm for each, why each of them could be a good topic personally and socially, and how each relates to the wider framing of the semester's theme. [EX: if one moment of great transformation for you was the transfer from high school to college, then a topic of Education will be very useful; if the mobility is concrete, like moving from another country, then migration or diaspora could be productive topics].

3) *Research Question* (henceforth RQ): This auto-ethnographic research question will serve as a guide to collect data and will be answered in draft of report, it is the skeleton of your project, without this you won't be able to finish a good final report, nor a good grade in the course. Here is a way to generate the question: Choose one of the topics in part#2, considering that area, explain what is it that you would like to investigate, what you don't understand about the transformation that inspired you to think of topic. Formulate the question in one sentence (does not need to have a question mark, but sometimes that helps). Do this exercise for each of the potential topics. When you are done with the 3 versions, choose the topic and RQ that resonates the most with *where you are*, in your life path, this semester (the one that seems the most urgent for you to research first).

TIPS TO GENERATE GOOD RESEARCH QUESTIONS

Your research question should be auto-ethnographic, this mean you should be at the center of it, in first person (your answer will be broader, but your RQ should be specific). The most answerable questions are: what and how, why could be a bit challenging, question should be open ended—not yes or no answers—specific, yet non-judgmental, don't use adjectives and qualifiers, make it concrete enough to fit the kind of data you may need to answer it. Focus on positive or negative aspects of your topic, on tensions or conflicts, but also on solidarity and alliances). Here are some questions, to help you generate your RQ: How has _____ affected my _____? What is my relationship with_____ and how it affects my_____? What kinds of_____ have influenced my choice of_____?

WORKSHOP 2: Progress Report (data to answer your research question)

1) FORMULAS TO USE, IF YOU ARE STILL LOST IN THIS AREA [1 SENTENCE EACH]

TOPIC: _____, _____ and Racialization in Puerto Rico

RESEARCH QUESTION: How _____ has affected my racial experience?

2) MEMORY-DATA: HOW IS THIS PART GOING?
[writing about your past experiences of racialization in the past, choosing 5 main landmarks, interpreting and analyzing the transformations that you have experienced in how you perceive race, and how you self-identify racially]

3) ORAL HISTORY: HOW IS THIS PART GOING?
[Have you found someone to collaborate and did you get signed consent form? How is this person related to you? Where will you be meeting this person? Which 3 question are you going to ask?]

4) FIELDWORK: HOW IS THIS PART GOING?
[Where are you doing your "deep hanging-out"? [could be a virtual place], How are you: documenting your daily routes? writing fieldnotes of your observations about your present experiences of racialization?]

5) REFERENCES: RESOURCES RELATED TO YOUR TOPIC [LIST & EXPLAIN HOW IT HELPS]
[Academic and other sources or references about your topic, including articles that give you data, history and critical analysis, to help you contextualize socio-culturally your personal experience [can be interdisciplinary]

WORKSHOP 3: Data Evaluation and Preliminary Analysis
THEME OF SEMESTER: PLACE AND EXPERIENCE

Purpose of the Workshop: (a) To help you evaluate the quality of the data that you are collecting (in particular primary sources from fieldwork); (b) To develop skills to edit and select passages from the data to use in your report; (c) To practice *critical* analysis of your data, using concepts learned in class and reading, to use as evidence in the answering of your research question. Fill out this exercise in class, then revise and bring a typed-printed copy to class to discuss in the next workshop.

1. *Sample Data from your Auto-ethnographic fieldnotes:* Cite yourself, select a short passage, representative of the notes you have been taking (could be a fragment of "memory-data" or from your deep hanging-out with yourself). The example should contain description and reflections about your observations and experiences. After the quote, use brackets [] to analyze and speculate about what this passage reveals to you, which direction it is pointing, to help you answer your research question?

2. *Sample Data from your fieldwork documentation:* Select and insert here, a short description, photo or any image (such as graph, table, map, cartoon, etc.), that best represent some aspect of what you have documented, noticed or understood from doing "deep-hanging-out" in your household, neighborhood and local routes. After the document, use brackets [] to analyze and speculate about what this passage reveals to you, which direction it is pointing, to help you answer your research question?

3. *Sample Data from the Oral History, from your collaborator's POV:* Select and quote a short narrative passage example from the oral history, showing your collaborator's perspective about your research topic (based on their experiences). If possible, include the question that generated this passage. In brackets [] give a preliminary interpretation of this passage, speculate how this perspective compare with your own perspective, and what are the different identity positions that might explain the differences and similarities. Explain what this passage reveals to you, which direction it is pointing, to help you answer your research question?

FINAL PRESENTATION POSTER RUBRIC

OJO: *REMOVE ALL INSTRUCTIONS!!!* You could do poster in Español or English [make it consistent with your final report]. Please, use this template to structure your poster. Bring 2 printed copies to class, for day of oral presentation [8 ½ × 11" paper; B&W or color].

[2 PART TITLE: first part more personal, second part should refer to your project topic keywords, see this example of title below (draft different versions for in-class workshop]

"La Prueba del Perejil":
Personal Routes, Blackness and Haitian-Dominican Solidarity in New York City

[Your full name here]
Depto of Sociología y Anthropología

Universidad de Puerto Rico-Recinto de Rio Piedras
[course code and name, current semester/Prof. Marte]

[USE A PHOTO YOU HAVE TAKEN, WITH CAPTION AND DATE TAKEN. YOU COULD USE OTHER KINDS OF IMAGES, SUCH AS MAP, TABLE, GRAPH OR CARTOON, AS LONG AS IS RELATED TO YOUR TOPIC. IF YOU GOT IMAGE ONLINE INCLUDE SOURCE HERE]

Abstract/Resumen

Include a summary of 500 words or less (12 o 14 font, single-spaced), describing your auto-ethnographic research project: (a) Project Topic: Describe your topic (under the semester's theme of Racialization); (b) Research Question: Which main question guided your research, and which answers have you found so far?; (c) Which 3 landmarks racial experiences (associated with institutions, communities of practice or places) have been the most important in your socialization/enculturation process? How do you self-identify racially in the present, and how has that changed over time, and how does that compare with official national racial narrative?; (d) Summarize your findings, in light of the poetics and politics of race in Puerto Rico, and discuss the effects on your community, and any implications for public policy, as related to your topic; (e) Evauate your project and your experience using the auto-ethnographic methodology; did your experience any "rich point" (unexpected insight), list any other challenges, skills or benefits gained from your research.

RESEARCH HELP AND FORMS
FREE-WRITING!
(This is a rapid-writing strategy to set you free …)
BENEFITS OF THE FREE-WRITING PROCESS
Never face a blank page again or suffer with writing projects …
The more you practice, the more it flows at ease, with pleasure …
You will learn how to trust your original powerful voice and refine it …
No one needs to sweat and suffer to become a good writer [left-brain lies!]

1) SET TIMER FOR 15 MINUTES & WRITE: Open a blank document in the computer (or write by hand). At the top area of your page write the topic of whatever you want to write about. Start the timer, and begin writing fast, in any order that comes to you; allow yourself to write freely, without censorship or corrections, and keep going until timer stops. Have fun with this!

2) STOP, TAKE A BREAK, CELEBRATE!! You have accomplished your first free-writing, congratulate yourself on this achievement. If feel fired up and still inspired to write more, re-set the timer for another 15 min segment. Do this as many times as you want, until the inspiration dies up, or until you finish 3 pages, single-spaced. Do stop at some point to celebrate!

3) READ WHAT YOU WROTE & CORRECT IT: As soon as you return from your celebration break, make a copy of your free-writing file, save it in a separate folder named Free-Writings for Project (save your wonderful poetic original, without changes, just in case). Work with the copy that you have made; finish incomplete sentences, delete vulgar expressions and repetitions, revise the contents for clarity, re-organize the order of paragraphs and correct spelling and grammar. Now you have a workable raw draft of whatever you wrote, this is the seed to develop further.

4) EVALUATE YOUR RAW DRAFT: Once your document is coherent and readable, decide if you want to use it for your project, if you do, then rename your file to identify the project, and rename the heading of your document to indicate which part of the project you wrote about (EX: Draft of introduction). If you are working on a short writing assignment, continue revising this raw draft until you are done, or save it to continue expanding with more writing as for a larger project.

NOTE: You could also begin first with a concept mapping or branching graphically by hand; use only 1 side of a page, start with a circle at the center and use arrows with keywords to explain whatever you need write about (don't spend more than 10 min). Then, you can use this graphic outline, to begin your free-writing. Writing with "your whole brain," requires dividing your writing projects in parts; separate the moments of brainstorming, research, drafting and editing/correcting into stages, this reduces stress and makes more efficient use of your imagination, creativity and intellect. Here is an example of the writing stages: (a) *First*, "download" from your mind what you already know, your ideas for the project, related memories, etc. using this rapid-free-writing exercise, this SETS YOUR MUSE FREE and liberates space for your original insights to flourish and to develop, otherwise they get scared or fly away; (b) *Second*, clean-up and correct what you have done, and expand the writing using your research documentation; (c) *Third*, develop your writing contents further; edit, expand, delete parts, create arguments, etc. Then revise and correct your document, as many times as you can, until you have a final draft (there are no finished products, everything in life is just a final draft, we can always keep refining, if we don't have a due date).

****

ORAL HISTORY REDUX

Quick Guide to collect Oral history for your Auto-ethnographic Project

[OJO: Read and Explain the consent form to the potential collaborator, before you conduct the Oral History. Follow this ethical procedure and guide below, even if the person is your 80-year-old grandmother]

1. Choosing your Collaborator

Clarify your research topic and your research question and write a final version that sounds coherent. This part should be clear in your mind, before you ask for anyone's collaboration. To choose the appropriate candidate, make a list of three people, well known to you (family, friends, peers, neighbors, etc.). It is good to choose someone that has some connection with your topic, and who could provide a different perspective, given some identity difference in relation to you (age, ideology, gender/sexuality, class, race, nationality, ethnicity, etc.). EX: If your project is about education, identify who has been important in your educational experience or who is connected to any aspect of your current career path. Once you have a list of three persons, meditate carefully with whom you want to collaborate, as it could be an intense emotional process. If you have challenges with the person you want to collaborate, you can still do the oral history with them, if you prepare to be open and avoid harsh judgment [in fact that tension might enrich the collaboration and the testimony you gather for your project].

2. Consent Form and Ethical conduct

Once you have a list of three individuals, contact them and ask orally to collaborate with you in your project, explaining briefly, for example: "I would appreciate your help and time, telling me about your experience in the past and present related to [here put your topic]" and explain to them that they need to sign a written consent form. Do not assume that all would say yes, ask each, and then decide which person you wish to work with. Once you have a verbal agreement, make an appointment with the person, to fill out the *Consent Form* [posted in Moodle under TOPIC 5], print two copies (one for you and one you give to your collaborator). Read it aloud this form to your collaborator, and then explain to them your project in more detail, and what kind of help you need from them. Do not assume they understand, ask if they do, before you ask them to fill out the form. It might be necessary in some cases to do the whole process only orally, and for you to fill out the form for them. If they are not literate, they can sign with an X. It is also possible to work with someone at a distance, and use any communication technology, in those cases, send the consent form to them in advance and let them ask you question (meetings by Skype or Zoom or even by WhatsApp or cell phone are acceptable. You could also send the consent and your questions for the oral history by email. Make sure all parts of the form are filled out (you will need to include a copy of this form in your Final Report).

Read the *At-ease-Handout* [Game of us and them, in Moodle], to refresh your disposition, and to be mindful of any stereotype or prejudice you might have, about your collaborator. Examine also the inevitable ethnocentric views that we all hold about our way of life. Being mindful of our cultural filters helps us to conduct better research and maintain an ethical behavior (e.g., we might hold stereotypes of what it means to be an older person above 70, not only the usual prejudices of race, ethnicity, class, gender/sexuality, etc.). Once all the logistics have been worked out make appointment with your collaborator. It is best to meet at least three times with this person, to make sure they feel comfortable and for you to have a chance to get responses to your questions. If you are meeting in person, arrange to meet to do "deep-hanging-out" with them, before you record anything. The location and time should be chosen by the individual who has agreed to help you. Explain to them that you will go to them, preferably to meet in place that is familiar to them and where they feel more comfortable (such as their home, in the kitchen, backyard, etc.). You can also accompany the person to run any errands they need to do, so meeting while in transport is acceptable and might be very productive. Be gadget ready, bring an audio recorder, or use your cell phone, and load your bag or pockets with a notepad and pen (or any tech gadget to write with) for taking short notes of words, or anything you notice in the place or environment where you meet, that you wish to remember, to describe later in your report. Prepare 3–5 informal, open-ended questions, related to your topic, to ask the collaborator (about their experiences related to your area of research). These should be tailored to the person style of communicating, not full of academic jargon that we use in class. Since you know this person, find the best way to ask them what you need to know, without making them feel uncomfortable, or less smart than you.

3. Conducting Oral History and "Deep-hanging-out"

For appointments, confirm in advance, be punctual and bring your questions and equipment ready to record [but always ask for permission before each section, and stop recording, if asked]. In your first meeting, explain to the person what that an Oral history is NOT an interview; it is a form of cultural documentation, centered in storytelling or narrative, guided by informal questions. The goal is to understand the collaborator's perspective, personal experience and history, in relation to your particular topic, not to collect objective data. Oral history meetings give you a great opportunity to do short periods of ethnographic "deep hanging-out" (fieldwork) with your collaborator. This includes observing, listening, conversing and participating, if necessary, or helping the person, in any way you can, or they allow it. We do "deep hanging" in *ethnographic mode;* this means that we are not in a hurry; we are open to feel/appreciate our environment and others, using all our senses, as appropriate. When someone decides to help you with the project, by giving you of their time and energy, this is a gift and a gesture of solidarity, thank them, at the least provocation, and treat them with respect and kindness. Be humble, listen and respect whatever the person expresses, it doesn't matter if you think differently or don't think that's the "truth." Our job as ethnographers is to *understand* first, not impose our own point of view. Once you are writing your report you can be critical and analyze their narratives, but not while you are documenting the oral history. However, it is ok to ask for more details of anything you have doubt or want them to explain in more detail, is also ok to ask why, to any answer they give. Do not write down what the person is saying, listen. At the end of the first meeting, ask the person for some biographical data, such as region where they grew up, when they were born, and where they live in the present, if they are single or have partners, and finally how they identify in terms of race-ethnicity, class, gender/sexuality, educational level, etc. (this part will depend on your topic, ask only what is relevant to the question you asked them).

Arrive early, greet and converse informally; *be present*, attentive to the person, to the context where they are and to what is happening there. When appropriate, show a copy of your 3–5 questions to the person, explain that they do not have to answer all of them, and that you will make them one by one depending on how long they are available. When the person begins to speak, listen, with all your being, to pay attention to the content, but also to how the words are pronounced, the voice and inflections, and the non-verbal gestures. Let the person narrative rhythm come to a pause (or a crucial point on which you need clarification), before you ask for more details, or move on to the next question. Do not be distracted by writing, it is more important to listen, see and feel. If the collaborator give you permission, and at the end of each section, take at least 3 photos, one of the person (does not have to show the face), doing something is always better, a close-up of some object-artifact related to oral history or to your project, and another photo—wider angle-of the context in which you met with the person [place, environment, space]. Sometimes if it is an older person may want to show you a photo album, and old ID or other documents, photograph those, never take anyone's original treasures. Once the appointment is complete, type in free-write or record yourself, to document your impressions about the session (these are fieldnotes you will need later). Then, begin transcribing the narratives that you recorded for the oral history.

4. Transcribing and Editing the Oral History Audio-Recording

Once you have all the materials for the entire oral history, organize them in a separate folder, and listen to the oral history fragments collected. Organize by date, if you met more than once, and have the questions that you asked ready while you listen. You don't have to transcribe everything, but you need to write enough under each of your questions, to have the passages that you need to complete your final report. You were present in oral history, and now you listen with other ears, at a distance; both of these moments will help you to understand your collaborator's perspective and personal experience, and will bring up other useful insights for your report, so be ready to transcribe and below that, in [] or in a different font, add any comments that occur to you as you listen. The first time you hear each audio segment, is more important to listen, than to write; just take brief notes about anything that catches your attention [note the audio sequence, so that you can return to it EX: 14:23, it indicates 14 minutes and 23 seconds of the total you recorded]. The second time you hear the recording be ready transcribe the passages that you need, those that reveal the person's POV, and that you want to use as data or evidence in your draft and final report. Once you identified which passages you need, transcribe those passages *faithfully*, listen to the segments several times until you are sure that you got every word, exactly as they pronounced. While listening, and if you remember the context, write notes about gestures and other details that give a sense of the environment where the person was when you met. At the end of each paragraph, in parentheses, identify the passages with the name that the person gave you permission to use in the consent form, plus include date and place where the audio was collected. If you have other documents, related to oral history—videos, photos, scans of old documents, maps, recipes, plants, copies of photos on albums, etc.), examine those carefully, name them in the digital files and select images of those that you want to use in your Final Report.

5. How to Represent the Oral History Narrative in your Report

Once you have typed the oral history narrative passages that you want to incorporate in your report, read each one, to decide the order in which you will present them, remember to put the block of text in quotes. Once you understand how the collaborator perspective, you will know how it compares with yours and will be able to analyze the differences and similarities. Remember to include a summary in 1–2 paragraphs describing the person biographically, then you can proceed to include the passages, in their own words, and then interpret those passages, analyzing critically what they mean, and explain what kind of data or insight this offers, to help you answer your research question.

*****

Consent Form for Auto-ethnographic Fieldwork
(Undergraduate Research Project)

Dear Participant:

I am a college student at _____. Through this form I ask for your collaboration for my Auto-ethnographic research project, for one of my courses this semester (semester and year). I would appreciate if you allow me to do *fieldwork* with you and to record an *oral history* about your experience, related to my topic of study. We will meet at your convenience and in a location of your choosing. I will explain, orally, my project to you and give you more detail about your participation, as well as to answer any questions you might have, before you decide if you wish to participate. If you decide to collaborate, please fill out and sign this form to give your consent. Thank you very much for your time and kindness.

Student's name _____

Brief description of Topic of my Project:_____

_____
_____
_____
_____

Important Note: You have the right to withdraw your participation at any time and for any reason. My first duty is to protect your identity and not cause you harm.

For the Oral History, you can use your real me or an invented one. Please, specify your preference. Our professor has provided a guide for how to work in an ethical manner and provided a written guide to conduct the oral history. If you have any additional concerns, you are welcome to communicate with my professor (contact is included below).

Consent Authorization
[Please, mark items with an X and sign]

_____ I have read this form, and listened to the student oral description of the project. I understand what has been explained to me about my participation in this academic study.

_____ I consent to participate, I give this student permission to conduct fieldwork and oral history with me and/or my organization.

I give the student permission to record: Audio Only ___ Video Only ___ Audio-Visual ___ No recording allowed ___. I have been assured that this documentation will be used only for educational and cultural purposes.

_____ I ask that my real name be used when referring to my person in writing.

_____ I do not wish to be identified with my real name, I have chosen a name below.

Participant's Name: _____
Participant's Signature: _____
Student Signature: _____

Academic Contact:
Prof. Name /Phone Number and Email Address/Professor's Affiliation

2) Coursework and Classroom Exercises

These are examples of coursework, which serve to supplement and support the development and completion of the project. As explained in Chapter Three, the coursework is related to a particular *framing theme* which changes each semester. The Critical Responses are assigned ahead of time, for students to get inspired to read before class discussion. The *Toolkit for Critical Analysis* is assigned to all basic courses, as these concepts are essential to produce *critical* auto-ethnographic reports (here I only include examples of four of the handouts). These materials are available to students digitally early on, through the online course management system. Assignments are completed online, unless students have specific challenges to do so. In such cases, we come up with alternatives, students can bring paper copy to class or drop in my mailbox.

RUBRIC GUIDE FOR CRITICAL RESPONSES (CRs)
[Use this document as a template, Upload file to Moodle or copy & paste your text]

INCLUDE THE CR# & TITLE + LIST THE RESOURCES ASSIGNED (AUTHORS OR LINKS)

1) *Initial reactions:* Share your first impressions of the readings or other resources assigned for this CR. Evaluate the degree of difficulty, familiarity, emotional impact, etc. of both format and contents. This initial paragraph allows you to get off your chest whatever you need to express in form of a like or dislike opinion, it is an informal reaction, don't analyze here. [5 points]

2) *Interpretation & Main Concepts:* Briefly discuss what the assigned materials were about, compare what they have in common and how they complement each other. Select at least one concepts from each resource, explain what you understood it meant and apply the concept, using concrete examples from the readings or from your daily life or past experiences. Evaluate the degree of difficulty of the contents and any challenges you had or critiques about the arguments. [15 points]

3) *Relevance for semester's theme and for your Project:* How do these resources help us understand our semester theme, what do they contribute to our ongoing class discussion? How do any of these resources help you in developing your research project? (as possible reference, example of composition or author's voice, or form to organize the writing). [5 points]

NOTE: This rubric is for All CRS. Answer under each question (you do not have to write a coherent essay), maximum of 1 page, single-spaced, 12 pts. You can answer in Spanish or English. Do not write a full summary nor do external research to answer these questions (Wikipedia or googling definitions). The idea is to know what he learned, what concepts are not clear, what difficulties you had understanding the materials, and for you to practice doing critical interpretations and evaluating references. The CRs will also help you practice consistently your writings and to develop in time an awareness of your own author's voice (your preferred style of writing and to discover your talents for expressing yourself), all of this will greatly benefit the quality of your final report. Additionally, by analyzing lectures assigned in class, you already have what you need if you decide to use them as references for final report. [**OJO:** Do not these instructions in your response].

Co-curricular Event 1: Critical Review for Workshop on Global Food Crisis
[Total 75 points—10 pts attendance/make review
no longer than 3 pages/Submit to BB]

For both assignments: include your name + assignment name and convert your file to PDF. There might be an additional standard rubric for grading the workshop—I will keep you updated once I get confirmation—in the meantime you can use this template to organize your draft.

1. Introduction: Event Description [10 pts]: a. Walk readers through the experience from the moment you arrived at the location; Briefly describe the type of workshop you attended (format and contents). b. Examples of activities or descriptions of activities, film, speakers, etc. c. Describe how you engaged with activities offered. Which country/region/goal table were you assigned to?

2. Critically analyze the *contents* and *format* of this Workshop—UN-MDG-Children—[45 pts]: a. Which were the guidelines and major tasks given to your team or table? Which strategies did your group used to find consensus for what to do?; b. Describe the region, situation, group or issue your group worked on. Which solutions were proposed, and why? Which perspectives or alternatives were not considered at your table or at the workshop?; c. Share some insights gained from your participation in this event about the effects of globalization on children food security, and about the ambitious UN goals. [if necessary, add here additional writing required by the official rubric.]

3. Critical assessment [10 pts]: a. evaluate the usefulness of this event for our course, for your research or for your education or personal life more generally; b. How do co-curricular activities like this enhance what you are learning in CULF 3331; c. Was this mandatory event worth your time? Evaluate what worked—or not—for you and why? and suggest constructive ways to improve the workshops and this assignment.

Co-curricular Event 2: Critical Review of Elective Event

[Total 25 pts—5 pts for attendance—with proof-/2 pages max/Submit to BB]

1. Introduction [5 pts]: Share free-form impressions about the event or experience. **a.** Name and describe the event attended (format and contents), and explain motivation for your choice; **b.** Give examples of what was done, shown, speaker name or film title and basic info, etc; **c.** Describe how you engaged with particular event and activity.

2. Critical assessment and evaluation of experience [10 pts]: a. Share free-form impressions about the topic and list 3 insights you gained from the *contents* of this event. Did it help you gain a different perspective about the food security or other related issues?; **b.** What did you find particularly effective about the *format* and how the topic was presented?; **c.** Summarize your critical evaluation of what worked or not for you, and why.

3. Relevance & lessons [5 pts]: a. evaluate the relevance and usefulness of your choice of event for our course, the workshop [CC#1] or your research; **b.** Do you feel you learn well through this kind of assignments; is it worth your time? Explain answers.

WHICH DOOR WOULD YOUR ENTER?...
BLACK ONLY WHITE ONLY

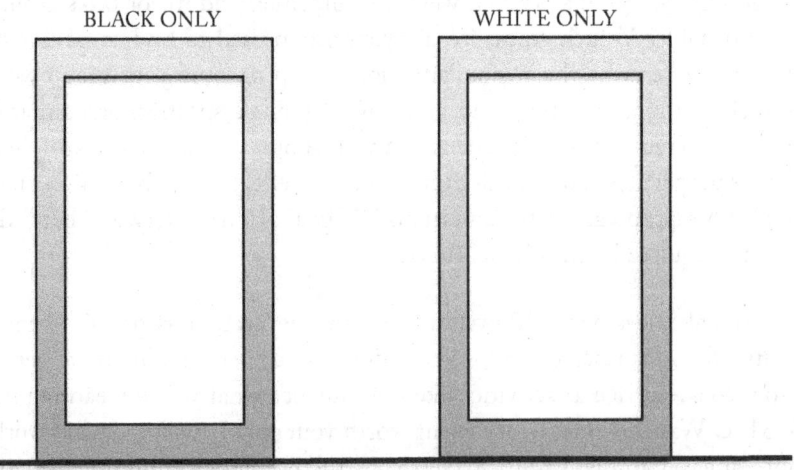

MARK WITH AN X YOUR CHOICE. EXPLAIN BRIEFLY BELOW YOUR REASONS FOR THAT CHOICE. IF YOU WANT TO CREATE

A DIFFERENT CHOICE, NOT GIVEN HERE, DO SO AND EXPLAIN WHY. ARE YOU AWARE OF THE HISTORICAL CONTEXT THAT THIS EXERCISE IS REFERING TO?

FOUR EXAMPLES OF HANDOUTS FOR THE TOOLKIT FOR CRITICAL ANAYSIS

The game of "we" and "them":
Strategies for Everyday Negotiation of Difference

This handout offers quick insights—that require constant practice—for navigating our way through human interactions and intercultural communication with less stress and more ease. The stages discussed below are in reverse order, towards the goal of compassion. The process of getting to understand the socio-cultural process and to help us relate to others does not have, of course, any stages; the ones below are for clarity's sake. How we react depends on context, situations and each person's agenda. Life is messy and we cannot know what anyone else is going through internally, or what kind of disastrous day they are having, a compassionate perception can help us recognize this and decide to be patient with others as we wish they would be with us.

1. *Discrimination to prejudice:* At the discrimination stage we take action that harm others, based on their perceived differences. At the prejudice stage you might have not questioned the prejudices against those that you consider "others" [out-groups] that you acquired throughout your life. You may agree with media representations of other groups in US society as if these portraits were truthful. You may have had some unpleasant experiences with individuals of particular groups, which influenced your view of the whole group [this is a very common form of generalization, which saves us from feeling guilty, and is a form of dismissing the uniqueness and complexity of individuals from out-groups].

2. *Rejection to stereotype:* At this stage things are getting better, yes, there are some lingering unfounded dislikes, but these superficial stereotypes are more a form of resistance to PC expressions or a desire to appear more ideologically pure—if on the right. Sometimes our perception of others is influenced by language and ideology; someone's accent, gestures and/or use of certain words could trigger negative associations in us that have nothing to do with the particular person we are interacting with. Remembering that individuals do not represent a whole group—even when they may claim they do—help us here not to extend judgment beyond the situation at hand. Identifying some of the stereotypes that others hold about people in what

you consider your in-group is also very helpful and humbling. It could show you concretely how you react to damaging representations of your community or group.

3. *Ethnocentrism to tolerance:* Ethnocentrism is the illusory perception and conviction that our in-group or our way of life is the best, truthful or "right" one, anything different is wrong, we judge others based on our own practices and experiences. This stage is common to all humans, we all do it; the problem is not feeling this way, but when this perception is not recognized, questioned or re-evaluated. We can watch ourselves go there, then instead of continuing to stereotype, we can recognize that everyone has their own perspectives and judge reality from that "situated knowledge." We can, indeed, learn to postpone judgment, even if briefly until we have more information [giving others a chance, as we wish others would for us]. As long as we recognize when our ethnocentrism is becoming a barrier to understanding, we will be skillful at relating to a diversity of people without feeling threatened by their "difference."

4. *Empathy and Compassion:* Tolerating others is good, but why stop there?... We can Learn to perceive, appreciate and value differences as resources rather than obstacles, and to use this understanding to create more collaboration and alliances across social categories. To get here you need to be open but also interested in going beyond the surface of human interactions. Understanding other perspectives or points of view is the key; it is also helpful to try to imagine others' experiences and predicaments, to place yourself in someone else's shoes. This recognition and interest in the lives of others could take many shapes such as reading-researching, watching films, attending their events, sharing time with them, or anything that could help us find out more about the complex stories behind the appearances. Only when we make this commitment to understanding could we begin to feel compassion. We could now begin to appreciate differences—ignoring difference is as bad as labeling them—without fears, accepting the problematic yet marvelous differences that make our lives so culturally rich and our interdependent survival in this planet possible.

Bonus Track: Code-Switching and Loving Perception

Once we reach a stage when we can create a bit of distance from our egos—at least in certain contexts—we begin to recognize our own reactions and cultural filters. But we begin to recognize also our agency, that one has a certain degree of choice in the way one performs multiple identities. In the same manner so do other people, so what we see is not necessarily what we get, we cannot pretend to know someone else's experience just from looking at them or exchanging few words.

Code-switching is the practice of shifting from one language or dialect to another (Ex: shifting between standard English into slang or a less prestigious dialect and accent) according to context and according to our agenda in a particular communicative exchange. According to the scholar Maria Lujones, code-switching could be extended as a metaphor to include any cultural shifting such as dressing the part or performing different aspects of our identity depending where we are and in whose company. Lujones identified code-switching as a playful, yet critical, way to interact, work and collaborate with others, to create common grounds, even if those alliances are temporal. In order to code-switch effectively you need to become aware of yourself and of how you behave in the multiple social spaces or contexts that you navigate often, or what Lujones calls "worlds."

World traveling is hence the shifting between these diverse social spaces. Some of the worlds we intersect might be hostile to us others friendly and welcoming and yet others are sanitized and homogenous, with very formal interactions such as hospitals and courts. World traveling also requires attention to where and when other people are, which requires paying attention to place, situations, and time—both in daily cycles and in sense of history—to help us ground what is going in the context in which it is occurring. Learning how to world travel helps you primarily to be comfortable in your own skin, and to recognize the power and responsibility that comes from the histories and experiences that made you possible.

World traveling as a conscious shifting practice between your many intersecting worlds (or communities) makes you flexible and supple but also sharp-wise as a snake and gentle as a dove. Code-switching and world traveling allow us to rescue some playfulness and humor in the usually heavy forms of human interactions. Imagining, for example the mundane things we share with so many others (how everyone needs to go to the bathroom, or sleep, or brush their teeth, or had a mother, or will die like everyone else) helps release some of the serious burden of judging and being judged, the miscommunication and the times of outright conflicts and violence.

Once you master being conscious of your code-switching and world traveling it will be easy to feel compassion for others through what Lujones calls *loving perception;* avoiding arrogance, giving everyone at least one chance, of defeating our stereotypes. At the stage of loving perception, we become more patient and at ease with ourselves and with others, wasting less energy and time judging others a priori. This perception is a form of compassion that takes—one situation at a time—to deal with our complex human interactions. Lujones assures us that through constant practice of code-switching and loving perception we can learn how to "navigate-at-ease all our multiple worlds."

Representation Redux

(This summary has been edited from diverse sources, see references at the end)

Representation: Some dictionary meanings

1. An Image, likeness, or reproduction in some manner of a thing; a material image or figure; a reproduction in some material or tangible form; in later use, a drawing or painting. (of a person or thing); the action or fact of exhibiting in some visible image or form; the fact of expressing or denoting by means of a figure or symbol; symbolic action or exhibition.

2. The exhibition of character and action upon the stage; the performance of a play; Acting, simulation, pretense.

3. The action of placing a fact, etc., before another or others by means of discourse; a statement or account, esp. one intended to convey a particular view or impression of a matter in order to influence opinion or action.

4. A formal and serious statement of facts, reasons, or arguments, made with a view to effecting some change, preventing some action, etc.; hence, a remonstrance, protest, expostulation.

5. The fact of standing for, or in place of, some other thing or person, esp. with a right or authority to act on their account; substitution of one thing or person for another.

6. The fact of representing or being represented in a legislative or deliberative assembly, spec. in Parliament; the position, principle, or system implied by this; the aggregate of those who thus represent the elective body. from The Oxford English Dictionary

Representation has been since the 1980s a much-debated topic, not only in post-colonial studies and academia, but in the larger cultural milieu. As the above dictionary entry shows, the actual definitions for the word alone causes some confusion. Representations can be clear images, material reproductions, performances and simulations. These "likenesses" come in various forms: films, television, photographs, paintings, advertisements and other forms of popular culture. Written materials—academic texts, novels and other literature, journalistic pieces—are also important forms of representation. These representations, to different degrees, are thought to be somewhat realistic, or to go back to the definitions, they are thought be "clear" or state "a fact." Yet how can simulations or "impressions on the sight" be completely true? This questioning is particularly important when the representation of the "subaltern" [the marginalized] is involved. The problem does not rest solely with the fact that often marginalized groups do not hold the "power over representation" (Shohat & Stam 2014); it rests also in the fact that representations of these groups are both flawed and few in numbers. Dominant groups need not preoccupy themselves too much with being adequately represented. There are so many different representations of dominant groups that negative images are seen as only part of the "natural diversity" of people. The mass media tends to take representations of the subaltern as allegorical, meaning that since representations of the marginalized are few, the few available are thought to be representative of all marginalized peoples. The few images are thought to be typical, sometimes not only of members of a particular minority group, but of all minorities in general. It is assumed that subalterns can stand in for other subalterns ["they all look alike"]. A prime example of this is the fact that actors of particular ethnic backgrounds were often casted as any ethnic "other." (Some examples include Carmen Miranda in The Gang's All Here (1943), Ricardo Montalban in *Sayonara* (1957), and Rudolph Valentino in *The Son of the Sheik*). This collapsing of the image of the subaltern reflects not only ignorance but ignorance—or lack of respect—for the diversity within marginalized communities.

Representations are meant to relay a message and as the definition shows, "influence opinion and action." We must ask what ideological work these representations accomplish. Representations or the "images or ideas formed in the mind" have vast implications for real people in real contexts. Both the scarcity and the importance of minority representations yield what many have called "the burden of representation." Since there are so few images, negative ones can have devastating *effects* on the real lives of marginalized people. We must also ask, if there are so few, who will produce them? Who will be the supposed voice of the subaltern? Given the allegorical character of these representations, even subaltern writers, artists, and scholars are asking who can really speak for whom? When a spokesperson or a certain image is read as metonymic, representation becomes more difficult and dangerous. Focusing on whether or not images are negative or positive, leaves intact a reliance on the "realness' of images, a "realness" that is false to begin with. Both negative and positive representations, when they become stereotypes, are inadequate and dangerous. Positive stereotypes that exoticize, eroticize and romanticize certain groups or attributes are also creating a distance of an alien "other" (e.g., all black men are good at sports, all "Latinxs" are good dancers) ascribing characteristics as "in their blood," as biological rather than cultural and historical.

Representation implicates also "political representation," or a speaking for the needs and desires of somebody or something. Representation can also be defined as the act of placing or stating "facts" in order to influence or affect the action of others. Of course, the word also has political connotations. Politicians are thought to "represent" a constituency. They are thought to have the right to stand in the place of another. So above all, the term representation has a semiotic meaning, in that something [a sign] is "standing for" something else. These various yet related definitions are all implicated in the public debates about representation. Representing is thus "proxy and portrait," according to Spivak. Elsewhere, Spivak addresses the problem of "speaking in the name of": This question of representation, self-representation, representing others, is a problem." Spivak recommends "persistent critique" to guard against "constructing the Other simply as an object of knowledge, leaving out the real Others". Representations in one sphere—the sphere of popular culture—affects the other spheres of representation, particularly the political one: The denial of aesthetic representation to the subaltern has historically formed a corollary to the literal denial of economic, legal, and political representation.

Edward Said, in his analysis of representations of the Orient in Orientalism, emphasizes the fact that representations can never be exactly realistic: In any instance of at least written language, there is no such thing as a delivered presence, but a re-presence, or a representation. The value and apparent veracity of a written statement about the Orient [the East] therefore relies very little on the "real" Orient. On the contrary, the written statement is selective; it excluded, displaced, and includes only those views familiar to the authors, sometimes taken from other representations. Representations then can never really be "natural" depictions; they are constructed images, images that need to be interrogated for their ideological content. Theorists interested in Post-colonial studies, by closely examining various forms of representations, visual, textual and otherwise, have teased out the different ways that these "images" are implicated in power inequalities and the subordination of the "subaltern." If there is always an element of interpretation involved in representation, we must then note who may be doing the interpreting. Ella Shohat claims that we should constantly question representations: Each type of knowledge and public image must be analyzed not only in terms of who represents but also in terms of who is being represented for what purpose, at which historical moment, for which location, using which strategies, and in what tone of address.

Returning to Spivak, is relevant to bring up her, by now, famous question, "Can the Subaltern Speak?." In her essay of the same title, Spivak emphasizes the fact that representation is a sort of speech act, with a speaker and a listener. Often, the subaltern makes an attempt at self-representation, perhaps a representation that falls outside the "the lines laid down by the official institutional structures of representation" (306). Yet, this act of representation is not herd. It is not recognized by the listener, perhaps because it does not fit in with what is expected of the "other." The struggle to "speak for oneself" cannot be separated from a history of being spoken for, from the struggle to speak and be heard. It cannot be ignored that representations affect the ways in which actual individuals are perceived. Although many see representations as harmless likenesses, they do have a real effect on the world. It is obvious that representations are much more than plain "likenesses." They are in a sense ideological tools that can serve to reinforce systems of inequality and subordination; they can help sustain colonialist or neocolonialist projects. Yet, Subalterns speak not only for those in power that may or may not wish to listen, but they speak to other marginalized groups and individuals to their own communities and to express themselves. The work of various "Third world" and minority scholars, writers, artists, and filmmakers attest to the possibilities of counterhegemonic, anti-colonial regimes of representation. A great amount of effort is needed to dislodge dominant modes of representation. Efforts will continue to be made to challenge the hegemonic force of representation, and of course, this force is not completely pervasive, and subversions are often possible. "Self-representation" may be one of the few spheres from where to challenge the monopoly of official representations.

Media Representation: Representation refers to the construction in any medium (especially the mass media) of aspects of "reality" such as people, places, objects, events, cultural identities and other abstract concepts. Such representations may be in speech or writing as well as still or moving pictures. The term refers to the processes involved as well as to its products. For instance, in relation to the key markers of identity—class, race, ethnicity, age, sexuality, gender, nationality, etc. (the "cage" of identity)—representation involves not only how identities are represented (or rather constructed) within a particular media frame [or "text"] but also how they are constructed in the processes of production and reception by people whose identities are also differentially marked in relation to such demographic factors. Consider, for instance, the issue of "the gaze." How do men look at images of women, women at men, men at men and women at women? This "gaze" [or looking] is not generic, however, which kinds of men and which women, from which "situated knowledge," socio-cultural location and histories, needs to be asked also. A key in the study of representation concern which representations are made to seem "natural." Systems of representation are the means by which the concerns of ideologies are framed; such systems "position" their subjects in particular ways.

Semiotics, commonly defined as the study of signs and of systems, is a theoretic framework and qualitative method of analysis, useful to interpret representations.

Both Semiotics and Cultural Studies stress *representation as a verb and a process, besides a product*. This emphasis is based on particular premises, such as:

- Reality is always represented, what we treat as "direct" experience is always "mediated" by perceptual codes and technologies. Representation always involves "the construction of reality" not its faithful reproduction.
- All representations, however "realistic" they may seem to be, are produce or constructed, rather than simply transparent "reflections" of a pre-existing reality out there.
- Representations require interpretation—there are not innocent or transparent meanings.
- All representations are unavoidably selective, foregrounding some things and backgrounding others (inclusions and exclusions).
- Representations which become familiar, through constant re-use and repetition, come to feel "natural" and unmediated, and in time assimilated as "true."
- Narratives about reality are multiple and are produced from diverse perspectives; representing others is always a way of representing ourselves indirectly.
- A critical approach to representation, focuses on asking, whose narrative of reality is this, what or whom is trying to represent, how and by whom, and what is being said or silenced about them?
- Post-colonial and post-structuralist approaches propose that "reality" and "truth" are relative and partial, products of particular systems of representation, which generate an historically contingent narratives and discourses, motivated by particular agendas.

Useful references for further study

Dines, Gail & Jean M Humez (Eds) (1994) *Gender, Race and Class in Media*. Newbury Park: Sage.

Dyer, Richard (1990) *How You See It: Studies on Lesbian and Gay Film*. London: Routledge.

Ferguson, Robert (1998) *Representing Race: Ideology, Identity and the Media*. Oxford: Oxford University Press.

Friedman, Lester (Ed) (1991) *Unspeakable Images: Ethnicity and the American Cinema*. Urbana: University of Illinois Press.

Hall, Stuart (1997) *Representation: Cultural Representations and Signifying Practices*. Sage [This is a bible on the subject; has extensive analysis of colonial and media representations]

Hall, Stuart (2000) Cultural Identity and Cinematic Representation. In Robert Stam & R. Miller (Eds) Film & Theory. Blackwell, pp. 704–14.

Russo, Vito (1987) *The Celluloid Closet: Homosexuality in the Movies*. New York: HarperCollins [there is also a video based on this book, that includes lots of clips from mainstream movies]

Said, E. W. (1995). Orientalism: western conceptions of the Orient. *Penguin, 115*.

(1985). Orientalism reconsidered. *Cultural Critique: Race & class*, *27*(2), 1–15.

Shohat, E., & Stam, R. (2014). *Unthinking Eurocentrism: Multiculturalism and the media*. Routledge.

Spivak, G. C. (1988). *Can the subaltern speak? Reflections on the history of an idea, Post-colonial Reader*, pp. 21–78.

Tagg, John (1988) *The Burden of Representation: Essays on Photographies and Histories*. Basingstoke: Macmillan.

Critical Ethno-Semiotics Extra Redux:
Basic Tips to analyze ("read," decode, interpret) Cultural Representations

This handout gives you quick *semiotic* tips, to decode ethnographically, any representation you come across, including text and performance. Representation involves not only how identities, objects, places, events, etc. are *represented* (socio-culturally *produced*) but also how *meaning* is co-created by the producers and audiences who are exposed to representations. This analysis shows the diverse interpretations possible, according to the situated perspective of who is doing the analysis.

Basic Questions related to representation as *product* (decode within the frame)

What am I witnessing, which media is being used?—materials that is made of also
Which story is being told, and what (or whom) is being represented?
How is it represented? Using which codes, strategies or narrative expectations?
Who produced this representation, when and where and for what purpose?
What is included (or foregrounded), what is excluded (or backgrounded)?
How does this piece compare with similar representations (past/present), how does it differ?

Basic Questions about representation as *process* (contextualize outside the frame)

What do you need to know about the USA society and public culture to understand its meaning?

Which audience (s) is this representation targeting? How do you know?
Whose interests does this representation reflect—who benefits? How do you know?
How does it assume or suggests a sense of "we"—or boundaries of us/them?
How is the representation made to seem "true," "commonsense" or "natural"?
What does this representation mean to you personally, given your situated own knowledge?

Intersecting Identities Redux
[Adapted from diverse academic sources]

What does identity mean to you? When you think about yourself, do you think about gender, race, sexual orientation, age, hair color? Which do you think of first? Each of us have been socialized into adopting certain identities that shape our lives in profound ways, and these identities influence how we see ourselves and how other perceive and treated us and by society at large. Our identities with regard to age, gender, race, sexual orientation, disability status, and religion influence our place in the power maps of a society. These identities are multiple and intersect with each other, allowing individual social actors to make choices under specific circumstances. **Multiple and intersecting identities** allow us to negotiate with certain dignity the webs of connections between personal identities and the actual concrete life of the here/now.

Most of us experience ourselves as having multiple intersecting social locations, this is, the many conditions that come together to have an impact on privileged and a marginalization, the ways we are treated by others, and the way we experience our lives. *These multiple axes of identity reveal how intersecting systems of privilege and oppression mutually construct one another.* We "deploy" or choose to perform various identities, depending on social context and life circumstances in which we find ourselves. We could say that identity *locations* are an expression of our "situated knowledge" and our partial perspectives. Yet it is not only our location, but our unique **positionality** (how we choose to self-identify) that allows us to negotiate our relationships across many concrete and symbolic boundaries.

All actors in a society are domesticated and made to consent—in diverse direct and indirect ways—to define their own personal identities in relation to both the identities of the social groups to which they belong (or *in-group*) and other *out-groups* with whom they experience the greatest **social distance**. Yet how individuals perform these **social categories** assigned to them by society is not direct and total, but an *interpretive process* through which we pick and choose aspects of our identities that further our life projects or intentions. Defining identity is not necessarily a conscious process; it is a **lived experience** of relationships between individuals and their surroundings, between external and internal landscapes. According to anthropologist Dorinne Kondo, "Identity is not a fixed "thing," it is **negotiated**, open, **shifting**, ambiguous, the result of *culturally available meanings* and [of] power enactments of those meanings in everyday situations" (1990: 24).

Intersectionality theory is an analytic tool to trace how multiple social categories define who a person is, and how they negotiate the forms of power differentials as **social actors** through the **performance** of identities. The *multiple axis of differentiation* are not restricted to social categories such as gender, race, class, and sexuality, disability, religion, etc. but can include other categories such as of age, region, education, professional identity, etc. Because the concept of intersectionality challenges the category of identity as "one and invariable," it provides a good theoretical framework to understand the complex identity performance of subjects in a multicultural society, such as the US.

The intersectional model argues for new conceptualizations of social categories and their role in **identity politics**—the way groups and individual pressure to have their civil rights recognized in a society. The intersectional model helps us also to understand our *interconnectedness* not only to others, to our past history, but also to our environments and to our sense of **place**. The main goal is to understand how individual identities and group identities are used by people to *resist and accommodate*—depending on circumstances and goals—to **hegemonic norms** [what is defined by dominant groups at a particular historical time as the "normal" or standard-. For example, racial/ethnic minority women who come to identify as feminist, lesbians or socialists must confront not only the Anglo-hegemonic norms in US society, but also the prejudices and discrimination they experience within their own communities.

Analyzing identity and personal experiences **intersectionally** requires that we focus on: (1) **context**, or the specific circumstances, situations and interactions that people are experiencing. Context includes actual physical and social locations but also time-space and event—or what is going on—; and (2) *power/knowledge*, in the matrix of all social relations, this is the motor of change, that reveals we are not puppets, but constantly negotiate our needs, wishes and desires. **Agency** in particular refers to our personal *culturally constructed* will to act; the ways we negotiate our ability to take action given the circumstances (another way to understand agency is as **life project**). In this sense, everyone has power, because *everyone has agency*, and as such can exercise a measure of control, even if only over ourselves and how to react. Yet agency—as a form of power—is *partial and contingent* to situational contexts. We use the term **micro-politics** to speak of shifting micro-power relations in everyday life.

Avtar Brah's and Ann Phoenix's define the concept of intersectionality as "the complex ... and variable effects which ensue when **multiple axis of differentiation**—economic, political, cultural, psychic, and experiential—intersect in **historically specific contexts.**" This mode of examining identity helps us to become aware of the tangled threads in "different dimensions of social life [that] cannot be separated out into discrete and pure strands."

Most important, multiple shifting identities help us recognize, understand and appreciate **diversity** from the inside out. *Difference*—of identities, abilities, talents, personal histories, etc.—is not only at the core of our human condition, it is also a powerful **resource** and mayor evolutionary advantage of all life forms and ecological processes in this Planet.

****

RESOURCES: RACE WEBLINKS

Race The Power of An Illusion Season 1 Episode 1 S1E1 The Difference Between Us
https://www.facinghistory.org/for-educators/educator-resources/resources/race-power-illusion [OJO: YOU NEED TO REGISTER, CREATE A LOGIN]

Standing Rock: Healing on Wheels
https://truthout.org/articles/standing-rock-medic-bus-is-now-a-traveling-decolonized-pharmacy/

Maroons in Comics
https://truthout.org/articles/comic-details-saga-of-escaped-slaves-who-formed-autonomous-communities/

Race in the Curriculum
https://truthout.org/articles/black-lives-matter-in-our-schools-developing-an-anti-racist-pedagogy/
https://truthout.org/articles/teaching-for-black-lives-and-bearing-witness-through-poetry/

Food & Race
https://www.washingtonian.com/2018/08/10/dc-restaurants-to-white-supremacists-yes-we-will-kick-you-out/

Street Food—Feeding unrest in Cairo: The politics of bread
https://www.youtube.com/watch?v=O8LTMhQgy_c

A taste of conflict: The politics of food in Jerusalem—Street Food
https://www.youtube.com/watch?v=f9P5Phj0TFY

Findings: Anthropology's Persistent Race Problem
http://anthronow.com/findings/findings-anthropologys-persistent-race-problem

Colectivo ILÉ [PR]
https://colectivo-ile.org/

3) The Harvest: Sample of Student Works (La Cosecha)

The examples of students' works show their responses and engagement with assignments. Since I didn't get written permission from all the students in my list (I have lost contact with some) to get their consent, I have removed all the names. The examples of posters are for the auto-ethnographic project; these are used in final presentations and are also submitted as assignments for grading. The Critical responses—or CRs—have usually a 20–25 point value. The CRs are due before the resources are discussed in class. I count any in-class exercises towards participation points (value= 5–10 pts). Attendance, participation and CRs count towards "class contribution," a 25% of the total value for the course. Other examples from workshops and in-class exercises are included below.

STUDENTS' EVALUATION OF AUTO-ETHNOGRAPHY

[TAKEN FROM FINAL REPORTS CONCLUSIONS, ANSWERING THESE PROMPTS: (a) Evaluate your project: How well do you think you answered your research question?; (b) Evaluate your experience using the Auto-ethnographic methodology; How did you project change from proposal to final report?; (c) What was the greatest challenge, did you experience any "rich point" (unexpected insight)?; (d) What academic or other skills did you develop during the process?]

Process of Research Evaluation 1
Since I began working on this auto-ethnographic project, I was a bit conflicted because I didn't know how to even start. The free-writing assignment helped me shed a light on the subject when I saw my insecurities a Puerto Rican. Although content wise, it changed drastically from my initial plan, the topic remained the same. I loved the whole idea of exploring my journey as a Boricua, because even though it was in college where I began to truly feel that I didn't know anything, or at least acknowledge that I was feeling that way, I didn't know where those landmarks would take me. They "memory-data" transported me to times that I had forgotten. And although it was a little painful, it is a beautiful thing for me to be able to discuss this issue in this work. Something that I have felt for so long, I was able to put into words and write about it in a way that could help me understand that I will always be a Puerto Rican, no matter where I go. And I may not fit the

usual stereotype of a Puerto Rican, but my way of seeing life and living has made me who I am today ...

Process of Research Evaluation 2
My family created the perfect educational environment for me, sending me to a bilingual school, but not one to understand the issues affecting race in Puerto Rico ... The most challenging part in this investigation (the one I probably got super wrong) was the area of poetics and politics, it was the area where I most struggled with. Public policy needs to be designed in a way that it is not exclusive of any racial group, the issues of blackness in the University is an issue that strongly need to be spoken about and treated. Legislation and education in my opinion, are the most efficient way to attack racial injustices in society ...

Process of Research Evaluation 3
The way I managed to answer my question was by analyzing my past experiences and researching about the main topics of the investigation. This project helped me to get out of daily routine and experience new perspectives. Although I don't feel like I have fully answered my question, I feel that I could go deeper ... The auto-ethnographic method was very useful for this project because from my personal experiences I was available to get a better understanding of the Puerto Rican culture and how the social structure is in Puerto Rico. It was hard because writing is already hard for me and then writing about myself and my personal experiences even more. I do think that my biggest difficulty was to write and analyze what I wrote. But after I got to the "deep hanging-out" I experienced "a rich point." I learned a lot from this investigation especially through doing free-writings, things about myself that I never knew, this helped my project a lot ...

Process of Research Evaluation 4
It's been a challenging yet beautiful experience. The hardest thing about this auto-ethnographic investigation was remembering my past and seeing how those things have had their long-term effects on who I am today. Throughout the project I've really grown to know myself more and who I consider myself to be. It's helped me remember things that I had buried deep in my memory that I released in through the free-writing (for the memory-data). In the draft I learned to analyzed and go into depth about my identities. This project also allowed to practice my writing, to research topics, and finding articles that study what I've gone through (it was so nice to see that I wasn't going through it alone)...

Process of Research Evaluation 5
I would like to point out that during my long and hard research process, my "rich point" was to sit and listen to the full story of my dear grandmother's life. It was

at that moment that I understood that not only should I investigate from my perspective, but from the same point of departure I could find other perspectives that should be analyzed. At that time, I changed the course of the project, and all the pieces fell into place ... I am aware that there are many ways to study this topic and hope to have the chance again to explore other aspects of multiracial families ... Finally, I feel it was a privilege to be able to do this research about the identities that form me as a person, acquire new knowledge, skills, perspectives and the need to share this experience through other forums ...

Process of Research Evaluation 6
I can say that I could find the answer to my question through this work and that now more than ever I want to fight my community stereotypes and racism, seeing the devastating result that has in us and our future, and since I am already a father, I want my daughter to get a different education ... At first, I couldn't find the necessary data for my research, so I had to read the educational reports for what was hidden away, between lines ... My biggest challenge was the search for the necessary information on the subject, because there is almost nothing official to breakdown the problems caused by racism in the universities of PR and almost no academic studies. I can say that I developed research and writing techniques with this work, and to apply what I learned in class, adding the point of view of others and finally applying to my own experience ...

Process of Research Evaluation 7
In order to answer the research question, I had to do my own analyses related to my physical appearance and field observations in my social networks. Comparing this final report with my first "free-writing," I notice changes in my topic, from general appearance to focus more on the hair. Analyzing was the biggest challenge for my work, I could say that it was the selection of references to support my arguments that made it difficult for me, incorporating the references in the report. Through this writing I think I had the opportunity to develop, personally, a criterion for analyzing future experiences related to the racialization that occurs every day in Puerto Rico, and in different parts of the world ... sometimes we are not conscious because we do not want, in my opinion, to see the existing reality because we want to live in a perfect world ...

Process of Research Evaluation 8
In finding Van Dijk's research helped me greatly to answer my question, gave me evidence that the media greatly influence racial ideology. I completed my finding incorporating data from what I observed in my "deep-hanging-out," this helped me to answer it more easily. I felt a little weird, doing auto-ethnography, because

it's something that you're not used to, usually you are told that you can't talk about yourself. However, I liked it ... by the time of the draft I had to write the question shorter, simpler and in a more detailed way, but I kept the same topic ... My biggest challenge was when I thought I didn't have all the references that would help me answer my question, none of them were relevant to my topic. So I had to look all over again, homework that took me several extra days. For this work I developed, the task of dividing a long project into sub-topics and putting the information in a coherent way, and to relate what was found with what I wanted to answer and present. Also, I developed more the task of looking for information, because I had to search a lot and read a lot until I found what was necessary.

Process of Research Evaluation 9
I managed to answer my question after long readings and reflections during the course of the investigation ... The conversation with the oral history collaborator helped me a lot to relate to some situations, for example, it is no coincidence that both of our father figures told us that we should "improve the race" since we were "jinchos" [too white]. It was also an experience of discomfort to express myself about these personal things, but always with the intension and the position of being agent of change, that is a motivation to overcome this challenge and for which I decided to continue the project ...

Process of Research Evaluation 10
Two rich points for me happened when I was confused how to introduce the acceptance of my appearance as a Puerto Rican woman, who felt I was ugly and inferior ... And another point was on 3th of April, when I cut my chemically straighten hair, to start leaving my hair grow natural ... it was an intense emotional moment of self-acceptance, to make this decision, in spite of my family's opposition ... my project changed after that, my writing improved, I wanted to see the report finished, for me, not only for the course ...

Process of Research Evaluation 11
My project almost completely changed from the free-writing assignment to the final report ... I really wanted to do with this work, but I was so confused, between what was my question and what was my topic ... After I changed the 5 landmarks to those related to rap music and I read them and noticed that since my early age I identified with African-American culture, then everything clicked, my research question became clear to me ... My biggest challenge in this work was to be able to search among all the music that I listen daily, to find the artists that have influenced me since my childhood to the present, and to research their era, race and gender ... In this project I developed skills of doing an investigation. I learned

how to make a graphic outline and how to ask guiding questions with my outline to search for information. I finally learned how to choose a research topic and ask a research question ... this has been the hardest and most fun project that I have ever done in college ...

Process of Research Evaluation 12
I have to point out that finding the answer to my question was not easy; I know that there is still information that could help me to answer it and that everyone perceives what is mentioned in this writing in a different way. During the draft I was able to modify my most relevant intersecting identities (I was so confused about that), in order to complete a better final report, which I was passionate to complete. The biggest "rich point" I had was when I asked my maternal grandmother for an oral history, because I thought I would find more racism in her day than in now and that was not the case, backwards, it was totally the opposite (at least according to her). Finally, I am happy to have come out of this research process with new perspectives of the world and with new communication skills, in specific when talking with my relatives ...

Process of Research Evaluation 13
To answer my research question took a long time and self-analysis to choose which data of all those that I gathered to use in my report ... During my deep-hanging in my daily life I constantly analyzed my actions and thoughts to check my emotional state and in this way I saw how the animé films have always been linked to my way of interpreting the world. My project was originally going to focus on the communities that exist within the video games, but did not feel a connection to this subject; It wasn't auto-ethnographic, once I began the memory-data, I saw how my room, since I was a child has been full of animé memorabilia ... My biggest challenge was to define my 2 other identities and relate it to my racialization, because I thought race only means focusing only on blackness, which is wrong. In this auto-ethnographic work I developed writing essays skills and how to use socio-cultural academic terms, something that I have been interested in learning for a long time ...

Process of Research Evaluation 14
Thanks to this auto-ethnography I have discovered a sense of belonging, that has led me to know more ... From the experiences lived from an early age to what I am today, coffee consumption have led me to develop a community at the university, and to relate to a diversity of people of all colors ... I am part of the beautiful subculture of coffee ... I didn't realized that was so important to me until I had to do this project ...

Process of Research Evaluation 15

At first, I didn't think much about the effect that video games, a mode of entertainment for many, would have on the development of my identities. In doing this research, I found that video games are a central piece in all my identities ... My mother also played video games, they were different than the ones today ... Although this is the final report, this version of my project is not going to be as complete, I will continue this project as an independent study, and I hope to add more sources in my analysis, which has been one of my biggest challenges because it is not a well-researched topic in the Caribbean ... I liked to read or listen to the testimonies of other brown Latina women in this gaming community, positive and negative, in addition to learning about my own family history through the testimonies of my parents ...

Process of Research Evaluation 16

This auto-ethnographic project is responsible for my understanding of various events that I have been through in my life. This work is also responsible for my understanding of essential factors in the development of my racial identity. Identifying those factors that affected my racialization was one of my greatest challenges ... Prior to this auto-ethnographic project I had never taken the time to reflect on my experiences ... I am satisfied with the findings I have obtained, although I understand that this topic offers much more to explore ... Despite being so, I feel a little bit more at peace with myself, and to be aware that my identities will continue to change over the years ... If it had not been for this process of research, perhaps I would have traveled all my life without knowing that part of me, there is some power to know where you stand ...

Process of Research Evaluation 17

I think the church has influenced me much more than just my racial identity, growing up in the Pentecost church taught me everything I knew about life, and now as a college student I can all of that ... The memory-data writing was challenging, as I got to visit some of painful roots, the struggle everyday with my sexuality, parts that I consider beautiful and what I consider grotesque ... This project definitely helped me to develop a critical analysis, to be able to see beyond the wounds and the painful experiences and to engage in a conversation with my family. I have now a desire to observe more and to listen, to pay attention ...

Process of Research Evaluation 18

I have to admit that although I do not have the same opportunities as those of higher status in society ... Through this project I discovered that I feel extremely privileged to have received a private education that not many could have ... it made me more aware that other students do not have the advantage of thinking for themselves ... I have been able to analyze all this looking for references in different databases. I have learned more about my identity during this process, than ever before ... Racism and the little chance that black people have in getting an appropriate education has been part of the problem in our society for a long time ...

Process of Research Evaluation 19
I managed to answer my research question by analyzing the memories of when I was little, talking to my mother and noticing many things that previously I did not see as bad, such as racist language and prejudice ... The free-writing for the memory-data helped me to remember many things to apply to my work and helped me understand and analyze many things I had not understood before ... The biggest challenge was to understand that not everything I was told was right; since I was small I have been carried away by the advice and opinions of my adult relatives, now that I am older I realize that I am not always in agreement with them ... it was a challenge for me because we usually think that our parents always make the best decisions for us, but as for my hair I do not agree to treat it with chemicals, that it was hard for me to refuse ...

Process of Research Evaluation 20
This project has led me to develop new research strategies. For example, how to do an oral history in an appropriate way that is not disrespectful ... It has make me question things like the inculcation of values that comes from the different relatives, and are sometimes racist ... I understood this thanks to another point of view provided by my neighbor (visibly black)... This was my biggest challenge, to go out and work with someone to talk about how their skin color has affected his life ... My project evolved since my free-writing, this is because I was able to get a greater volume of secondary and primary sources ...

Process of Research Evaluation 21
In conclusion, I was able to answer my question ... skin color does play a role in the consumption of clothing ... mostly for women, to satisfy the aesthetics established by our society ... I found that society manipulate us in so many ways that we sometimes let them think for us ... This was the first time I began to question what I like and why, and how much I care about how others judge me ...

Process of Research Evaluation 22
By answering my research question I was able to use references that contributed to my work ... It is was difficult to talk about myself and to feel exposed, but when we get out of that bubble and see beyond, we want do it to help others who may

feel the same way ... It takes empathy, to be able to understand others and to know there is no superiority on one side ...

Process of Research Evaluation 23
In conclusion, I think it was good to get so many sources, even if I did not add all of them to this report ... I found interesting to see how the male dress has transformed and compare with the trends in music of many generations ... I never recognized how my style changed from regular to cross-dressing and painting my nails ... and I never asked my girlfriend how she felt about my appearance ... I understand that if I were a black young man my dress wont be taken as something interesting or innocent, it is risky, I might get in trouble with the police ....

Process of Research Evaluation 24
My auto-ethnographic experience really was enriching ... At first it was tedious to do the deep-hanging-out and find the references, but once I got my research question I enjoyed it and learned a lot about my life ... My biggest challenge was to find the references, I had to go to the library to ask for help and devote a lot of time to the search ... My answer was based on the information I found in the articles and reading everything I had written in my memory-data and fieldnotes ... in addition, through the deep-hanging-out with my family, I realized that in all my important decisions in life, I counted on my mom ... Lastly, with this project I learned to do "free-writings," to compose in the first person, professor always ask that it be in third person ... I also learned how to do deep-hanging-out with myself, not only with the others ...

Process of Research Evaluation 25
It was possible to answer my research question through my own experiences, the oral history and the references ... it pleased me to see those combinations of ideas materialized in a fluid report ... The free-writing was a good practice for my writing ... My biggest challenge was to find a way to organize everything ... I learned how to connect all the ideas into one academic paper ...

****

EXAMPLE OF POSTERS FOR FINAL PRESENTATION
Two poster Post-Maria Hurricane

A cuatro meses de María:
Caminando a Ciales, mi pueblo de valerosos

Depto. of Sociología y Antropología
Universidad de Puerto Rico-Recinto de Río Piedras
ANTR4225-2U1-2017S1 / Prof. Marte

Foto tomada por: Ray A. Huertas Padilla –Río Grande de Manatí en Ciales, 2017, Hombre pescando días luego del pase del Huracán María-

Resumen

El huracán María fue una experiencia inusual para mí, ya que la mayoría del tiempo estuve tranquilo durante y después del huracán y la considera más educacional. En Ciales hubo varios derrumbes, puentes, casas y caminos que fueron destruidos lo que hacía difícil la movilización de las personas. La mayoría del tiempo leí libros en mi casa más los periódicos y caminando por las calles de mi pueblo. Gracias a los racionamientos de alimentos, baterías y linternas entregados por de FEMA, Cruz roja y el municipio, se nos facilitó la vida durante los días de oscuridad en la isla. Mi amigo Joel Villafañe y yo caminamos el pueblo y Bo. Hato Viejo después del huracán que fue una grata experiencia conversar con personas luego del huracán y es una que no olvidaré. Fue justamente con él, quien a diferencia de mí, lo pasó en un área rural donde hubo más daño, comparado al casco urbano. Luego, nos dirigimos al Paseo Lineal Juan A. Corretero. Sinceramente no estuve atento a la poética de este tiempo y las pocas que pude ver fueron por la calle, como "#Puertoricoselevanta" o el de las banderas en los carros. En la política tuve un poco más de atención; realmente me gusto como el gobernador manejo la situación con el toque de queda de las 6pm. Luego de esto no hubo un buen manejo de la política sobre la crisis. Mi experiencia fue educativa, ya que mantuve una paciencia sobre lo ocurrido y gracias a los libros encontré un gran amor a mi patria. Mi único conflicto fue la falta de comunicación. Pienso que la reforestación, la cual ya empezó es un buen método para revitalizar el país. Este trabajo fue interesante por las razones que reflexione sobre lo ocurrido, lo cual no había hecho. Me gustaría compartir este trabajo con una maestra que me dio clase en la High, por las razones que siempre me ayudó mucho y me gustaría saber qué pensaría sobre el auto etnografía.

"Bajo todas cirscunstancias llegamos a nuestros hogares": Como el Huracán María reestablecio lazos familiares y comunitarias olvidadas en Puerto Rico.

Z   s
Depto of Sociología y Antropología
Universidad de Puerto Rico – Recinto de Río Piedras
Antropologia de las Ciudades, Primer Semestre 2017-2018, Prof. Marte

La primera foto a la izquierda fue tomada por Cheery Viruet (residente de Manatí, PR.) el jueves 21 de septiembre, 2017 en la carretera #2 hacia Barceloneta. La segunda foto, de izquierda a derecha fue tomada por Matt Black el 9 de noviembre de una familia lavando ropa en un arroyo. La foto fue recuperado del website New York. La tercera foto fue tomada por Carmen González (residente de Barranquitas) el jueves 21 de septiembre de la entrada de su casa.

Resumen

La experiencia que tuve con el huracán María fue llena de ansiedad e inseguridad por la destrucción a nivel isla. Pasé este fenómeno natural en Río Piedras con mi pareja, Edwin Rolón, y nuestros familiares lo pasaron en Manatí y en Barranquitas. El día después del huracán, sin conocer el estado de destrucción de las carreteras, nos tiramos a nuestros pueblos natales para asegurarnos que nuestras familias se encontraran bien. Ellos no sufrieron daños físicos en los hogares, pero el impacto de las condiciones dejó una huella en todos. Por la domesticación de los medios ante los huracanes, entiendo que eran pocos los que estaban preparados mental y emocionalmente para las circunstancias que nos dejó María. Sin embargo, fue una oportunidad para reestablecer, según Safa 2011, las rupturas en el *sentido de pertenencia comunitaria* puertorriqueña que ha dejado la modernización de Puerto Rico del siglo 19. En sí, esto ha sido uno de los mayores regalos de este evento, porque pude ver como en los tres comunidades: Río Piedras, Manatí y en Barranquitas volvían a interactuar entre sí. No obstante, uno de los retos ante la situación fue el mal manejo de la emergencia en la isla después del huracán. Por tal razón, es fundamental conocer como *se supone* que se lleve a cabo este manejo y, a base de esta experiencia, encontrar como mejorarla. Primeramente, se tiene que hacer un análisis comparativo del manejo que fue llevado a cabo y contrastarla con las acciones tomada luego de María. De tal forma, podremos presentar los hallazgos ante el gobierno puertorriqueño como sugerencias para mejorar el plan de manejo de emergencia ante un huracán. Aprendí como expresar las experiencias que he vívido de manera académica y me gustaría publicar un trabajo basado en este, en algún futuro.

EXAMPLE OF POSTERS FOR FINAL PRESENTATION
The girl sitting in front of the Xbox:
Video games, Gender and Racialization in Puerto Rico

Official Logo of ND games. This was one of the first games I saw my mom play when I was 6 years old. Taken from www.herinteractive.com

Abstract

My research was focused on observing the relationship between video games, gender and racialization in Puerto Rico. The question that guided my research was: How did my "gamer" role has influenced my racialization? Based on this question, I would say that the main answers have been, the way the characters are presented in the games, which have mostly been white men or white women, and the interactions I have had with other players, either online or face to face. Among the experiences that have influenced the formation of my racial identity have been to hear the history of my family as told by my grandma, my mom and my dad, but especially through my interactions with communities of players in Puerto Rico and Youtube or Twitch.tv., where I was one of the few non-white women. Another experience would be the times I spent playing *Pokemon*, the series of *Legend of Zelda* and especially *Nancy Drew*, more recently *Final Fantasy XV*, among many others, where I watched how all the protagonists were mostly white or Asian with white features. Today I identify myself as a "Latina woman," although I have been called "Cream" or "cremita" at certain times. Although sometimes I have felt out of place in Puerto Rican society, because of my preference to speak English, I also felt out of place in some communities of players for being Latina. However, sometimes

I do identify as "Boricua" and feel that I am part of my culture. During this project, I learned how much influence the national narrative of racial mixture had on my way of identifying, because it was what was taught in my home and in the school, and reflected among my friends also. I would say that I have learned about how colonialism has influenced Puerto Rico's racial discourse, as racism is normalized in words and images that we see daily. I also learned about the reality of women in a macho society, which is observed in some player communities too. One of the rich points of my research was learning about the origins of my family in greater detail than before, which I consider to be part of the memory-data and oral history. This research has helped me in my writing skills, especially the use of "free-writing," in collecting information about my family and personal history, and using refences properly.

"The whiteness of my education":
Education and its impact on Racialization in Puerto Rico

Abstract

The main focus of my investigation was to see the relationship between my private education and the affect it had on me regarding race and racialization. I focused on the way my accent influenced my racial experiences in Puerto Rico and outside of Puerto Rico. Social classes were also one of the main topics in this investigation. The research question was: "How has my private education and accent affected my racial experiences in Puerto Rico?" From the information gathered, I can say that my private education did have an impact on my racial experiences. One of them being the lack of diversity in my high school and even now at the university. My racial identity has no changed while doing this investigation, I still identity has a "white Puerto Rican," since my past experiences lead me to identity this way in my classroom, where classmates and teachers would point out my light skin. I noticed that the impact of race in Puerto Rico, does have a big effect on the access to private education and not many have the opportunity of getting a good education. I did manage to learn a lot from this project, it helped me to get out of my daily life routine and see another perspective.

In Black & White:
Rapping, Music and Racial Formation in Puerto Rico

(Photo taken in "Club 77" at a rap concert on February 13, 2018)

Abstract

My project is an attempt to answer the question: How did Rap music contributed to my racial formation, to lead me to identify myself as a black man? In order to answer this question, I chose five Rap songs (e.g., the one in my title, "in black and white" is a rap song of Intifada, one of the groups of rap that I studied) that I heard in five moments that I consider racial landmarks in my life, and that helped me to identify myself this way in the present. In addition, I found works by anthropologists to analyze the songs in depth and thus to write about its political-social implications in Puerto Rico. The three identities that I chose for the auto-ethnographic analysis are black man, musician and Puerto Rican. The collaborator for the oral history was my great-grandmother, who unlike me identifies herself as an accountant, "white" and American. I must point out that despite our differences in identity, my great-grandmother also chose music as an important element of her racial formation. However, unlike me, the musical genre she chose was sacred (Christian) music. After analyzing, I came to understand my cultural background and the privilege of my middle class, but the oppression that I live in the present due to my skin color. Also, based on my racial experiences I wrote about recommendations I give for with public policy and for changing social norms in the island. In relation to the national identity, racial mixture (the three races) that I was taught growing up, as if that was the only racial identity of Puerto Ricans, I see now that is a very convenient myth for those close to "whiteness."

"It looks better straight":
Feminine Aesthetics, Professional Identity and Racialisation in Puerto Rico

(Photo retrieved from #tallncurly in Deskgram. Published on April 28, 2019)

Abstract

My focus on this research is aimed at answering the question: how does the representation of women in the media affect my racial experience? I found preliminary answers that the media do have an influence on what is presented through product ads and famous women, among others. Within my development, seeing these women has affected my way of thinking about women's beauty and what is supposed to be a "professional" image. Since Elementary school, I was taught that we are a mixture of three races, but I look more like the Spanish despite having curly hair and a wide nose. I have faced pressure from my relatives to remove the curls, because that way I would look more professional. In Addition, my friends are impressed that I am allowed to keep my natural hair at my job (I work in a store for tourists in Old San Juan). Perhaps because of my skin color I might be considered a white woman, however, I have always been clear that we come from a mixture and that I cannot say that I am of a single race when my traits prove otherwise. With this project, I have been able to study directly the poetics of representation and how that has a great influence on society today. The media reproduces the thoughts that there is a superior race, the closer to white the better. While in politics it looks a little more explicit, seeing that there are really not many politicians or influential people in PR that are black. The process of completing my project has been long and of much uncertainty. I discovered after I had read all the items to find the possible answers to my question, none worked for me, and I had to start that process again, but then I found very good resources. For this work I developed the skill of organizing my writing and to search and evaluate academic information.

"The Black Girl of the neighborhood":
Matrifocality, Family Narrative and Racialization in Puerto Rico

Photos by author: where I was born, raised and still live, with extended family.

Abstract

The topic of my research was based on identifying how I live in a matrifocal home, which was the only space of total acceptance of my blackness, especially having another side of my family where they make many racist comments. My investigative question was: How do my family's comments about my skin color have influenced my racial identification? I discovered that my family has been my greatest source of knowledge, values, beliefs, etc. I had always identified myself as black, but only because of my color, I don't have a choice, but through my mother's side of the family I learned to know my roots and I am proud. The most important landmarks in my process of racialization were: when I realized that my brother and I were the only blacks in the neighborhood, because the main adjective they used to refer to us was the "blacks." The second is when my mom had to give a talk to my brother about important black people in history, because he felt inferior, and third, when I started to accept my hair, because when I was little I felt uncomfortable having it natural, I felt out place in my school group. According to Llorens, Grodeau and García-Quijano (2017), we know that there is racism in Puerto Rico, even if it is officially denied. I think it is important that we continue to educate on this subject. I think the greatest problem of Puerto Rican society, is that racism became tradition, and is camouflaged behind our daily speech and actions, even if it is unconscious. I hope many others in can identify themselves as black and contribute to eradicating racism in the Island one day at a time, one comment at a time, one person at a time, with love and respect. My auto-ethnographic experience was enriching, although, at first, I had problems getting the references and with doing the "deep-hanging-out." Finally, with this project I learned to make a "poster" of my research, to improve writing in a first voice and to spend quality time getting to know myself, not just understanding others.

¿*Gringuiqueña?*:
Nationality, Diasporic Experience and Racialization in Puerto Rico

I took this picture as the plane started descending towards Puerto Rico in 2016. I was on my way back after spending all summer in the US, visiting family ... and I had never been so desperate to come back home.

Abstract

My auto-ethnographic investigation was about how my diasporic experience has affected my nationality and "race." How moving to Puerto Rico affected how I view myself nationally and racially is what I was questioning, and throughout the research I have realized that my diasporic experience has been an eye opener in so many different ways. It has completely transformed how I view myself racially and the nationality I identify myself with today. It has been the most important thing in my entire life in terms of growth and transformation. I discovered this through my landmarks. My three most important landmarks were #1: the one in which I was faced with the horrible truth that my birthmother was indeed racist. She wouldn't allow me to have playdates with my grade school best friend Brianna because she was black. I had never realized this before, but once she told me that I couldn't go to Ronda's house because her family isn't like ours, because they aren't safe when never actually meeting them, I realized that there were differences between my best friend and I, and sadly I associated it with skin color. #2: was when I moved to Florida because of my father's very progressed cancer. I remember living with my uncles and their children and how they were all very "latino." They were very submerged in Puerto Rican culture, even though they had lived most of their lives in Orlando, FL. I remember eagerly wanting to be part of this culture and telling all my new friends at my new school that I was "Puerto Rican." #3: was when I moved to Puerto Rico, after my father's death, to live with my aunt. When I got to Puerto Rico I realized how NOT Puerto Rican I was! How I was lying to myself about my national identity. I was a white "American." I was so incredibly white and I hated it. These landmarks helped me understand who I was and helped me see the transformation that I have undergone in my life. I would definitely say that this project has helped me get to know myself in a way I had never thought to know myself before. It was hard writing about past experiences and being vulnerable on paper, but it was totally worth it, because now I see myself, others, and the world in a whole new way.

EXAMPLES OF PEER REVIEW

Peer Review for Socio-Cultural Anthropology Course
1) Evaluate the Draft in light of the rubric for Final report: Which parts do you think are most complete and clear of your peer's document, and which parts you think are incomplete, confusing, or simply crooked? What about the title?

The only incomplete parts are the findings and the conclusion. Everything else is pretty well developed and is concise and straight to the point.

2) General Feedback on draft status: Is it finished, advanced, which parts need urgent help? How is the format, are references used in the text? Give any additional advice you want, if you have time.

The most urgent thing is to finish, you are doing well in all the other parts, you also need to delete repetitive use of words and concepts within a single paragraph. Also repetition of same stories in different parts of the draft. You still need to include your references. I left you more comments in your file, about other things you could fix in terms of grammar and syntax of your writing, in your document in Google Docs.

3) Findings: After appreciating the content and format of this work, evaluate from your perspective as a reader, how well your peer answered the research question, and how critically has author analyzed the findings? Offer concrete examples of your answer, whether yes or No.

I love the fact that without knowing we had quite similar topics, as we both talked about the standards of beauty in Puerto Rico and touched the theme of "Bad hair." This has been very useful to me, but I can't find your answer to the question, that part is missing, I think you hint at answers when you tell stories of your experiences, but they are not put together in the part required in the final report rubric. I hope you finish soon it is a nice project.

Peer Review for Caribbean Course

1) The topic of and the research question are clear and explicit. I consider that this work is well structured as I think it is going to be done well; the author is following the rubric to complete every part requested, and the topic is very relevant to the semester's theme.

2) She chose Cuba and Puerto Rico as countries to contrast but part of the references is not complete, missing references for access to education in Cuba. What is written so far is good. My peer justified very well her relationship to her topics and to these countries. So I think there are several parts of the research well accomplished, such as the memory-data, Introduction, methodology etc. and others incomplete, like references for the findings.

3) I really liked your topic because I think that is really important, and it helps in my work, the way you have structured your writing and order of ideas.

4) The Title I consider very relevant to the topic that she selected, just missing the "cultural flavor" that the professor wants ... My peer fulfilled most of the promised points.

Peer Review for Metropolitan San Juan Course

1) The topic and the investigative question are well done, but have of the draft is missing, the peer has a note saying he still searching for data ... I noticed that he used the rubric to organize the parts, but apart from the intro, the rest is incomplete ... I found many grammatical errors.

2) I think the draft could be very good once is done ... my peer makes it clear that it is in process.

3) As we exchanged drafts, the peer said that mine helped him see how to do the parts that he was confused about ... His topic seemed pertinent to our social reality, he has a good question and an outline of what to do next, just need to hurry up to get the data to answer his question. We still have few more weeks to complete the work. [there is no title to answer #4]

EXAMPLE OF FULL PROGRESS REPORT
ANT3500: Caribbean Counterpoints

Working Title: "Trini Food Shopping: The Industrial Foods That Feed Trinidadian New Yorkers And Their Evocative Symbolism."

State your revised *Topic:* Industrial food items associated with Trinidad & Tobago, and the means and reasoning behind their consumption by New York City based Trinidadians.

State your revised *Research Question:* Why are Trinidadians in New York purchasing and consuming industrial food products relative to Trinidad & Tobago, even though said products are typically more expensive and difficult to obtain than their American counterparts? Why do I consume these products and what do they mean to my family?

1) *From your Auto-ethnographic Fieldnotes*
Documented: March 24th, 2013
"What is the significance of "familiar foods"? Is it related to taste as my mother says, or is it simply nostalgic? Are New York Trinidadians eating a bounded diet? Sorrel from Utica Avenue versus sorrel from Spanish Harlem, which mom claims is not "dark enough." The sweetness of the beverage is also significant not just to mom but to grandma; both say that Trinidadian drinks are meant to be sweet. Mom says sweetness in juice is needed in Trinidad because of the hot climate, so the drink would has a lot of ice in it, and the ice melts and dilutes the juice with water, weakening the sweetness of the drink. What's the necessity of sweet drinks in cooler climates like New York? My grandmother just called to remind me that she is coming over on Easter Sunday and she'll be bringing my favorite drink: mauby. After telling me that she's busy boiling the mauby bark while on the phone, she also informs me that since she changed jobs last year, it's been difficult getting to her favorite shop on Utica Avenue to buy her "little things." It's as if she's rubbing it in my face; she wants me to know how hard it was to buy the mauby bark, so I'd appreciate the sweet beverage even more."

[*This passage is significant to my research because it exposes a second reasoning for why New York Trinidadians go out of their way for Trinidadian products, which is the taste of something familiar. The extreme "sweetness" of a drink like mauby or sorrel identifies it as Trinidadian, because the sweetness reveals something about the island's warm climate.*]

2) *From Fieldwork*

"That's a real Trini beer!" My mother Joanne is cheering at the visual of Trinidad's Stag Beer in the music video from Trinidad by-way-of Atlanta, Georgia rapper Trinidad James. James has been the center of much debate for my family, who still cannot decide if he positively or negatively reflects Trinidadians. "You can't get Stag anywhere in New York, that's how you know he's in T&T." In the video, the rapper is roaming a shantytown in St. James while sitting on a truck with some barely dressed Trini girls, and a Stag beer.

[*The significance of the Stag's presence in the music video is rehashed later that night, when my mom calls her boyfriend Frank to talk about Trinidad James' new video and the great job the rapper did with "showing some Trini culture." This exchange aligns with the seemingly impressive nature of Trinidadian products (whether in origin or association) to New York based Trinidadians, who go out of their way to obtain these items, sometimes solely for nostalgic reasons. I can recall sitting on a beach in Trinidad with my mother in 2005, drinking Stag beers like water. The Stag's significance diminishes with its' abundance in Trinidad, but in New York it becomes a treasure my mother actively searches for. I want to know why memories of life on the island are implanted onto products like Stag Beer, which are not only difficult to find in NYC, but are not tastefully unique in comparison to counterparts easily found in New York (for Stag Beer, a Heineken is an acceptable alternative).*]

3) *From Library Research*

Errol A. Simms and Marilyn Narine, *A Survey of Shopping Behavior of Consumers in Trinidad and Tobago: The Case of Grocery Shopping* (Social and Economic Studies, Vol. 43, 1994), 107–37.

This paper offers statistical analysis of grocery shopping trends in Trinidad, particularly in the economically varying neighborhoods of Valsayn, Morvant and Trincity. I thought this would be a useful source since it shows a difference not only in the types of products purchased by Trinidadians of various economic classes, but it also outlines the shopping days prioritized by each economic group. The prioritizing of grocery shopping is something I have been observing in my own research, and it correlates with my theory that shopping for Trinidadian industrial products, especially in markets that claim to specialize in West Indian goods, is an almost ritualistic behavior of New York based Trinidadians. This paper also has some insightful information on consumer preferences in relation to can foods vs. fresh foods.

Jacques M. May and Donna L. McLellan, *The Ecology of Malnutrition in the Caribbean* (Studies in Medical Geography, Vol. 12, 1973), 423–75.

This source is a bit dated, but I found that it is a useful counterpart to the Simms and Narine survey, since the information aligns with my mother and her boyfriend Frank's (a second consultant) generation. In the chapter outlining nutritional patterns in Trinidad and Tobago, during the 1950s and 1960s, there is an observed disparity among the diets of Afro-Trinidadians and Indo-Trinidadians. This exposed a gap in my theory and research, which was that I had been observing behavior among Afro-Trinidadians exclusively, and making value judgments on Trinidadians as a whole. In the source, researchers noted that Indo-Trinidadians consumed more fruit, vegetables and skim milk than Afro-Trinidadians, who consumed larger amounts of bread, red meat and pork, and condensed milk. After noting this ethnic food consumption disparity, I've decided to visit specialized markets in predominately Indo-Trinidadian neighborhoods like Richmond Hill and Jamaica in Queens. And I am also planning on interviewing two Indo-Trinidadian friends of my mother, who moved to New York City in the mid-2000s.

EXAMPLE OF IN-CLASS WORKSHOPS AND EXERCISES

Nahirily M. Orona Cosme
ANTR 3006-005
Prof. Marte
Mapping #4

Research Question
- How important, and which are the diverse uses of water, in my artistic processes?

Data Update
- While I already have my working space prepared and ready, I still need to continue to take notes.
- I have a freewriting regarding my past relationship with my topic, but I still need notes on my current relationship with art and water. Lots of field notes are still needed, as well as various useful references. I need to change the various ways to work, e.g. watercolor, acrylic, in order to get a deeper understanding about how water is connected to both and in general. I need to finish my constant one-week field notes and begin my month of fieldwork. I need to also write some field notes, instead of just recording. I've been planning to try and get some statistics regarding the amount of water the processes take, after my fieldwork finishes.
- As aforementioned, I still need references. I've been trying to go to Lázaro and other libraries but I've not much luck as of yet.
- I've talked with my teacher, and while they are available, I've yet to legally get their consent (by signature, I mean.)

Progress Report
- I have had three problems so far:
  - First, I have had trouble finding good references and resources so bring a more serious aspect to my project. Art by itself is, most often than not, found as a tentative subject not necessarily worthy of being studies as a profession. While there are great references about art in general, it is rare to find articles and texts talking about the intricate relationship that art has with water. If not much be found, I'll have to go talk with the teacher regarding this problem.
  - The process of art-making varies depending on the artist. In my case, I'm mostly silent. I've had trouble concentrating on doing both: painting and taking notes. Nevertheless, I'm adapting.
  - I love art, but it is time consuming and sometimes, even frustrating. I've found difficult having to make time for it and also juggling around with the constant accumulation of university work and trying to also squeeze in some periods of free time. Again, I'm adapting.

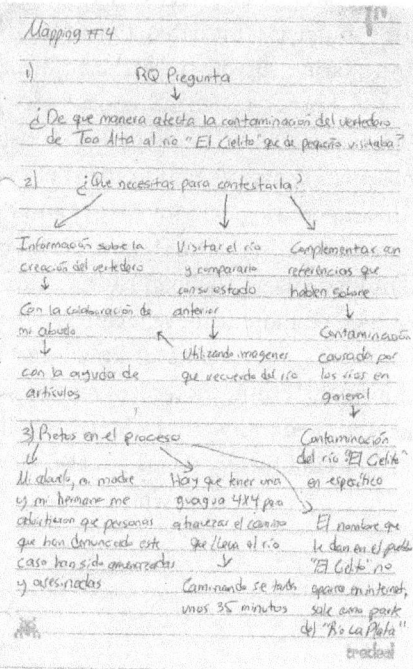

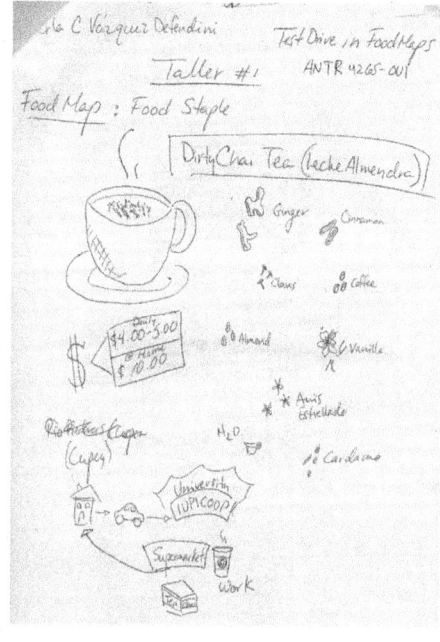

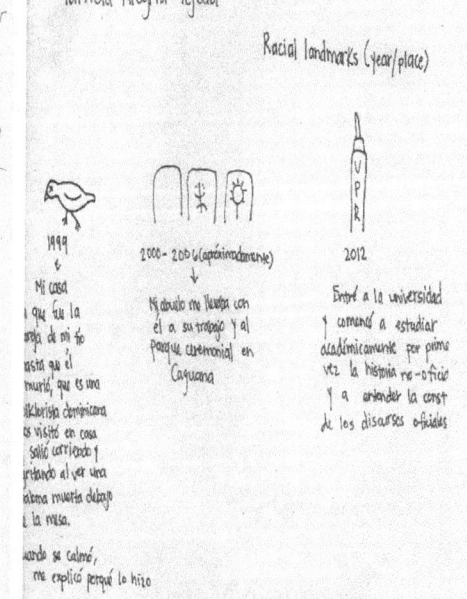

SAMPLER OF STUDENTS CRITICAL RESPONSES

CRITICAL RESPONSE #3: DISCOURSE ON COLONIALISM (CUNY-2013)

The reading was an essay by the author Aime Cesaire on the effect of colonialism on the colonizer (European civilization) and the colonized. In his analysis Cesaire shows that through their (colonizers) concerted efforts to show their superiority over the colonized, they have become dehumanized in the process ... Three points I found useful for the class and that may also be useful in my research are: That black identity was a European creation; it was never a negotiated agreement on what it means to be black. (a) Acknowledging our past to move forward, (b) a theory proposed into creating a new society, (c) Creation of an identity that the colonizer previously denied ... The most challenging part from the reading were the long arguments and references made to both Greek and European scholars, who used scholarship to systematically negate the knowledge systems, heritage and culture of the people in colonized areas of the world.

UPR-2018: CR#14: BLACKNESS & BELONGING IN PR
Resources: TED talk Y tu Abuela donde está? Arroyo and poem "Yo Soy Negra" Abadia

STUDENT 1
I understand that everyone in Puerto Rico should talk about blackness and deconstruct the misunderstandings of society. Arroyo TED talk video was really inspiring, her stories of the women ancestors in her family make me think how I don't know my family's history ...

Abadia-Rexach's poem touched me more than I could possibly think. All these abusive words that we use and do not realize how offensive they are, until we read this poem that makes us think before using a racist vocabulary. It has been 144 years since slavery was abolished in PR and still racism exist ... Both readings are relevant to our project. The point is that we use an inclusive language in it, and that we are aware that it is necessary to deconstruct it. We're doing an auto-ethnographic research, and these stereotypes must begin to break down somewhere. The Academy is too important for the conscience of society, and if we continue to promote racism, it will never end. We must be more aware of how we speak, and how we write because we do not know who we are going to offend ...

STUDENT 2
The first thing I saw was the video (TED talk). From the beginning it caught my attention and I think it was cool to have integrated narration of the work

with Children's tales. The most interesting thing was the story of the braids, since I would never have imagined that they originate from slaves escape attempts. The "Yo Soy Negra" poem, surprised me as I discovered several racist expressions that I also use in my daily life. This resource was easy to understand and its title represented the reading totally ... The video was about how it is necessary to tell those stories of our rebellious grandmothers and their struggles to know our history. Two important concepts are history and narration. What she said first, I understood that it was the official story, which is selective, while the her narration is that ability to tell a story that is invisible. Abadia's poem offers examples of different expressions that are racist and that we use daily. These expressions imply that we associate black as: Bad, dirty and ugly. I realize that all my life I have used some of these expressions and although I had no idea, it contributed to racism ... Relevance: These resources help me to better understand racialization in Puerto Rico by understanding that racism is not only acts, but also words. Also, just as I realized that certain expressions were racist, there may be many other things that I do constantly and do not notice. For my project, it helps me to better analyze the national discourse and how it influences my racialization.

STUDENT 3

I found very interesting this CR, especially the video which motivates us to find those stories hidden in our family that we do not know. Arroyo in the video says, knowing who your ancestors were helps you understand yourself and know who you really are. I personally consider myself "white," but my grandmother is black, she doesn't talk really about his past because it was a sad and she suffered a lot of violence, now I'm motivated to look more about her story. I want to know more about my great-grandmother now, where I come from, what my roots are. I found these resources easy to understand and interpret, now the challenge is to find more about my own roots and see where I come from ... In the poem "I am Black," the author shows through a few sentences that, although it is said that there is no racism, all at some point in our lives, even without realizing it, we have spoken in a racist way. It is very true that for a long time many Puerto Ricans spoke with this jargon, but definitely does not justify the racist language with which we express ourselves most of the time. The black color has always been related to the negative, the ugly, the bad, etc. and it is amazing that we still continue to carry out this practice, both in our actions and in our daily vocabulary ... I definitely feel I could use these resources for my project as I thought I plan to do the oral history with my grandmother, and I would like to learn more about her parents and about her grandparents. My grandmother never had an education because she was raised working the land, I want to see how the times in which she lived made her the strong person ...

STUDENT 4

The two resources communicated their ideas in a very effective way and I could easily understand them. First of all, Arroyo's Ted talk was very interesting given the narrative character of the presentation, she spoke about the educational project on Afrodescendencia that she created ... These are very relevant and useful to me, considering that we have to do an oral history (for the project about our racial identity)... the video talk served as an example for me to get ideas how to present the oral history in my report ...

STUDENT 5

These resources help us to understand our topic of the semester and the development of the research project because as Arroyo says in her Ted Talk, to know the history of our country, we have to know the history of our families, to know the history of those who are closer to us, to know their struggles, their victories and their losses; In some ways those stories help us to know ourselves ...

STUDENT 6

I liked the poem "Yo Soy Negra" because it talked about the racism that we have in our language and how we normalize this and just associate everything that is bad with the color black. Abadía-Rexach talks about the internal racism that still exist in our language even though slavery was abolished more than 100 years ago ... I found the video by Yolanda Arroyo Pizarro very informative because she said that we need to know the history of our past family members and know where we came from. We cannot be ignorant about our history ... She talks about the importance of knowing the history of our grandmas and great-grandmas. She also talked about an organization she is hosting and what they do there as well. The common topic of these resources is blackness in Puerto Rico and how people tend to either forget or be ignorant about it ...

STUDENT 7

The resources assigned have great relevance, for our project, so we tell our story, that has been silenced since centuries ... These resources are relevant to the theme of semester since it speaks about race and the human inequality. Personally, these resources help me in my project to tell those stories of my "kinky" hair and its beauty that have been marginalized, like me. These resources are very close to my topic and give me an example to develop my voice as author and a way to organize my writing and references ...

STUDENT 8

The resources given for this Critical Response spoke about the racial discourse in Puerto Rico. Bárbara Abadía Rexach poem "Yo soy negra" addresses the suppressed problems of racial aggression in colloquial Puerto Rican dialect and how it perpetuates racism in our island. Micro-aggressions have been inserted in our vocabulary, and it translated into the conversations that we have with our children, our mothers, our friends and everyone who surrounds us ... The video speaks about our black ancestry and tries to bring our blackness and our history to the present, instead of leaving our blackness as only part of our history. These resources show the silence around discrimination in Puerto Rico ... and acknowledge how the black body has been ignored in Puerto Rican national identity ...

STUDENT 9
The Cimarronaje is also invisible in the history of Puerto Rico, and the stories of Arroyo Pizarro wants to rescue there struggles of resistance and blackness, especially that of the black women who are forgotten in our present ... to break with the victimization and recover the power that has been stolen. The Tedtalk makes me want to do to have my grandmother's oral history and rescue even a portion of the thousands of stories she has of my family. The poem made me more aware of racist words and also provides me with the right alternatives to use ...

STUDENT 10
The first resource, by Yolanda Arroyo Pizarro, is a very special one. I was extremely impressed by her stories, her tranquility and her clear narrative. The poem by Barbara Abadia, presents us a great literary piece that speaks of racial pride and denounces racist stereotypes. At first it looks like a simple poem, but when read carefully I appreciate the frustrations of the author with the racist vocabulary ... Returning to the video, the phrase that made the most sense of all her presentation was "We have people who do not know the history of their country because they do not know the history of their family." This phrase I get very strongly, because I am constantly asking my parents and grandmother about things in our family of our past and through that narrative is that I know as their lives were in the past ... In conclusion these resources help us to understand the history of Puerto Rico from a racial perspective, through the voices of brilliant, strong, and determined black women. These people are examples that in PR there is a lot of racial difference but also that they have not let that overshadow them, but become stronger, something we must do all of us, to learn to understand and love our "differences" to be stronger ...

STUDENT 11
I believe the main link between the resources Abadia's poem and the Ted talk by Yolanda Arroyo Pizarro center on one of main problem in our society: the negation or covering of our roots, specifically our African roots. They do it differently,

of course, the poem taking a more direct approach to the subject, claiming a black identity and establishing its prevalence in our culture as well as the fact that it is widely rejected; and urges to reinstate the importance of our African roots in our culture and ourselves as individuals. Arroyo Pizarro's Ted Talk, takes the common saying *"y tu abuela, onde tá?"* and exposes Puerto Rican rejection of the African roots in our culture. The saying is present in poetry, music, children's literature and the such, having a widespread outreach. This question directly asks for the roots of the individual in question, your grandmother as an equivalent for your ancestry, your foundation as an individual ... There is no doubt that there is an overwhelming white-washing of our culture and identity across generations; however, the questioning that occurs in these times is a way of bringing back all that has been rejected in the past regarding our roots ...

****

Yolanda Medina and Margarita Machado-Casas
GENERAL EDITORS

Critical Studies of Latinos/as in the Americas is a provocative interdisciplinary series that offers a critical space for reflection and questioning what it means to be Latino/a living in the Americas in twenty-first century social, cultural, economic, and political arenas. The series looks forward to extending the dialogue to include the North and South Western hemispheric relations that are prevalent in the field of global studies.

Topics that explore and advance research and scholarship on contemporary topics and issues related with processes of racialization, economic exploitation, health, education, transnationalism, immigration, gendered and sexual identities, and disabilities that are not commonly highlighted in the current Latino/a Studies literature as well as the multitude of socio, cultural, economic, and political progress among the Latinos/as in the Americas are welcome.

To receive more information about CSLA, please contact:

Yolanda Medina (ymedina@bmcc.cuny.edu) &
Margarita Machado-Casas (Margarita.MachadoCasas@utsa.edu)

To order other books in this series, please contact our Customer Service Department at:

peterlang@presswarehouse.com (within the U.S.)
order@peterlang.com (outside the U.S.)

Or browse online by series at:

WWW.PETERLANG.COM